RANDOM ACCESS MEMORIES (RAM) OF A LIFE WELL SPENT

PHILLIP L HIXSON

Copyright © 2023 Phillip L Hixson.

All rights reserved. No part of this book may be reproduced, stored, or transmitted by any means—whether auditory, graphic, mechanical, or electronic—without written permission of both publisher and author, except in the case of brief excerpts used in critical articles and reviews. Unauthorized reproduction of any part of this work is illegal and is punishable by law.

ISBN: 979-8-88640-956-7 (sc)
ISBN: 979-8-88640-957-4 (hc)
ISBN: 979-8-88640-958-1 (e)

Because of the dynamic nature of the Internet, any web addresses or links contained in this book may have changed since publication and may no longer be valid. The views expressed in this work are solely those of the author and do not necessarily reflect the views of the publisher, and the publisher hereby disclaims any responsibility for them.

One Galleria Blvd., Suite 1900, Metairie, LA 70001
1-888-421-2397

Families used to tell stories to their children and grandchildren that provided some insight to the elders' lives. We don't do that much anymore, so this book is a means to pass on some of my life's stories that I want to share with our children and grandchildren. I hope they will do the same for their future families.

I dedicate this book to my wife, Shirley, our son Matthew and his wife Heidi, to our son Thomas and his wife Tia, and to the two most wonderful grandsons in the world: Briley and Keller.

TABLE OF CONTENTS

1. RAM—An Introduction..............................1
2. My Early Education 9
3. Off to College.....................................15
4. Mrs. Shirley Ann Hixson—My Best Friend 23
5. Our Boys—Matthew and Thomas 34
6. My Mother—Martha Elizabeth Hixson 45
7. An Eventful Afternoon In Norfolk, VA.................50
8. My Dad—Dr. Floyd M. Hixson 52
9. The Blue Creek Flood of '96 59
10. The Pizza Chronicles and Vermont's Pizza-Eatin' Mountain Man....................................67
11. The General Hixson Tree 73
12. Fond Memories of Hume Lake 75
13. Never, Never, Ever Pick Up an Injured Bobcat!...........82
14. A "Bucket List" Event 86

15.	Snakes In My Life	88
16.	Horses In My Life	95
17.	Pat and Babe, the Covered Haywagon, and the Party Barn	108
18.	Teaching Environmental Education	123
19.	Insurance For The Future	134
20.	OLE!	137
21.	Lava Beds National Monument	142
22.	Rob Zink—Interpretive Park Ranger, My Mentor and Close Friend	155
23.	Journey To Alaska	161
24.	Dreamland	197
25.	Canoes, Paddles, and Life Jackets	201
26.	Larry, Canada, and Me	208
27.	Health and Fitness	216
28.	Natural Resource Management in the Corps of Engineers	228
29.	Conclusion	249

RAM—AN INTRODUCTION

Any computer user will recognize the term "RAM" as an acronym for "random access memory." While searching for a title, it dawned on me that most of the chapters to follow were about events in my life that just popped into my head as I sat in front of the computer to jot them down. After the first few chapters, the remainder of the book is not in chronological order. Thus, I hit on the idea that this book is mostly a result of "Random Access Memories of a Life Well Spent."

No two people begin life in exactly the same manner. I was fortunate to enter life with two parents and a sister three years older than me. My maternal grandparents lived close by in my younger years, and they were a positive influence on my life. However, my grandfather did have a way of thumping me on the noggin and saying "cheese it" when I did something wrong.

My earliest recollection involves the scar on my nose. I received that while running up the steps of our front porch in Stillwater, OK, when I was three years old. All these many years later it is still with me. Along the way I've managed to collect many more scars from hay hooks, surgeries, falls, and an assortment of stings, stabs, lacerations, and scrapes. It is surprising how resilient skin can be. In my later years,

I've come to realize that many people have much of their life experiences recorded on their skin and in their bones!

My folks tell me that my first two words were "horse" and "no." I apparently used the word "no" frequently when being taken to the nursery at our church in Stillwater. "Horse" was an appropriate word for me as my first name, Phillip, is derived from a Greek word meaning "lover of horses." That love for horses has stayed with me throughout my life. However, I was never to own my own horses until I was in my late forties, when Pat and Babe, two beautiful Belgian mares entered my life. More about them later.

After my dad earned his BS in Poultry Husbandry at Oklahoma A&M in Stillwater, we moved to Manhattan, KA, where he worked on his master's degree at Kansas State University (KSU). Upon completion of his master's, it was back to Stillwater where he taught at Oklahoma A&M. We subsequently moved back to Manhattan where he began teaching at KSU while starting the process of working on a PhD in Genetics. All this moving happened by the time I was four years old.

In 1951, we moved to Fresno, CA, where my dad began teaching in the Agriculture Department at Fresno State College (FSC). Several years later, he became the first professor in the department to earn a PhD.

By this time our family had expanded when a younger sister arrived in 1951. When we landed in Fresno we moved into a house in a middle-class development near Fig Garden Village in northwest Fresno and there my oldest sister, Joyce and I began school. For her it was second grade, for me it was kindergarten. Our teachers were Mrs. Mann and Mrs. McMann. After only two weeks of school, the deal on our house fell through, so we moved to the old Army Air Corps barracks at Hammer Field east of Fresno next to the airport. This was probably a good thing for my dad since it was just a stone's throw from where the FSC poultry farm and Ag Department classrooms were located.

Kindergarten was not a high point in my life. I had a crush on my teacher (I don't even remember her name). One day I got upset with my folks, so I told them I wanted to go live with my teacher. So, they helped me pack a suitcase and my dad drove me out into the country within a quarter of a mile of her house. He said, "There's her house. Hop out, this is as far as I'm taking you." That's when I realized I wasn't even able to carry the suitcase by myself, let alone drag it all the way to her house. After reconsidering the situation, I decided to stay with my family.

That same year, my cousin, Kay Patterson, came to stay with us so she could attend kindergarten. Apparently there was no kindergarten available where she lived in Pomona, CA. That was okay with me until she told my folks I had received a spanking at school one day. The rule around our house was if you got a spanking at school, you would get another one at home. After that, I wasn't too keen on having Cousin Kay around for the rest of the school year.

After living in three different apartments at Hammer Field over the next five years, my folks found a small house in a new development in nearby Clovis, CA. It was only about 1,100 square feet with four bedrooms, one and a half baths, a kitchen/dining area, a living room, and a one-car garage. We moved to 1297 S. DeWitt in 1956. By this time, I had three sisters and while living there I finally got a brother.

My brother's life definitely started out differently than most people's as he was born in our 1951 Studebaker sedan near Starlight Theater while my dad was trying frantically to get my mom to the hospital in time for a more "traditional" delivery. My dad tried to get the hospital to reduce its medical bill since the baby wasn't born in the hospital. They disagreed of course.

Our house was awfully crowded with seven of us occupying that small space. At one time we also had five other kids living with us temporarily due to divorced parents needing some child care support. Seems we had bunkbeds everywhere during that era!

In 1956, Clovis was a good six miles from Fresno. It was what most people would call a "rural" community of four thousand. The two towns were far enough apart that Fresno State College moved its main campus and the agricultural facilities between Fresno and Clovis since there was a considerable amount of agricultural land available between the two towns. Today, you can't tell when you leave Fresno and enter Clovis and the entire college (now California State University at Fresno/FSU) is completely surrounded by housing and business developments.

Our house was right in the back of Sierra Vista Elementary School where my older sister, Joyce, and I would continue our early childhood education, as did our three younger siblings later. There was an alley between our house and the fenced schoolyard. The schoolyard was about five feet lower than the alley, so we had a great place to dig caves back into the slope between the playground and the alley. Since the school grounds were usually locked during non-school hours, our folks would not allow us to climb the fence and play on the playground. So, we spent much of our time digging our caves (which we were told not to do).

Our caves became forts. If you had a fort, you needed to defend it. That's where grape stakes from the vineyard across the street—another place we weren't allowed to go—came in handy. These stakes were merely laths that could be easily sawed or broken to form swords or daggers with which to conduct "war" on our enemies. Of course, we were short of "enemies" so our best friends and siblings had to serve as the "enemy."

Speaking of best friends, one of mine was Harold Bradford who lived just four houses down the street. He and I had a way of getting into a running fight that would last all the way home each afternoon after school. However, the next morning, having already forgotten what we had fought about the prior afternoon, we always went back to school as best friends!

In the third grade, I met a boy who would be a best friend throughout the rest of his life. Glenn Henshaw and I always seemed to end up in the same classes each year as we progressed through grade school and junior high. While we didn't always have the same classes together in high school, we remained good friends and both of us ended up as managers of the Clovis High swim team for the last three years of high school. Glenn was a football player and I was in our high school a capella choir, but every day outside football season, we were together at the end of the day with our swim team chores (which also included getting to swim every day during swim team practice). More about Glenn later.

Across the street from Harold and east a few houses lived a boy named Vernon Reader. Vernon was the kind of kid that bullies loved to pick on. We had been in the same classes from third through sixth grades. Vernon had a bad case of asthma that kept him from participating in most physically demanding activities. That just caused the bullies to pick on him even more. During the summer following our sixth grade, Vernon passed away. It was my first encounter with the death of someone I knew well and it really shook me up. I just couldn't imagine school starting without him.

About this time, my dad was introducing me to a "work ethic." He would often take me to the college poultry farm with him so I could keep records while he was weighing and banding chickens. Because of the extreme heat during the warmer months in the San Joaquin Valley, we would perform this work starting about 4:00 a.m. in hopes of beating the heat of the day. Sometimes we would do this in the school year, so we had to be done in time for me to get to my morning classes. At other times I also helped gather eggs, clean chicken houses, feed, clean eggs, and somewhere along the way I learned to drive a tractor.

At the beginning of my seventh grade year, I contracted a most obnoxious respiratory disease. Laughing, bending over to tie my shoes, or just having a "tickle" in the back of my throat, would suddenly send me into an unending coughing fit. I would turn bright red, tears would well up in my eyes as the coughing continued unabated. I ended up missing a lot of school over the next three months. My cough had all the doctors baffled. They tested me for tuberculosis, rheumatic fever, scarlet fever, and a host of other such diseases to no avail. Finally, thinking it might merely be an allergic reaction, they drew a grid on my back and placed various allergens in each square to see if they could find the culprit that was torturing me. Nothing! This malady had hit me hard and fast, and just as fast, it left me one day. Still, the doctors could not figure out what had attacked me.

Some twenty-plus years later while studying to get my Emergency Medical Technician certification, I came across a respiratory disease called Valley Fever. As I researched this disease, it became apparent to me that it was in fact what I had contracted as a seventh grader. It seems this ailment is caused by a fungus in the soil (remember my dirt caves?). So far it had only been identified in the soils of the San Joaquin Valley and in the soils of Central America. Another thirty-five years later, a friend's son-in-law who was living in Phoenix, AZ, contracted Valley Fever and almost died because of it. So it appears that Valley Fever is very mobile, more well-known, and a very active disease today.

Summer was my favorite time of the year. It meant two things would happen: 1) we would go visit our grandparents in Oklahoma; and 2) from the age of nine to sixteen, I got to go to Eureka Springs summer church camp up in the cool Sierra Nevada Mountains about six miles south of Yosemite National Park.

The trips to Oklahoma were especially fun when my grandparents still lived on the farm halfway between Stillwater (where I was born) and the small rural community of Perkins (where my mother was born). It was great to be out in the country since we lived in town the rest of the year. My grandparents' propane tank that we were forbidden to play on always made a nice pretend horse for us to ride—yes, we would get in trouble later. There were plenty of trees to climb and a variety of farm animals to get acquainted with.

One summer we were warned to stay away from the young bull calf in the corral by the barn. Unfortunately, it was not within our power to deny ourselves the opportunity to rope him and try to ride him while he was tied to the corral fence. We seldom managed to get on his back before he would knock us off our feet. None of us were destined to become professional bull riders. At least there were no broken bones or visible scars as a result of this venture.

The road leading to and away from my grandparents' farm was made of concrete. During the warmer parts of the year, the tar between the concrete slabs would ooze up from the cracks between the slabs. Every time a car passed over these strips of tar they would make a "thud" sound. So at night, while trying to go to sleep, you could hear cars coming from several miles away. The rhythmic, thud, thud, thudding of their tires would tell me a car was getting closer and closer until finally it passed and I would hear the thuds fading away in the distance. It was kind of a soothing sound that would eventually lull me into dreamland.

We seldom ever experienced thunderstorms in the San Joaquin Valley, so the frequent summer thunderstorms we encountered in Oklahoma were always thrilling for us kids. Before the storms, we often laid out on the lawn and tried to visualize various animal and geometric shapes in the huge cumulus clouds. Once the storms started, we would retreat to the house where we would watch the lightning strikes with great interest and thrill to the thunderclaps, booms, and low rumbles. One such storm dumped six inches of rain in less than a day turning the streets in town into rivers.

Grandma had an old ringer washing machine that she used every week. Next to it she would set a large metal tub on a wooden bench to put the clothes in after she rung them out and subsequently hung them to dry on a clothesline. One day, my siblings and I got the bright idea to set the bench on the lawn and take turns hurdling over it. I made the mistake of jumping onto the bench rather than hurdling it. Of course, my momentum caused the bench to tip forward while I fell backwards. The result was immediate—I had broken my right arm in two places as I used it to try to break my fall. Joyce ran over to me, lifted my arm off the ground, yelled to my mom that it was broken, then suddenly dropped my arm back to the ground. Then things got even worse. My granddad seldom ever drove his red and black '53 Buick over twenty-five miles per hour whether in town or on a country road, but while driving me to the hospital in Stillwater about twelve miles away, he was doing sixty! My arm quit hurting enough to allow me to worry more about living long enough to get to the hospital!

When school started that fall, I showed up with a cast on my right arm from just below my right shoulder all the way to my fingers. My friend, Glenn, chose that same summer to break his leg, so we were both in casts. His problem: while visiting his grandparents in Oklahoma, he was "surfing" down a metal storm cellar door when his foot hit a bolt that turned his leg breaking it in two places. And yes, he had been told to stay off the cellar door. Seems it wasn't a good summer for fun-loving boys to visit Oklahoma.

Church camp at Eureka Springs was always a high point of the year for me. It was a young active boy's heaven in part because it meant no baths for a week, although we were forced to put on clean underwear a time or two. The kitchen cooks served pretty good food and lots of it. There were church services to attend, badges to earn, a cabin to keep clean, crafts to be made, and a campfire at the end of the day for sitting around and singing campfire songs while roasting marshmallows.

Much of the fun didn't begin until after "lights out" in the cabins. As we each hunkered down in our sleeping bags on our bunkbeds, we took turns adding to a story that the high school-aged cabin "counselor" usually started. The darker the night, the more scary the stories became. All sorts of weapons such as knives, guns, baseball bats, and pitchforks would be added to the story to make it really scary. Of course, the whole idea was to make the story more and more frightful till we could hardly go to sleep! Despite this ending to each day, we managed to get enough rest each night to go full bore the following day.

I really enjoyed being in the forested mountains and was always excited to see what wildlife we could find. There were butterflies, beetles, chipmunks, deer, frogs, quail, woodpeckers, and a host of other critters to observe. This probably had something to do with my decision to major in biology in my college years.

There were always some "summer missionaries" (young college students) who would come to help with summer camp. They were usually from somewhere in the south. One summer, I fell madly in love with a sweet young lady (about twice my age) named Annabelle. Being from Mississippi, she had a wonderful Southern accent, something you seldom heard in the San Joaquin Valley. It really hurt to leave camp knowing I would probably never see her again. However, I did survive.

One of the male summer missionaries liked to play tricks on us boys, so several of us decided to get even with him. The only shower in camp was outside with a canvas curtain hung around it. The water was provided by a cold mountain spring. That water was not heated, so it was exceptionally cold. If you showered in it, the objective was to get wet, soap up, and rinse off as fast as possible. Several of us boys decided to fill our buckets with some of that same cold spring water and heave it over the shower curtain onto our target. His screams were of epic proportions. He spent most of the rest of the day chasing us down to give us a spanking!

MY EARLY EDUCATION

I attended elementary, junior high, and high school in Clovis, CA. While my elementary and junior high years were not much to take note of, I do have some good memories of my high school years.

During the fall of my freshman year, our PE class did cross-country running every day. We would circle a baseball field, run the outside of our oval track, head for the race car track beside the high school, climb the steps to the top of the stadium, circle the rest of the car race track, run the outside of the high school track once more, then do one more lap around the baseball field for a total of two and a half miles. There were about thirty of us in the class, but four of us always ran together and visited with each other until that last lap around the baseball field. That was when the other three always took off and left me. I always ended up fourth after that final lap.

I was not an athlete, but our coach saw some potential in me for something else. As track season was about to begin in the spring of my freshman year, I was invited by Coach Stark to serve as a manager of the track team. That kept me busy after school doing such things as taking inventories of equipment, helping runners with their starting block practice, setting up hurdles, announcing events at track meets, and keeping lots of records.

Coach Stark was quite an athlete in his younger years. He told us about the time he beat Olympic athlete Rafer Johnson in a 100-yard dash while they were both in high school. Johnson, then a student in nearby Kingsburg, CA, apparently tripped on his own shoelace and fell, allowing Stark to coast to a win. They raced against each other several more times during their high school years, but that was the only time he ever managed to defeat Rafer Johnson. Years later Rafer Johnson would become an Olympic decathlon world record holder.

For the next three years, I would serve as a manager of the swim team along with my best friend, Glenn Henshaw. I wasn't a strong swimmer, but I got to swim every day during team practice. Coach Don Utter soon learned that I had some strong teaching abilities, so he would have me take some of the promising new swimmers to another area of the pool and have them practice the same exercises he was putting the more mature swimmers through. When he thought "my students" had progressed sufficiently, he would allow them to practice with the rest of the team. Again, there was a lot of equipment to keep track of and records that had to be kept.

My work ethic was further enhanced while in high school by working for a family friend, Mr. Lyle Golden. He was a carpenter/builder who attended our church. He would frequently hire high school-aged boys such as myself to hang sheetrock, wrap houses for plastering, and shingle roofs—all for only a buck an hour (in the early 1960s).

My first two days on the job with Mr. Golden found me helping install cedar shake shingles on a two-story cabin with a half-pitched roof in the Sierra Nevadas northeast of Fresno. I spent most of those two days hanging on to anything within reach in hopes I would not slide off the roof! It was slow going nailing those shingles when I was focused on remaining safely on the roof.

Later that summer, we shingled some roofs with a lesser degree of slope, but this time we were working on the west side of the San Joaquin Valley where the temperatures could easily hit 105–110°F each day. So, once again I was up early in the morning so we could get our work done and escape the hottest part of the day. The temperatures on the roofs would definitely exceed the reported high for each day. The one "benefit" of working in such a sunny intense environment was that we had terrific tans by the end of summer. Of course, that might pose some problems later in life since we later discovered that such tanning can lead to skin cancer.

During my senior year, Coach Utter started varsity and junior varsity water polo teams at Clovis High. The only opponents we had were at Bullard High in Fresno, and a high school in Visalia, CA. So, he reached out to the colleges in the area and we ended up playing JV teams at Fresno City College, College of the Sequoias, and Fresno State College. No, we didn't win any of our games, but it got us started. It was the only sport in which I competed and actually received a high school "letter" for my participation.

I was also fortunate to participate in the Clovis High A Capella Choir under the direction of Mrs. Mercedes Edwards. She was a very demanding music director who knew how to bring out the best in us. When we weren't making the effort to perform as she wished us to, she would slap the top of the piano and shout, "Bad words!" That was our signal to stay focused. Our choir consistently rated the highest score available at music competitions all over the state.

We traveled to various locations in California to participate in musical competitions. One very memorable trip was when we went to the University of California at Berkley (UCB). We did our singing in the morning and then were able to attend the UCB versus UCLA football game that afternoon.

We spent the night at the Whitcomb Hotel on Market Street in San Francisco. We were actually "turned loose" for a few hours that evening to explore the city. Eight of us decided to take a trolley to Fisherman's Wharf on the San Francisco Bay waterfront. We eventually settled on dining at Exposition Grotto No. 9. I'll never forget the barbecued swordfish steak I had that night.

We were supposed to be back at the Whitcomb Hotel by 11:00 p.m. That wasn't going to be a problem as the place to catch the trolley was less than a block from our restaurant. Unfortunately, when we arrived at our anticipated departure point, we discovered the trolleys stopped running at 10:00 p.m. So we did the next best thing we could think of—we started following the trolley tracks. That introduced us to another problem when we realized the tracks didn't all keep heading directly back to Market Street. There were many intersections where tracks spun off in different directions. Needless to say, we did not meet our 11:00 p.m. curfew. We didn't get the chewing out we expected, probably because the choir director's daughter was in our group.

My junior and senior years I served as the second tenor section leader. When the California Music Educators Association met in Fresno, I was one of several from Clovis High who were invited to sing in the Central Valley High School Honor Choir where we would sing Schubert's Mass in G accompanied by the Fresno State College Orchestra, and directed by Lara Hoggard, then director of the Houston Symphony Orchestra.

Mrs. Edwards invited a select group from the a capella choir to perform as the Madrigals. In my sophomore year, I was selected for the Madrigals and continued with that group for the rest of my high school years. We voluntarily practiced during our lunch break each day and stayed an extra hour every Monday night after the a capella choir practice. We performed at a wide variety of functions including the Farm Bureau's annual Thanksgiving Dinner, garden clubs, service organizations, for visiting dignitaries, and on local TV stations. I mention the Farm Bureau because of the fantastic "turkey with all the trimmings" meal they provided each year when we performed for them.

My family remembers our Madrigal's TV appearance best because during one performance, I followed Mrs. Edward's directions so precisely (keep your eyes on me) that I found myself "hypnotized" by a bright stage light immediately behind her. I eventually passed out and went over backwards. I came to as soon as I hit the ground and got back up and kept on singing. However, I was down long enough that my family noted my absence when the camera panned my side of the group. They always accused me of having to go to the bathroom during the performance.

Between my junior and senior years of high school, I went to California Baptist College (CBC) in Riverside to work on the facilities and grounds crew in hopes of earning money to help pay my future college tuition. We did everything from mowing lawns, to bucking hay, tending the college-owned black angus herd, stripping palm fronds off trees, plowing weeds in the orchard, and general planter bed maintenance. It was hard, dirty work, but once again I was happily making a buck an hour!

I graduated from Clovis High School in June 1964 and went straight to Riverside, California, the following week and began working on the facilities and grounds crew at CBC once again. The second half of that summer was spent at the Southern Baptist Conference Retreat at Glorieta, New Mexico. I took a Greyhound bus to Santa Fe. With only one dollar in my pocket, I bought a small carton of milk when we stopped in Flagstaff. It wasn't until I started to drink it I realized it was one of my least favorite drinks—it was buttermilk!

While the pay at Glorieta was almost non-existent, I did get to meet and work with some very wonderful college-aged young people. My job was to help set tables for 1,500 people to eat at one time and to clean up afterwards or wash dishes. We had lots of free time on our hands, so I was able to do some interesting things. I hiked to the top of Mount Baldy once and rode a horse to the top later. From Mount Baldy's peak, you can see at least a hundred miles in every direction.

Glorieta is in a forested area, but it is very dry. However, almost every day at about 4:00 p.m. we could count on getting a little thunderstorm that would normally only last about fifteen minutes. It always freshened the air and we usually got a nice lightning show for a few minutes.

One especially fun excursion involved a short bus trip to Santa Fe where we treated ourselves to some great Mexican food. We also bartered with the Navajos for jewelry and other items that they offered for sale on the front porch of the old Governor's Mansion on the main town square. The Navajos would merely spread a blanket on the ground and lay out their wares for people to shop.

I should note that I worked in the counseling office one period a day during my last two years at Clovis High. I would help schedule students for counseling sessions and ensure that their teachers knew when the students should appear at the counseling office. During those two years, I was never scheduled to sit down with a school counselor to discuss my future plans after high school. No one ever mentioned to me that various scholarships might be available to help pay for my college education. Fortunately, I was already forging ahead with my own plans to attend college.

Grades were not especially important to me during my first two years of high school. Passing classes with a "B" or "C" meant to me that I was doing okay. My parents kept asking me why I couldn't get grades as good as my older sister Joyce's. So, during my junior and senior years, I decided I should probably work a little harder on my grades. I wish I had started a little earlier as I missed being a lifer in the California Scholarship Federation by only half a point!

OFF TO COLLEGE

In September 1964, I began my freshman year at CBC. During the two previous summers, I had earned enough money to pay for tuition, room and board, books, and other educational materials for only one semester.

Although I did not want to work that fall semester since I needed to buckle down and tackle my college courses, when offered a job washing dishes part-time at a retirement village immediately east of the campus, I decided to give it a try. I started the week before school was to begin. I had been told I would be paid $1 per hour plus a free lunch every day I worked. I would only be expected to work twenty hours a week. That sounded okay, especially with the free lunch thrown in.

I referred to my boss as a "dirty-mouthed Greek" who berated me for everything I did. His concept of a "free lunch" meant he would prepare my plate, usually with smaller portions than what he gave the people in the dining room. There were never any seconds. His idea of "part-time" turned out to be thirty-six hours that first week. I ended that employment immediately. There was no way I was going to be able to keep up with my studies working that many hours per week.

An interesting course I took that first semester was Psychology 101. Other than trying to understand the statistics involved in the subject,

I rather enjoyed the course content. I'll never forget what one of the questions on our first exam was: "Who is the author of your textbook?" Most of us didn't get that one right, but I learned to always know the name of the authors of all of my textbooks in the future in case I was ever asked that question again!

We were assigned to write a ten-page term paper based on a book on the subject of psychology. The paper was due right after Christmas break, so I had almost three months to tackle this assignment. Just before Christmas break, I ambled over to the school library where I stumbled onto a book entitled *Psychoanalysis and Group Behavior* by Dr. Saul Scheidlinger. On one of the last nights of our Christmas break, I finally sat down to read it and found the first chapter quite difficult for a first year college student to understand. So, I skipped to the last chapter which sounded pretty much like the first chapter; at least all the "big" words were the same. So, I dug out my typewriter, typing paper, carbon paper, and "white-out" (obviously a pre-computer age eraser) and went to work. Somehow I managed to write the entire ten pages that very night. I merely compared the first chapter to the last chapter. I was hoping to at least get a "D" on the paper so I could pass the course. To my great surprise, I received a "C+"! To this day, I've never read the rest of that book, nor do I intend to do so anytime soon.

At the end of that term at CBC I returned home to Clovis since I was totally out of funds for tuition, books, and room and board. Moving back in with my folks, I began attending Fresno State College (FSC in those days) for the second half of my freshman year. Unlike a lot of private schools, I did not receive any financial advantages just because my dad taught at FSC.

This was during the Vietnam War era, so I decided to sign up for Air Force ROTC in hopes I would not get drafted while working my way through college and I really did want to be able to fly. I was in the first-ever draft lottery and my number was 72, so I knew there was a good chance I would get drafted and not have a choice of which branch I would serve in. I was assured by an Air Force recruiter that I would be able to fly even though I did not have twenty-twenty vision.

We had a uniform day once a week when we were to attend class in our full Air Force uniform. My feet were small and very narrow, so they told me to wear whatever black shoes I owned since the Air Force did not have in stock any shoes that would fit me. On one uniform day, one of the upperclassmen in ROTC was performing an inspection to see that we were wearing the uniform 100 percent the way it was supposed to be worn. When he got to me he asked a very simple question: "Why aren't you wearing regulation shoes?" Thought that was easy enough to answer, so I started to say, "They don't have any shoes that fit me." Before I got halfway through that sentence, he yelled at me, "No excuse, sir!" Thinking he might not have understood me, I started to repeat my answer, but was once again rebuked with a response of, "No excuse, sir!" It finally dawned on me that this "jerk" wanted me to tell him a lie by saying, "No excuse, sir!" So I yielded to his superior way of handling my situation by repeating his words. This was the first sign that I might not do well in the military.

Halfway through the semester, I was reading my Air Science 101 textbook, furnished by the US Air Force. Contrary to what Major Snow, the recruiter and course instructor had told me when he was trying to recruit me, I came across a sentence that said one had to have twenty-twenty vision in order to fly. On the next "uniform" day, I went to see Major Snow. I saluted the major and asked permission to approach his desk. He allowed me to do so. I plopped down my textbook on his desk. I had underlined the "vision" requirement sentence in bright red ink (this was before highlighters). I asked him to read that sentence aloud to me. Although his eyes scanned it, he did not say anything. I asked if that sentence meant what it said. After he started to stammer a bit, I merely said, "I'll be checking out of ROTC at the end of the semester, Sir." Picking up my book, I saluted him, spun around, and exited the room. Despite that, I ended up getting a "C" in the class.

During the summer of 1965, I returned to CBC and hoped to land a job to support myself. I decided to take a couple of courses during summer school, one of which was English Literature. Since these courses are condensed into six weeks, I had the same classes five days a week. On the first day of class, our instructor assigned us to read "Beowulf." Since it was only a fifty-page reading assignment, I chose to go out on a date that evening and did not return to the dorm until 11:00 p.m. What I had not realized was that "Beowulf" was written in

Anglo-Saxon and about every fifth word was footnoted so you could learn what it meant. I spent the next five hours plodding through the poem as we were to discuss it in class the next day.

I was able to land a job at a Sears Roebuck Store in Riverside, CA, about the time fall classes began. I was immediately assigned to be the "Head Man" and was then making $1.60 per hour. That title meant I had to clean all the public and employee male and female restrooms in the entire building every morning between 4:00 and 8:00 a.m. My dorm roommate didn't really appreciate my obnoxious electric alarm going off at 3:30 a.m. But I got pretty good at jumping out of bed and shutting it off in a matter of a couple of seconds.

It was a two-mile drive through city traffic to get from Sears to the CBC campus. I would change my shirt in the car at stop lights and splash a little Aqua Velva aftershave on my face so I would be a little more presentable in the classroom.

One of the janitorial crew at Sears drove past the Green Turtle (GT) on his way to work every morning. The GT was both a restaurant and a bakery. They actually produced donuts twenty-four hours a day. California law required all donuts made before midnight had to be sold as day-old donuts as soon as the new day arrived. So our janitor friend would stop and pick up a dozen donuts on the way to work about 3:30 a.m. each day. Since they were day-old, even though only a few hours old, we paid a mere $1 per dozen. Occasionally, the whole crew would go to IHOP on Saturday mornings when we got off work. On Saturdays they had "silver dollar" pancakes; all you could eat for a dollar! I'm sure they lost money on us.

After completing my sophomore year at CBC, a friend, Randy, and I decided we wanted to go to Oklahoma Baptist University in Shawnee, OK. We decided to drive to Randy's sister's in Oklahoma City while we searched for a job. We weren't aware that by the time we got out of school in California, the Oklahoma students had been out of school for a month. Therefore, they had sewed up every part-time job within a hundred miles.

Randy and I finally got a two-day job picking up and wheelbarrowing rocks from a rich guy's five-acre front yard that he intended to plant with grass. It was a back-breaking job that didn't even pay well. That was about the time I decided to go up to see my grandparents in Perkins, OK, where I might find employment for the rest of the summer. While driving to Perkins, I had to change my route in order to skirt a tornado heading in my direction. Even though it was several miles away, it was quite a frightening sight to see.

Well, Oklahoma State University was only about twelve miles away from Perkins and it was obvious that their students had also grabbed all the summer jobs before I arrived. So after visiting my grandparents for a few days, I decided I had to return to Clovis where I could live with my parents and attend FSC again.

I heard years ago that the average college student would change his/her college major at least three times before graduating. Well, I took a simpler tactic. I merely took very general courses that could apply to most any field for the first three years of college. It was finally time to commit to a major field of study as I began my senior year at FSC. I had noticed that a lot of the biology students were forever going on field trips up into the Sierra Nevadas or out to the wildlife refuges in the valley. That appealed to me, so I declared to work on a degree in biology.

At the time, FSC required two years of foreign language for a major in biology. I had already completed two years of Spanish in high school. In my freshman year, the Spanish teacher taught Castillian while in my sophomore year, the teacher taught Tex-Mex. There was quite a bit of difference between the two.

At CBC I decided to try German for a year. The instructor was easy to pull off the subject, so we ended up listening to his experiences growing up in Germany during World War II. I still can't count to ten in German.

So here I am at FSC being told I had to have two years of foreign language and I am already in the first of my two senior years. The head of the Biology Department, Dr. Woodward, insisted the two-year requirement was going to be around forever. If I passed the Spanish proficiency test, I could forego the two-year requirement. I failed it miserably! So I had to start all over. My first semester Spanish instructor was from Barcelona. In Barcelona, the Spaniards spoke with a "lisp" as one of their kings had a speech impediment and spoke that way. I made it safely through the first semester. The second semester instructor was a former missionary from Quito, Ecuador. Her Spanish had acquired somewhat of an Ecuadorian Indian flavor to it. I took the last two semesters during summer school. Being short on Spanish instructors that time of year, one of the French teachers was recruited to teach summer school Spanish. Somehow I managed to complete the two years without learning how to speak the language. I can read some Spanish and can sometimes even understand it if the person speaking speaks very slowly. That fall they dropped the two-year foreign language requirement to one year!

Several years later while teaching sixth graders, many of whom were from Mexico or at least spoke Spanish at home, I called one of the boys an "abuela." The Spanish-speaking kids seemed to be laughing more than I thought they should, so I asked them what I had called him. They said I called him a "grandmother." Oh, I meant to say "guajolote" which means "turkey."

I have yet to meet anyone who has a degree like mine, a "Bachelor of Arts in Biology." The reason being that I had so many units in Humanities it was easier to go with the arts degree, rather than with a bachelor of science degree.

The National Park Service seemed to be pulling at me, so with a degree in biology, I thought being a park ranger would be a good way to go. But just in case that career wasn't available to me, I also began working on a teaching credential hoping to be able to teach high school biology.

I was able to take ten units of education coursework during my second senior year at FSC. If I could not have a career in the NPS, I decided to prepare to teach high school biology. It was only at the end of my senior year that I was told education classes completed before graduating could not count toward the thirty units I would need to obtain my secondary teaching credential post-graduation.

The one class I took during that time that was truly beneficial was Classroom Observation. I had to attend a certain number of junior high and high school science classes to observe teachers performing in the classroom. It was very interesting to see how the fifteen or so teachers I observed handled their classroom duties.

Off to College

Upon graduation from FSC, Mr. Silas Bartsch, superintendent of the Kings Canyon Unified School District in Reedley, CA, offered me a position as a fifth grade teacher at Great Western Elementary School in a rural area five miles north of Reedley. It was an internship that allowed my first year of teaching to count as my student teaching. I would be supervised by the on-site principal and a retired teacher working for the Fresno County Schools District. I was required to complete thirty units of college education coursework in two years. By taking classes during summer school and during the regular school year, I was able to complete twenty-seven of those units the first year. While teaching and working on my required coursework, I was also working for a friend's janitorial service three nights a week from 6:00 p.m. to midnight! The nice thing was while other future teachers were paying $600 per semester to do their student teaching, I had signed a contract to earn $6,000 in my first year of teaching! WOW! That was big bucks for me back then as Shirley (my wife) and I together working part-time had only been making about $5,800 a year.

During the eight years I taught at Reedley, I was still required to take a certain number of education credits every three years in order to keep my job. I found most of these classes to be of little to no direct value to prepare me for teaching in the classroom.

One professor had videotaped how he worked with a third grader one-on-one showing us a new teaching technique. Unfortunately, the student did not perform as the professor expected him to. So after watching the training video for about forty-five minutes, the professor proceeded to explain to us what he had hoped to accomplish with the student. After listening to his "jibberish" explaining what went wrong with this new teaching style, I raised my hand and said something like, "Dr. . . . , if you couldn't get this teaching technique to work when you were one-on-one with a student, how do you expect us to make this technique work in a classroom of twenty-five students?" After attempting a feeble explanation, class was dismissed for the rest of the day.

Most of the education classes for teachers were conducted on a Friday evening and concluded with an all-day Saturday session. One could usually count on getting a grade of "A" just by sitting through the two sessions. However, one professor came up with a writing assignment that had to be completed in order to get an "A." The assignment was so ridiculous, I refused to do it, but because I had attended the class sessions, I still earned a "B." That may have been the only postgraduate education course in which I did not get an "A."

MRS. SHIRLEY ANN HIXSON—MY BEST FRIEND

My dad always seemed to be finding students at FSC who could use a little financial help to get them through their college years. Such was the case with a young lady who attended the church I grew up attending in Clovis, CA. Frequently my dad would hire students to work for him at the college and would pay their salary out of his own pocket.

While attending CBC in Riverside, CA, I would occasionally catch a ride with someone or drive myself to go visit my folks and friends back home for a weekend. On one such weekend, I went to church with my folks and noticed a new face in the choir. I still remember she was wearing a white blouse and a green skirt. After church, my mother introduced us briefly and then ushered me off quickly as I had to drive home to Riverside (three hundred miles) that afternoon. I later learned that the girl in the choir was one of those students who did work for my dad at the college. That was his way of helping her to pay her way through school.

Soon after that chance encounter, I wrote to my mom and asked her if she thought the "new girl" at church would go out with me the next time I was in Clovis. A couple of weeks later, she sent me a postcard and said I had a date with "Shirley" the next time I was in town. I immediately wrote back and asked, "Who's Shirley?" as I had not remembered the new girl's name.

When people ask us how we ended up together, we always say it was an "arranged marriage" because of my mother's involvement in introducing us and setting up our first date.

That date involved attending my alma mater's football game at Clovis High the next time I went to Clovis. We seemed to get along well. I remember she was wearing a white blouse under a plaid jumper-type dress. I was wearing slacks with a shirt, tie, and a blazer. I was probably the only one there wearing a necktie. Why I remember these things is beyond me. Must be my RAM!

Over the remainder of the school year, I made several more trips home and each time went out with Shirley. On one of those weekends, she invited me to her home for lunch after church on Sunday. She was living with her grandparents, Hayden and Zula McPhetridge, at that time while attending FSC. I'll never forget that we had both a cherry cream cheese pie and another fruit-flavored cream cheese pie for dessert. To this day, cherry cream cheese pie has always remained my favorite dessert.

That summer was when I made the disastrous trip to Oklahoma and I ended up broke and without a job. Having very little money left in my pocket, I decided to head for home in my trusty little red 1965 Datsun pickup. The first night out, I actually found a motel to stay in for only $6 a night in Dodge City, KS. While in town I visited the Long Branch Saloon where I purchased two little green glass kerosene lanterns as a gift for Shirley.

Once I was back in Clovis I decided to continue my education at FSC. I was visiting the personnel offices of United Airlines and Sears Roebuck in Fresno each day as they were the two most promising places for me to land a job. Fortunately, Sears finally hired me to work in the boys' clothing department. The very next day, United called and offered me a job. Since I had committed to Sears, I decided to stick with them. Having worked for them in Riverside, they seemed like a pretty good company to work for. Over the next three years, they allowed me to work hours around my college courses and all day each Saturday.

Since I was back in Clovis, Shirley and I began dating on a more frequent basis. However, Shirley's grandfather thought that seeing each other at church a couple of times a week was enough dating! Friends at our church, Bob and Jody, invited us to go for a picnic up in the Sierra Nevadas at Bear Creek Meadow one Saturday. While there, I proposed to Shirley and she accepted right on the spot without even hesitating! The next thing I had to do was to ask her grandfather if I could marry her. Fortunately, he agreed to let me do so.

We bought engagement and wedding rings and announced to everyone on my grandmother William's birthday, July 9, 1966, that we were engaged. We married four months later on November 4, 1966 in the First Southern Baptist Church of Clovis, CA, where we first met. On that day, Shirley was nineteen and I was just barely twenty. It was a rather simple wedding as we didn't have much money to work with. It probably didn't cost $500. Shirley made her own wedding dress on her grandmother's 1931 White treadle sewing machine. I used my Sears employee discount to put a simple dark brown suit on layaway and paid it off in time for the wedding.

Shirley's grandparents had introduced us to a couple, the Watsons, who lived out in the country east of Fresno on their own acreage. They had a small house for rent at the back of their farmhouse. They offered to rent it to us for $25 a month if I would mow the lawn and help take care of their animals. The price was right and we both preferred living in a rural area, so we jumped at the chance. A side benefit was that Mr. Watson didn't have time to exercise all his horses as much as he would have liked, so I was told I could ride his palomino, Sandy, any time I got a chance. Often I would come home after my classes and go for a ride for an hour or two along the irrigation canals and country roads. I loved it!

We had no furniture, so we were happy to buy my older sister's living room sofa, chairs, TV (with rabbit ear antennae), and lamp for only about $100. Sears was having a sale on unfinished furniture, so we bought a kitchen drop-leaf table, six chairs, a desk, a chest of drawers, and a bookcase for about another $150. We worked hard to get the unfinished pine furniture finished with a maple stain before we married. We still have all those pieces except the bookcase which we sold to friends and four chairs that had become unstable. In fact, Shirley is sitting at the drop-leaf table sewing as I write this some fifty years later. Our first rental house was quite small—probably less than seven hundred square feet and was much in need of some paint on all the interior walls. So we took that chore on also. One of Shirley's telephone operator coworkers gave us a double bed which pretty much filled our dinky bedroom.

My dad's office partner at FSC was Dr. Wilbur Ball. He and his wife, Martha, owned a rustic cabin at Hume Lake up in the Sierras and they agreed to loan it to us for our weekend honeymoon. When we arrived at the cabin about 11:00 that night, there were a couple of deer standing on the back porch. My first chore once we got inside was to find the valve to turn on the water since the cabin had already been winterized.

The weekend we married just happened to be the week before midterms. So, I had to study for my Chemistry test scheduled for the following Monday. Yes, I managed to pass the test!

We were both attending FSC that year and barely squeaking by on our combined incomes from our part-time jobs. Shirley was working as a telephone operator for Pacific Bell in downtown Fresno. We might spend $5 one week for groceries, then $10 the following week. Going out to eat was a very rare event. When we did eat out, we could get a good, inexpensive meal at Happy Steak. It was always a real treat when my folks or Shirley's grandparents would invite us over for a home-cooked meal. Because of our economic situation, we had to borrow $150 from my dad for our tuition and books in the Spring of 1967. That was the only money we ever borrowed while in college. We paid $64 each for tuition and had a little money left over to buy a few books.

Shirley was majoring in home economics which at that time was not considered an "academic" subject worthy of a college major without also having an academic minor. So when I decided to major in biology, she decided to minor in the same field. Because of our economic situation, Shirley decided (and I concurred) to drop out of school for a year and work full-time as a telephone operator while I completed the second of my two senior years. When I started teaching in 1969, she was able to return to FSC full-time and complete her degree over the next two years.

We both are attracted to outdoor activities, so much of our spare time was spent taking day trips into the Sierras anywhere from Yosemite to Kings Canyon and Sequoia National Parks. We often hiked all day then returned home that night. If we were in the Shaver Lake area we would frequently buy a loaf of freshly baked raisin bread at Angelo's Bakery (it was absolutely the best). A favorite meal after a day of hiking included fried breaded shrimp and a green salad, along with the raisin bread of course.

While I was teaching near Reedley, CA, Shirley began substitute teaching. We were finally "rich enough" to rent an apartment in town. Our only vehicle was a 1969 Chevy pickup that we bought brand new ($2,600) in March of 1969 just before I graduated from FSC. Our green and white pickup was parked between gold and silver Porche Targas at the apartments. Beside one of the Targas was a Mercedes. I'm sure we lowered the rating of those apartments due to our vehicle preference! We sold that pickup forty-two years later for $1,000—it was in great shape even then.

It was while living in the apartments that we welcomed our first son, Matthew Phillip Hixson, into our family on October 31, 1974. As the time for delivery arrived, Shirley had to go to the doctor to see if she needed to head to the hospital. It was decided the delivery would be by Caesarian Section since the baby was headed in the wrong direction for a normal birth. She picked me up after school and said we needed to head to the hospital in nearby Sanger. So we rushed home, grabbed what she would need at the hospital, and headed for Sanger. When we arrived in Sanger we realized that neither one of us knew where the hospital was. Since this was pre-GPS, we looked it up in a telephone booth phone book (ask your parents, they'll know what I'm talking about) and soon arrived at the hospital.

We walked into the hospital and saw no one at the reception desk. Finally a nurse showed up and asked if she was Mrs. Hixson. Shirley answered affirmatively and the nurse told her to hurry down to her room as her dinner was there waiting for her. Why dinner? The next thing they did was to give her an enema!

Matthew arrived the next morning. Yup, he is a "Halloween Baby." That always made it easy for Shirley to decide how to decorate his birthday cakes each year! I was afraid they had made a mistake at the hospital as the only other baby born there that day was a very light-complected Mexican girl (that was before the word "Hispanic" had entered our vocabulary) and Matthew was darker than her and had very black hair.

Hospital administrative people can often become somewhat "compulsively anal" when checkout time arrives. We had excellent insurance at that time and had previously made a pre-payment to the hospital. So we were sure the hospital would get paid whatever was due. Three different times the person with the clipboard and paperwork told me we needed to pay the hospital an additional $400 before they would let Shirley and Matthew leave. Each time, I replied that our insurance would be paying the bill. I guess they didn't want to get charged with kidnapping my wife and baby, so they finally let me take them home. A couple of weeks later, we had not heard anything from the hospital, so we decided to drop in and see if we owed anything. No, we did not . . . but they did have a refund check of $200 waiting for us! They must not have had our address or they would have mailed it to us I'm sure!

Babies were not allowed at our highfalutin apartment, so we were asked to move out when we went to work at Crater Lake in the summer of 1975. When we returned in the fall, we lived with Shirley's grandparents for a couple of months, then moved in with my folks for a couple more months before we bought a house on the Kings River about halfway between Clovis and Reedley. We found the house about the time the framing was being completed, so we were able to choose the carpeting, counters, and other minor features. Our living room window looked straight out at the Sierra Nevadas. It was perfect for us. A side channel of the Kings River actually flowed through our backyard. In fact, the thing that sold us on the house wasn't the design, but rather it was the beaver dam in the backyard!

Three years after Matthew was born, while living in Cottonwood, AZ, where I worked as a park ranger at Tuzigoot National Monument, we welcomed Thomas Phillip Hixson into our family on December

2, 1977. Again the baby would be taken by a Caesarian delivery. The doctor was anxious to go on a hunting trip to Texas, so after doing a test to see if Thomas's lungs were ready for birth, he delivered the baby, then headed for Texas.

Somewhere in here, I need to interject that Shirley's home ec major was perfect for her. She really enjoyed her clothing construction (even made her own synthetic "camel hair" coat) and cooking classes. We've always had a mutual "problem" in that Shirley is into "experimental cooking" and I've always enjoyed "experimental eating." When we first met we both weighed about 125 pounds. As my career took me on a path to more and more desk work, I began to pack on the pounds. By the time I retired, I was a little over 200 pounds. Way too much. I am now diabetic and have made some changes in my life to adapt to that challenge. I now eat less (darn!) and I play pickleball or swim most days. I've managed to shave off about 40 pounds in the last couple of years.

Shirley complains about her weight, but she still looks great for someone about to turn seventy-five this year. While the boys were still at home she participated in Jazzercise for about seven years. She has not turned into a frumpy little overweight granny with a blue hair bubble. She is still quite slender and has maintained most of her beautiful shoulder-length gray hair. She is always getting compliments on her gorgeous hair. She still loves to do the experimental cooking which I still enjoy sampling, only now I can't eat as much as I would like to. While living at Stoneridge in north Idaho, she was named "Baker of the Year" when we had a community-wide baking contest. A local master chef says she is the best "baker" he knows. He once had her help judge a Christmas Desserts baking contest.

Before moving to AZ, while still living in Reedley, we attended the Mennonite Brethren Church. It was a large congregation with several hundred members. Having grown up in Southern Baptist churches, I found the Mennonite church to be a German form of Baptist. We really liked the people there. The music was fantastic. The assistant pastor even played the bass in their small orchestra. Shirley and I were both involved with teaching, so it wasn't long before we were roped into teaching middle school-aged boys and girls. I was soon asked to serve as the junior department superintendent in Sunday school. During my seventy-five-plus years, I always look back on this church as my very favorite. Both of our boys had their baby dedications there.

This is turning out to be a long chapter, but after fifty-six years of marriage, it is hard to know what to add in and what to leave out.

After both of our sons were in elementary school in Clarkston, Shirley decided to go back to school and get her teaching credentials. She had already been working at a preschool and as an instructional aide at one of the public schools in Clarkston. She wanted to be able to teach home ec, so she met with an "old maid" home ec professor from Washington State University to see what courses she would have to take to get her credential. The "old maid" had the audacity to tell Shirley that since she had been "out of her field of study" for so long it would be kind of tough. In fact, as a mother and wife, unlike the "old maid," Shirley had been sewing, cooking, and raising two boys (called early childhood development in her field of study). In other words, she had been applying her home ec skills ever since leaving college some fifteen years earlier. The only thing the "old maid" had been doing was teaching at the university level. I call her the "old maid" because she had never been married, never had children, and therefore appeared not to have been doing much in the way of practicing in her field for the past thirty-some years.

Shirley would drive up to Pullman, WA, several days a week, and after one year she received her credential. It was a one-hour trip both ways and sometimes not under the best weather conditions. At one point she was concerned that perhaps the boys didn't like her being away so much and therefore not fixing the great meals she normally made. Those fears went away when Matthew, used to eating only homemade bread, said, "Mom, did you know they have already sliced bread at the store?" She was no longer worried.

Shirley worked in the Primary Intervention program for a couple of years before being hired to teach first grade for two years at Grantham Elementary School in Clarkston, the same school our boys attended.

When we moved to Walla Walla in 1992, Shirley kept trying to land a full-time teaching position but ended up doing several long-term substitute positions and short-term subbing instead. She also team-taught in an elementary school for part of one year when the other teacher's husband passed away.

We were at Stoneridge Resort in north Idaho in August one summer when she got a call asking her to come to Walla Walla for an interview for a permanent elementary teaching position. She made the four-hundred-mile round trip by herself and was confident she got the job. However, she was a runner-up for that position. She continued to substitute teach that year. The following year she received another call asking if she would be interested in a one-year appointment to teach kindergarten. However, the very next day, the principal who had offered her the position called to say she had just seen an announcement for a home ec teaching position at Garrison Middle School. Since school was about to start they were desperate to get a home ec teacher on board. She was offered that teaching assignment and she very quickly and willingly accepted it. That was exactly the job she wanted, so two weeks later, she started teaching middle school home ec.

Shirley loved teaching middle school kids, especially since she was teaching home ec. Her students rotated throughout the year. She had sixth graders for seven weeks, and seventh and eighth graders for nine weeks. That means she had about five hundred students in twenty-six classes each year. She had a budget of $2,000 per year which amounted to only $4 per student. The sixth graders were taught sewing and cooking. Seventh graders were taught nutrition, sewing, and cooking. Eighth graders were taught early childhood development, sewing, and cooking.

Of course, it was the cooking the kids all wanted to do. Cooking necessitated cleaning up, so she taught them how to leave the kitchen clean when they were through cooking. She would use her allotted funds carefully to ensure she could purchase all the ingredients necessary for her cooking classes. We ended up supplementing those funds with our own money to the tune of several hundred dollars each year.

The kids all did a sewing project. She ran into one of her former students who was working at the local hospital as a nurse several years later. He showed off the smock he was wearing as he told her he made it himself. We later encountered one of her former students working at a local hotel cooking a Sunday morning brunch.

Shirley was forever giving kids "fifty extra credit points" for doing something related to home ec at home. For instance, they might fix dinner for their family, iron some clothes, sew a button on a shirt, do some house cleaning, wash the dishes, or bake some cookies. Whatever the chore, they only needed to have their parents sign a note explaining what they had done. And, voila, they got the fifty extra credit points. The points were only applied if a student was on the borderline for getting a higher grade. Someone in my office accomplished a difficult task one day, so I wrote on our office whiteboard that he got "fifty extra credit points"! He could use them any way he wanted to.

We gradually began traveling a little more after the boys left home. We started exchanging our Stoneridge Resort units for stays at other resorts around the country and in Canada. That allowed me to take Shirley to some places I had been to while traveling with my work. Other times we got to visit places neither of us had ever been to. From 2002 to the present, we've visited over forty different resorts in Canada and the US, several of which have been in Hawaii.

The year I retired, Shirley continued to work. We banked all of her checks that year to see if we were going to be able to live on my retirement income alone. It worked. To lighten her load a little, I would often do the laundry or have dinner cooked when she came home from work. I even did the dishes sometimes.

In 2009, while building our new house at Stoneridge near Blanchard, ID, we lived in a condo just about a third of a mile from our building site. We had looked at many different places to retire, but land and house prices seemed way too high for us. We had a contractor friend, Paul Schaub, in Walla Walla whose wife, Carol, had passed away a year or so before we moved north. They had been living in the apartment above our garage which they had completed constructing for us.

We had observed Paul's exceptional construction capabilities, so we coaxed him into coming to Stoneridge with us and serve as our on-site contractor. We shared a condo with him, so we saw him every day. In fact, Shirley would make us a super supper every evening. We would discuss with Paul what we needed to be doing next in order to keep our project moving forward. Paul, Shirley, and I would frequently make day trips to look at various contractors' workmanship, or to select building materials such as flooring, paints, cabinets, hardware, doors, windows, plumbing fixtures, and everything else needed to complete the house.

Shirley adapted to retirement far better than I did. She had a fantastic new kitchen and she had thousands of recipes she wanted to try before she expired. She was still sewing aprons for everyone. She volunteered in the first grade at Idaho Hill Elementary School once a week during the school year when we were home and when the roads were safe enough to drive on during the winter. She spent a lot of time decorating our new home at Stoneridge. It seemed she had different decorations for every season. She also served as the secretary for the Lakes and Forest Stoneridge Property Owners Association Subcommittee. We had a neighborhood "Coffee Connection" that met every Thursday morning, so she always had a new dessert recipe she wanted to try out on our neighbors. She's afraid she'll die before she gets to try all the recipes she has collected over the last fifty-plus years. Me . . . I just continue to enjoy the experimental eating!

Through the fifty-six years we've been married, we have continued to be best friends; although she has accumulated a number of female BFFs (best friends forever) over the years. I can't think of anyone I would rather have spent my life with. She has supported me in all my career efforts and was one of the best teachers the Garrison kids could have ever had.

OUR BOYS—MATTHEW AND THOMAS

Matthew and Thomas are very special boys (men now) to us. I won't pretend to say everything has been smooth sailing while raising them, but we had some wonderful times together.

Matthew won't remember this, but when he was less than two months old, we drove from Reedley, CA, to Houston, TX, to visit my Uncle Maurice and Aunt Elva. There we were in our '69 Chevy two-wheel drive pickup with Matthew strapped in the passenger side seat with only a seat belt around him. He was a great traveler—slept all day! We were afraid he would keep us awake at night, but at that young age, he was a sleep specialist. He seemed to wake up only for eating or a diaper change. We look back on that trip and think how lucky we were not to have to drag along all the baby seats and other paraphernalia that young couples today have to contend with.

On the return trip along I-10, we stopped for breakfast at a motel where we planned to eat quickly and keep driving west toward home. The only table open was one that had been used but had not been cleared yet. We kept waiting for someone to come by and clean the table so we could order our food. After about half an hour, I finally stopped an employee and asked if they would clear our table and take our order. The employees had apparently thought we had already eaten and just hadn't left our table yet!

By then we had lost over an hour of travel time. We had not gone far before we encountered a "Blue Norther" winter storm coming down from Canada. It was an icy snowstorm moving south across our path. I first noticed we might have problems when we crossed a bridge that had already iced over. Our Chevy pickup did not respond well on ice. Having to slow down, it took us hours to get from one town to the next. We tried to get a motel in El Paso, TX; no rooms were available. The same thing happened in Las Cruces, NM. By this time we were seeing many cars and semi-trucks stuck off the road and only one lane of the highway was still open ahead of us. We kept going at much slower speeds. Twenty miles before we reached Tucson, AZ, the snow stopped and we finally found a room at a La Quinta for the remainder of the night.

No, I haven't forgotten we have another boy. Thomas was born in Cottonwood, AZ, on December 2, 1977. Our two boys could not have been more different from each other. Thomas was always a "socialite." He was funny, talked too much, and was often the center of attention within his group of friends.

Thomas was also "creative" in his own way. When he was about three years old, his Aunt Mary had given the boys several Bible storybooks that came with tapes. That way they could "read" the book while listening to the narrator. One of his favorites was about Samson and Delilah. He was having trouble finishing his dinner one night and he knew he could not have dessert if he didn't finish eating his peas. Finally, he looked at his mom and quoted Samson, "Let me die with the Philistines!" Shirley asked him if it was really all that bad. When he replied in the affirmative, she allowed him to move on to dessert. At least we knew he had been listening to the Bible stories.

Both of our boys had the same three teachers in kindergarten through second grade. Their kindergarten teacher was Mrs. Rodgers; their first grade teacher was Mrs. Rogers (no "d"); and their second grade teacher was Mr. Rodgers (who was married to their kindergarten teacher). By then they were beginning to think all teachers' names were just a variation of "Rogers."

Matthew's third grade class was preparing a program to present to the PTA, but he did not want to be on the stage. Fortunately, his teacher decided that Matthew, being an excellent reader, would be a good narrator who would sit behind a curtain and speak into a microphone. He had the largest active part in the program, but he was happy not to have to appear on a stage in front of a bunch of people.

Matthew had a habit of spreading his school materials all over his desk, so in the fifth grade his teacher, Mr. Havens, moved him over next to a countertop where he could continue to spread his papers and books.

That was the same year that Pauliina, our Finnish exchange student, came to live with us for a year. By that time we had a Blazer and a seventeen-foot Road Ranger camp trailer. Just a few days after Pauliina arrived, we all piled into our Blazer and took her to see Glacier and Waterton National Parks on the US-Canadian border. When we got to Customs on the Canadian side of the border, Pauliina and I spent an hour being questioned about why we were taking such a young foreign girl into Canada. Fortunately, her passport was valid so they finally let us into the country. We were expecting to have great weather for our ten-day trip in mid-August. That was not to be as it rained seven of the ten days we were traveling and camping.

Since Pauliina was an only child, the boys referred to her as their "sister" who was an only child. Partway through the school year, Pauliina was told by her grandmother (via a phone call) that her parents were divorcing. That came as a real shock to Pauliina and it caused her to become somewhat not trusting of all adults, including us. Yes, it caused Shirley and me considerable trouble for the remainder of her time with us. Still, we had many positive and memorable times with her.

Pauliina was an excellent student. She spoke both Finnish and Swedish as those two languages were both considered Finland's native languages even though Swedes made up only 5 percent of the population. In third grade, students were required to start studying English. When she got to high school, she had to take a "foreign" language, so she took French. She almost never had to ask us what an English word meant as her vocabulary was quite extensive.

During Matthew's junior year at Clarkston High School, we invited another exchange student into our home. Philipp was from Fraubrunnen, Switzerland. He already spoke Swiss, German (very similar to Swiss), French, and English fluently before he came to us. Since Matthew had taken some German in high school, he and Philipp would stand in the school hallways and point to girls while saying such intelligent things in German as, "Is that a red car?" That was about as deep as the conversation could go with Matthew's limited mastery of the language. The girls, of course, thought they were talking about them!

One day, Philipp came home and showed Shirley his grade on an English exam. He announced that it was the highest grade in his English class. Shirley was congratulating him when he responded, "But no Mom, it's the other kids' language, not mine!"

Philipp has been back to the states to visit us several times in the last thirty-plus years. On one trip he bought a bicycle in Seattle, rode it all the way down the coast to LA, then rode it across the deserts and the Rocky Mountains before flying home from Denver. And that was in the middle of summer! Another time, he and three girls came over. They bought a beat-up, ugly, old Mercedes that they named "Timmy." They drove from Vancouver, BC, and all the way to LA. They had to stop frequently when climbing the mountains to let Timmy's engine cool down. Several years ago, he and some Swiss buddies were going to come to the US for a summer vacation. When he told me they planned to visit Florida, I suggested they not go there due to the heat and humidity at that time of year. They took my advice and went to New England instead. Matthew just happened to be in Massachusetts at that time, so he was able to connect with Philipp for a couple of days.

Matthew was taking a science class in high school and had a lab partner, Dan, who would occasionally pass out for no known reason. So the lab instructor appointed Matthew to serve as Dan's official "catcher" when it would look like his lab partner was about to pass out. One day Dan went down before Matthew could catch him. Matthew rubbed his fingers together and just said, "Butterfingers." To this day, Matthew is a man of few words.

Computers became Matthew's area of expertise. He earned an AA degree in Computer Sciences from Walla Walla Community College, then went to Washington State University, University of Idaho, and Central Washington University and continued to study computer sciences. However, each of those schools insisted at that time that he would have to get an engineering degree in order to study computer sciences. That's when Matthew decided to drop out of college and learn computer programming on his own. As he pointed out, the college professors were writing computer science textbooks that would take them a year or more to write, another year to get them published, and then expected the students to buy their books. The trouble with that plan was the computer industry was developing so fast at the time that the textbooks were two or more years out of date by the time they reached the students' hands.

While Matthew was still in junior high, we bought our first Tandy XS 1000, 8086 computer from Radio Shack. We subscribed to *Family and Home Computing Magazine* so we could start to learn how to use our new "toy." At the end of each issue, there was always something relevant to the season that one could type in the "basic" code to create things like a picture of Santa, or a pumpkin, or even a code that allowed the computer to play Christmas carols. We were really proud of him when we saw him take a hymnal at church and start writing something down in a notebook (during the sermon). He had taken piano lessons long enough to know what the musical notes were, so he was writing them down. By this time he had pretty much mastered "Basic" all on his own. When he got home that day, using his newly learned programming skills, he was able to have the computer play the hymns he had been studying in church.

We had a retired Park Service friend who spent many holidays with us. He was known by the boys as "Uncle Rob" although no relation. While visiting at Rob's place one day, Matthew became fascinated with an airplane program that Rob had purchased. Back at home, Matthew began to write an airplane program of his own. By the time he grew tired of working on it, he had designed the instrument panel of the plane and could make it look like it was headed down the runway for a takeoff! By this time we knew he was hooked on computers for life.

Matthew is now working for a government contractor on stuff we don't even want to know about.

Matthew is also working with some people who are trying to help save the "Right" whales off the eastern US coast. So many of these whales have become entangled in lobster trap ropes, that the population is now down to only about three hundred individuals. When people first started hunting them there were a thousand right whales off the Atlantic coast.

While still living in Clarkston, WA, we were on the western edge of an earthquake that began near Challis, ID, several hundred miles away. Having spent most of our lives in California, Shirley and I knew what to do. We ran into the boys' bedroom, yanked them out of bed, and told them to stand in the doorway (one of the safest places during an earthquake). I'm sure they thought we were crazy at the time. I doubt either of them knew what an earthquake was and they probably had not even felt it that morning.

Shirley and I have sat through hours of windy, cold, rainy, and snowy football games in support of Thomas and his Walla Walla High School (WA-HI) team. Sitting in those ice-cold bleachers had probably taken several years off our lives. The year after Thomas graduated from WA-HI, he and several buddies decided to go to a WA-HI football game supposedly to cheer for their former high school team. We were surprised when they were only gone about an hour before returning home. When asked why they were home so soon, they said it was "too cold to sit out there!" DUH! We thought of the many hours we had suffered through so much bad weather just to watch him play!

We came home from a trip to Hawaii one time to find that Thomas had invited a bunch of friends from town to come up to our home on Blue Creek where he had dug a hole in our backyard to use as a fire pit! Sometime later, my garden tractor lawn mower discovered one of the coat hangers they had used to roast marshmallows!

Thomas is a very compassionate person. He wanted to become a veterinarian so he could help animals. He was forever finding animals in dire need of his help. He once brought a kitten home and put it in a cage on our front porch. The poor thing was near death. By the time Shirley and I arrived home from work, there was a line of ants crawling across the kitten to get to the food Thomas had given it. Unfortunately, there was definitely one thing that was going to keep Thomas from pursuing a veterinarian degree. He could not handle "blood and guts."

We once rescued a female cat that became quite attached to Thomas. It would sleep in his bedroom and on his bed every night. When we realized she was pregnant, we told him to get a box and put rags in it for the day of delivery. However, "Kit Kat" decided to have her kittens on Thomas's pillow right next to his head while he was asleep! When we went in to wake him that morning, there were five newborn kittens on his pillow. One was born dead, so we immediately removed it. He had no idea what had happened just inches from his head.

The boys were still in grade school before we had our first real pet. The first time we saw this cat it had a gun pellet sticking out of its nose. We managed to catch her, wrap her in a towel, and while Shirley hung on to her, I pulled the pellet out with a pair of pliers. Mission accomplished, she took up residence with us. It wasn't long before that cat had kittens under our canoe in the backyard. There were two black and two gray kittens and a really ugly little white runt. We managed to give away three of the kittens, but one committed suicide under our electric garage door. We ended up keeping the "ugly runt" since no one else would take it. As time went on, that cat turned out to be a beautiful Siamese! Because of his light brown sides, we called him Smoky.

About the time Smoky was turning eight weeks old, we went to the Nez Perce County Fair in Lewiston, ID. We met a lady with a pen full of eight-week-old puppies she wanted to give away. She said they were a cross of shepherd, elkhound, and "Heinz 57 variety." We decided to let the boys pick one out to take home. She was a fluffy ball of fur at the time and showed characteristics of both a shepherd and an elkhound. We named her Sierra and promptly introduced her to Smoky. The two became best friends.

During the winter, Sierra would curl up on the deck with Smoky curled up on top of her. They spent a lot of time playing together in the backyard. Smoky would often want Sierra to play with him when she really didn't want to. So Smoky would reach up and slap Sierra with his paws (claws retracted) trying to get her interested in playing.

Eventually, Sierra would have enough. She would pick Smoky up by his head and would carry him to the farthest corner of the yard where she would unceremoniously deposit him before returning to the deck to rest undisturbed! On the way to the corner of the yard, we could hear Smoky making a muffled cat cry. Our neighbors later told us they always enjoyed watching as Sierra ended Smoky's harassment.

While the boys were still quite young, I saw a design for an outdoor jungle gym that looked like something I could build. It was mostly made of 2x4s, dowels, and some 1x2s. So over the next couple of weeks, the jungle gym began to come to life in our garage. When finished, we hauled it out to the backyard. It had a couple of "platforms" that the boys could move to different locations. It had a rope ladder that led to monkey bars. And it had a tire swing. Our boys became popular for having such a neat jungle gym in their backyard. We counted as many as fifteen kids playing on it at one time. One time some kids came over and asked if Matthew and Thomas could come out and play on the jungle gym with them. The boys weren't home right then, so they asked if they could play on it anyway.

Oh, back to the boys. It was not unusual for kids in high school to want to start watching a couple of movies at about 9:00 p.m. For some reason, Thomas and his friends seemed to prefer coming to our house to do so. Sometimes the living room noise would rise a little bit so Thomas would yell at them, "Be quiet, my parents are trying to sleep!" One young lady decided to pop some corn in our microwave. She let it run a little too long, so we had the smell of scorched popcorn in our house for the next several days.

Thomas always enjoyed a variety of sports. Through his elementary, junior high, and high school years he participated in soccer, flag football, wrestling, and eventually even tackle football. The Walla Walla High School (WA-HI) varsity football team made it to the state championships in his senior year. He was playing on the JV team at that time. His coach told the JVers that if they would continue to practice with the varsity team as they prepared for the state championship, they could go with the team to play in Seattle's Kingdome. Steve Largent of the Seahawks was Thomas's favorite football player. As it turned out Thomas got in for two plays during the game. He was wearing

Steve Largent's number 80 and was even wearing the Seahawks' colors, blue and white. While the team was riding home on a nice warm bus that night, Shirley and I were freezing to death in a Motel 6 in nearby Issaquah, WA.

Even today, Thomas keeps tabs on his favorite teams and players and occasionally takes his family to professional football and baseball games in Seattle.

We had encouraged Thomas to attend Walla Walla Community College (WWCC) for his first two years. We told him he could save a lot of money by staying at home, and all of his community college classes would be transferable to any Washington state college or university. Plus, it would be a whole lot cheaper to attend a community college. He knew we didn't know what we were talking about!

Thomas decided to attend a WWCC program during his high school senior year. It was aimed at getting students to attend locally. He came home all excited that night telling us that all of his classes would be transferable within the state, that it would be a whole lot cheaper since he could live at home, and that he could save even more of his own money by continuing to live at home! We thought that he had a great idea. However, after one year he went off to Whatcom Community College on the other side of the state at Bellingham, WA. He finished his education degree at Western Washington University in Bellingham.

As we raised our boys, we gave them a good dose of nature studies, hiking, bird watching, and just enjoying the out-of-doors. Matthew took up mountain biking while in high school and to this day he still competes in races. Matthew had a serious bike accident in Spokane just a month after graduating from high school. Not only did it mess up his bike badly, but he ended up with a broken right scapula (about the hardest bone in the body to break). It was late at night when we learned that he was in a Spokane Valley hospital, so we waited until the next morning to drive to Spokane hoping to take him home. When we arrived, he looked at us and asked, "What are you guys doing here?" I think there might have been a little bit of concussion there also! The previous night we had talked to him briefly by phone. When I asked to talk to the doctor again, he said his goodbye and hung up the phone.

I don't think he realized what I had requested. The doctor did say he should stay off his bike for a month while the shoulder healed.

At eighteen years of age, a month is a long time to stay away from your favorite pastime. We had hauled his bike to a local shop and they had it fixed in about a week. Ten days after his accident, he decided he wanted to "test" his bike to see if it was really fully repaired. That test ended up being a thirty-mile ride. Thirty days after the accident, he took third and fourth place in downhill and cross-country races, respectively, at Schweitzer Ski Resort near Sandpoint, ID.

Matthew has continued being an avid mountain bike rider and continues to compete in mountain bike races occasionally. He and his wife, Heidi, have done the Seattle to Portland (STP) ride a couple of times. That's a two-hundred-mile ride over two days.

At WA-HI, Thomas was active in wrestling and football. We made it to almost all of his wrestling matches. He was competing in a regional meet at the end of the season in Kennewick, WA, with us watching in the stands. His opponent's mom was sitting near us and kept yelling to her son to "Kill him!" We finally let her know the other wrestler was our son, so she toned it down a little. Thomas was not winning the bout and in the last round he was taken down backwards and broke his right elbow. The match was immediately stopped. We wanted to take him to a nearby emergency room, but he insisted he wanted to stay and watch the rest of the meet. Five minutes later, he asked if we could take him to the hospital to have his arm tended to. We did and the doctor saw to it that he would not be feeling any more pain the rest of the day. Whatever the doctor had given him knocked him out for the next couple of hours. I don't think he even knew Shirley and I had stopped and gotten something to eat before our hour drive home.

On 911 Day, Thomas was selling resource books door-to-door in New York City when the Twin Towers were hit by terrorists. He went to the area of the disaster to see if he could volunteer to help in any way. They actually turned him and others away because they already had too many volunteers. As usual, Americans tend to come together during times of disasters.

While at Western Washington University, Thomas met Tia Kutschia. Both were working on education degrees. Tia had also been involved with the door-to-door book sales for a couple of summers back east. Tia is very close to her family. In fact, her brother was her "bride's maid"!

Thomas has continued to work for Great American Opportunites for the past fifteen years. They are a company that helps with school fundraising events for choirs, sports teams, cheerleaders, and other school-associated organizations. He has become known as a very creative salesperson within his company. Out of over three hundred salespeople in Great American, he was ranked in the top fifteen in 2017.

Thomas and Tia, have two boys, Briley and Keller. Without a doubt, they are the sharpest and best-looking grandkids we've ever known! They are getting a good dose of outdoor experiences from their mom and dad. By the ages of eleven and thirteen, both boys had been involved in soccer, baseball, lacrosse, wrestling, and other sports. They enjoy camping, going to Hawaii every year for a few weeks, mountain biking, and occasionally visiting with Grandma and Grandpa.

Tia has definitely put her education degree to good use teaching her boys to be well-behaved young men who are eager to learn new things. Besides being a taxi driver for her boys, she is a great cook. She is currently the director of the music program in their church in Mount Vernon, WA.

When we are together, Shirley likes to help Briley and Keller make a "mystery dinner" for the whole family. They don't tell anyone else what it is they are preparing. Each boy has his own apron that Shirley has made for them. They usually spend the entire day in the kitchen making a delicious dinner for the rest of us. I always look forward to those meals.

Matthew met his future wife, Heidi, while both were attending WWCC. Heidi graduated with a BA in Psychology, Sociology, and Philosophy. Later she obtained her Master of Education degree at the University of Idaho. While serving as an elementary school counselor, she also completed a Doctor of Education in Counseling Psychology. She has a wonderful sense of humor and a great knack for telling stories of her experiences with parents and students at school. She and Matthew frequently take Briley and Keller on day excursions or weekend camping trips.

MY MOTHER—MARTHA ELIZABETH HIXSON

My mother, Martha Elizabeth Williams, was born to John Thomas and Olive L. Williams at their home near Perkins, OK, on March 17, 1921. I believe she was their sixth child, one of whom had already passed away. She had four sisters and one brother at birth, and one more brother was born later. Mama and her younger brother were born after her oldest sister started having children.

Mama's father was the local postmaster in Perkins. He used a one-horse enclosed cart to deliver mail to homes as far away as fifteen miles from town. He had two horses; one was left at a farm at the end of his route after he hitched up the horse he had left there the previous day. So each day the horses got a fifteen-mile workout.

Her mother was a stay-at-home mom who spent most of her time preparing meals, doing laundry, raising the kids, and doing all the things a mom did for their family back in those days.

Mama was raised near Perkins and attended all her schooling through high school in Perkins. I don't remember all the details of how she met my dad, but I know it was through a church friend.

While my dad was off to the Pacific Theater fighting during WWII, my mother was living with her parents in Stillwater, OK. She already had my oldest sister, Joyce, who was born in 1943. I didn't come along until October 12, 1946, the year after WWII ended. As I've mentioned elsewhere, we moved four times before I was five. My sister Mary arrived in 1951, followed by sister MyrnaLoy two years later, and brother Tom in 1955.

Mama's most memorable birth event had to have been when Tom was born. Daddy was driving her to a hospital in Fresno in our 1951 Studebaker sedan when Mama said the baby was coming. They were next to the old Starlight Theater on Fresno Street when Daddy pulled the car to the side of the road, parked, and ran around to the passenger side of the car to offer assistance. However, when he got there, Tom had already arrived. So he jumped back into the car and continued on to the hospital. Later he would try to reduce the delivery costs at the hospital since the baby arrived before they got there. Didn't work!

For the most part, Mama was a stay-at-home mom. With five kids to raise, we kept her very busy. Mama was not the best cook in the world, but she kept us well-fed. She made a lot of clothes for the girls and even made shirts for us boys occasionally. I often wore jeans that had those big iron-on knee patches to school (not really popular at that time).

The folks bought us a former Solo Concerto player piano in 1954. Although the player mechanisms had been removed, it was in good enough shape to play it. Each of us five kids eventually learned to play it. Mama made sure we practiced an hour each day (I think we did get to take off on Saturday and Sunday). Middle sister Mary may have been the smartest one of the whole bunch; to this day we all say she waited until time to do the dishes each evening for her hour of practice! She seldom had to do the dishes.

Our house was only about one thousand square feet in size, so we were pretty crowded. We had four small bedrooms, one and a half baths, a small living room, and a very small kitchen/dining area. We also had a one-car attached garage. Since it gets so hot in the San Joaquin Valley during the summer, we were very lucky to have an evaporative cooler on the roof. We often took our naps laying directly under the only vent from the cooler. Needless to say, it didn't provide nearly the amount of cool air we enjoy from our air conditioners today.

Mama and Daddy made sure we all went to church every time the doors were open. We attended the First Southern Baptist Church in Clovis about a mile from our house. If my dad had to work on a Sunday, we would walk to church. Mama would often drill us on Bible verses so we could compete in memory contests. I made it to the state finals a couple of times. I remember getting home from church one Sunday night before we realized MyrnaLoy was not with us. A quick trip back to the church revealed our youngest sister was asleep in the back row of the sanctuary!

Mama was a good singer, so she was always involved in our church choir. Several of us joined her in the choir later, and the three girls were frequently the church pianists.

Mama would occasionally help with record keeping and egg cleaning at the college poultry farm. Eventually most of us kids also got to participate in these activities. I think we all enjoyed helping out when Daddy was banding day-old chicks just coming out of the incubators.

I do remember Mama working at the FSC fruit packing shed one summer. They were packing mostly peaches for shipping to markets and fruit stands. She also worked with a lady who did re-upholstering of furniture. She got pretty good at this.

There were two times when we took in kids from parents who were divorcing. At one time, it seemed we had bunk beds everywhere. Despite the additional kids to care for, Mama kept us all fed and properly clothed.

We did not have an enclosed yard when I was growing up, so pets were pretty much out of the question. However, a stray terrier showed up at our place one time and I was allowed to keep it. We played a lot of cowboys and Indians in those days, so Mama made me a pair of chaps out of some burlap gunny sacks. I would wear them with my gun belt, cap pistol, and my cowboy hat. Thought I was really cool like my favorite cowboy at that time, Hopalong Cassidy. Unfortunately, after only a few days of getting to have a pet, the terrier attacked me and started tearing the chaps off me. My mother took that much more seriously than I did and insisted we had to get rid of the dog. I was heartbroken over the loss of my brand-new pet.

Mama had epilepsy from her early childhood. She was prescribed phenobarbital for most of her life to help control the seizures that usually accompanied epilepsy. It was not until very late in her life that her doctors decided that was not such a good medication for her. Thankfully, I never saw her have a seizure.

Mama began showing signs of some form of dementia as she progressed into her eighties. She and Daddy moved into a retirement home for several years before she had to be admitted to a 24/7 care facility.

It was very sad watching her change during her last few years. At Christmas time, Daddy would share all the recent Christmas cards that he had received so she could look at them. She would pick one up, read it, and set it aside. She would do that until all of the cards were stacked beside her in a neat little pile. After a while, she would notice the cards and start going through them again having no idea she had already seen them all. About the third time she would start to go through them, Daddy would take them away from her and tell her she had already seen them all. At least she seemed to be happy while looking at the cards both the first and second time.

When we would go to Fresno to visit the folks, Daddy had his own apartment in a retirement home. We would take Daddy to see Mama at her care facility. For two years she either called me Floyd (my dad) or Tom (my brother). She never once called me by my name. I just let it go as I know she at least recognized me as part of the family. One day when we went to see her, as she was walking (with her walker) down the hall toward us, she looked at me and said, "Phillip Lynn, what are you doing here?" That was the first time in two years she had called me by my name.

The weekend before Mama passed away, hospice had told us she had only a few days to live. One cousin, the five of us kids, and my dad surrounded her bed on a Sunday morning and sang some of her favorite hymns. MyrnaLoy had an app on her phone that allowed her to pull up numerous hymns, so we sang for about two hours. While singing "Shall We Gather at the River," I could see her lips moving as she was trying to sing with us.

Later a hospice nurse told us Mama had not eaten nor had anything to drink the last seventeen days of her life. When one of us would try to get her to at least suck on a damp washcloth, she would merely turn away from it. She may not have known what was coming, but it was clear that her body knew she was at the end of her life. Mama died five days before she and Daddy would have celebrated their seventieth wedding anniversary.

About thirty years later, we were visiting Philipp, our Swiss exchange student in Switzerland. He took us to meet his parents one evening. His mother's name was Elisabeth Martha Maeder! Just the reverse of my mother's first two names with an "s" in place of the "z."

AN EVENTFUL AFTERNOON IN NORFOLK, VA

I really didn't get to know Bob Rawson very well until that fateful day in Norfolk, VA. Both of us were chiefs of natural resources management in our respective districts. We had attended a Corps of Engineers Real Estate and Natural Resources Management Conference in Norfolk, VA, that ended earlier on the last day than we had anticipated. So Bob, two other attendees, and I decided to head on out to the airport to see if we could catch an earlier flight to our homes on the West Coast.

No such luck; so we hunkered down to await our late afternoon flight to Seattle. As we waited, we noticed the thunderstorm outside intensifying and no flights seemed to be coming or going. About the time of our late afternoon flight (4:00 p.m.), they announced our plane was up in the air so long, it had to divert to Richmond, VA, to refuel. It was not until 6:00 p.m. that we finally boarded our plane in a heavy downpour. The geese at the side of the runway didn't seem to mind the rain as they grazed on the infield grasses.

As we lifted off the runway, about a hundred feet in the air, there was an explosion on the left side of the plane and the cabin immediately filled with a smell of burnt wiring. The plane was full and we were climbing steeply when the pilot announced that we had apparently sucked a bird through the number two engine. He said he had shut down that engine and we would circle the airport and land. I was hoping we had at least two engines on the plane that were still functioning.

We didn't hear anything more from the pilot until just moments before we landed. I'll always remember his exact words: "You may notice a number of fire trucks along the tarmac as we land, but everything's . . ." That sentence was not finished and we never heard from the pilot again, not even after we landed. Yes, there were fire trucks along both sides of the runway! No, thank goodness they were not needed.

After a safe and smooth landing, we disembarked and were told to line up to reschedule a flight for the next day. While in line, Bob got the splendid idea to go call the government travel agency to reschedule. So, I held our place in line while he did so. When he got back, I went off and did the same thing. By the time we got to the desk, they merely had to print off some new tickets and return our luggage to us.

Our next action was to find a motel near the airport. A short taxi ride in the continuing downpour got us there quickly. It was then after 8:00 p.m., so once we got checked in and settled into our room, we decided eating dinner would be a nice thing to do. Even though there was a restaurant less than a hundred yards away, it was raining so hard that we decided we weren't going to risk drowning just to get dinner. So, as a backup, we ordered a couple of pizzas to be delivered to us at the motel.

While eating our pizza, we were watching the evening news. That's when we discovered that a tornado had actually hit the downtown area of Norfolk earlier in the afternoon while we were sitting in relative safety in the airport terminal awaiting our flight. Fortunately, we were able to fly out to Seattle early the next morning with no further incidents.

MY DAD—DR. FLOYD M. HIXSON

My dad's parents were Ovie Faubush and Lola Mary Ann Hixson of Holdenville, OK. He was the second of two sons they had. Their other son, Donald, was about three years older than my dad. Unfortunately, Ovie and Lola divorced before my dad was born.

Floyd Marcus Hixson, my dad, was born in Holdenville, OK, on May 15, 1918, around the time WWI was taking off. He never met his father who was killed in a car accident at the age of forty-one. He later learned that friends had known when Ovie came to town once, but for some reason they didn't think Floyd should meet him.

Lola later married Homer Christy and had several more children. But when my dad was three years old, she "gave" him to her mother. So Floyd lived with his grandmother until she passed away while he was in junior high school. He was then taken in by his neighbors, the Van Hoosers who lived next door. By the time he graduated, his brother Don had his own apartment in Holdenville, so he allowed my dad to live with him. Floyd attended Holdenville Business College for one year.

About this time, he met Martha Elizabeth Williams at a Baptist Young Adult meeting in Oklahoma. Although Martha lived about one

My Dad—Dr. Floyd M. Hixson

hundred miles away in Perkins, OK, they began to see each other. Floyd once rode his single-speed, "balloon tire" bike all the way to Perkins to see her. He managed to catch a ride with someone for the return trip home.

While growing up in Holdenville, someone gave him some chickens to raise. When deciding what he wanted to major in when he went to Stillwater, OK, to attend Oklahoma A&M, he opted for a major in poultry husbandry. He graduated with a BS in 1941. On October 25 of that year, he and Martha married.

Floyd had just started working on a master's degree when he was drafted into the US Army. He served in the Ninetieth Infantry Division until he was sent to Officer's Candidate School. Upon completion, he was made a First Lieutenant and sent to the Thirty-third Infantry Division at Fort Lewis, in Washington. His unit trained in the Mojave Desert of California. He would later serve in Hawaii, New Guinea, Indonesia, and the Philippines. His last nine months of active duty were served in Japan after the Japanese surrendered. His job was to destroy Japanese military equipment. He remained in the US Army Reserve until 1951. I remember going with him to his reserve barracks for some of his assignments. The place always smelled of canvas and other military equipment.

Floyd was able to move our family to Manhattan, Kansas, after the war. He started working on a master's degree in poultry husbandry at Kansas State University (KSU) while teaching several classes. He returned to Oklahoma A&M for about sixteen months before returning to KSU where he taught while he finished his master's degree. In 1951, he was hired to teach in the Agricultural Department at FSC where he taught for the next twenty-nine years. Before heading to Fresno, he had begun working on a doctorate in Genetics. While teaching, supporting a family, and being very active in our church, he managed to complete his doctorate in about nine years. He was the first professor in the Fresno State Agriculture Department to have earned a PhD.

College professors may have had highly respected positions, but they certainly weren't paid very well. So, with five kids, a stay-at-home wife, and often helping other kids afford to go to college, he managed to provide us a good home, clothes, and enough food to keep us healthy.

The girls even got braces; that wasn't important for boys in those days even though we could have used them.

We always only had one car as my dad was the only one who could drive. The first car I vaguely remember was a little Crosley. Just before we moved to Fresno, he bought a blue 1951 Studebaker. That's what we moved in from Kansas to Fresno. Fortunately, there was only my older sister, a brand new baby sister, and me to occupy the back seat. Seat belts hadn't been invented yet! We actually had a wooden bench between the front and back seats that allowed us to turn the back seat area into a makeshift bed.

In 1956, Daddy (as we always called him) came home driving a two-door white Ford Ranch Wagon (station wagon). That first evening he had my mother drive it down to the end of our block and back. That is the only time I ever saw her attempt to drive a car.

His next car would be a 1960 Studebaker Lark station wagon. He is the only person I have ever known who had owned two Studebakers. It was just a few years later that Studebaker quit producing cars. On one of our summer trips to visit my grandparents in Perkins, our engine "blew up" just as we were approaching Needles, CA. Seems we had to wait several days for a repair.

The big surprise was when he brought home a brand new bright red Dodge Dart, a four-speed, four-on-the-floor sedan sometime in 1964. It looked nothing like a family car. More like what a teenager would have wanted back then. I was driving by then, so I kind of liked its flashy look. The four-on-the-floor was really cool too! We all remember the day he brought it home as that very night he discovered the front doors had a very sharp frame around the glass. As he was opening the door, that sharp point caught him on the chin—he carried that scar the rest of his life.

When I went away to college, my dad bought a 1965 red Datsun pickup for me to drive while away at school. Wasn't near as "sexy" or flashy as the Dodge, but it was a set of wheels that I sorely needed. That brand-new truck, having just arrived from Japan, cost him a whopping $1,599.00! Most people had never even seen a Datsun pickup so it was interesting when people tried to pronounce it. Old men in town would stand around and discuss its size, shape, its probable gas mileage, and whether or not they thought this model would ever catch on here in the states. That little truck got me through the first couple of years of college. When we were finally able to afford a new vehicle, Shirley and I passed the little Datsun on to my middle sister and her husband who were attending college in San Jose. That's enough about vehicles.

Daddy had a very strong work ethic and he passed that on to each of us kids. He was often up and gone in the morning before any of us kids were up. He had the poultry department to run at the college and he had classes to prepare for. He often spent Saturdays working on the college poultry farm.

Floyd was also very active in the life of our church. On Sundays, he usually taught adult Sunday school classes. He served as chairman of the deacons for many years at our little church in Clovis. For ten years, he served on the Board of Trustees for Golden Gate Baptist Theological Seminary near San Francisco, CA. The California Baptist Foundation was based in Fresno and he served on their board for a number of years. He was also active with the Gideons who provide Bibles and New Testaments to many organizations. He served as chaplain for the local Veterans of Foreign Wars Post in Fresno.

My dad never sat down and talked about his time in the Army, but church friends would frequently come over on Sunday nights and the folks would play board games with them. Occasionally, he would tell his adult friends stories of the war. If we were in the living room, we could hear them. We could tell it was not a fun time in his life, but for four years as he moved around the Pacific, he carried out his infantry duties. On one occasion, he ended up in a hospital with yellow fever. He was presented a Bronze Star for his service.

Dr. Hixson was always helping various college students financially so they could continue their studies. I mentioned earlier that he had hired Shirley to do some paper filing at his office and paid her out of his own pocket to do so. He hired other college-age men and women to do work at the poultry unit, or directly provided finances to help with their college expenses. In 2011, a perpetual scholarship was named in his honor by the CSUF Agriculture Department.

Because of his commitment to his college and church work, Daddy didn't spend a lot of time with us kids. I was always happy when he got home from work early enough to toss a football or softball around with us. When I was in fourth grade, I had mentioned that I was the only boy who did not have a mitt when we played softball. He showed up at the school fence beside our house one morning and handed me a brand-new mitt! As I mentioned earlier, we didn't have a lot of money to spend on such things, so I wasn't too surprised to see it did not even have the lacing to hold the fingers together like all the other mitts had. But I was so happy to at least have my own mitt. I still have that mitt.

We had lived in Clovis for about six years before Daddy discovered his mother was living six miles from us in Fresno. Every once in a while, he would take us over to her house to visit Grandma and Grandpa Christy. We kids hated to go there. They had lived through the depression, so they had learned to live with a single twenty-five-watt bulb in the living room lamp. They never had any treats for us kids and they seldom even spoke directly to us. It was just a sad, depressing place to visit.

California passed a law that required the children of elderly people to pay for their parent's welfare if they were financially able to do so. Although several of Daddy's siblings who were actually raised by Grandma Christy lived in California at the time, my dad was the only one ordered by the state to pay her welfare because he had the highest income. He did so for some time before friends convinced him to challenge that order since she gave him away at the age of three and never cared for him ever again. The state finally decided he no longer had to pay for her welfare.

I actually sang "Rock of Ages" at Grandpa Christy's funeral. I don't believe they attended any church, so I was surprised when one of my dad's stepbrothers asked me to sing that song. My heart really wasn't in it as I didn't really care much for him or his wife. I only did it for my dad. A few years later as Grandma Christy was lying in a bed in a Fresno hospital, slowly dying, my dad and I went to visit her. By then her mental state was not so good. She ranted and raved, cussed at my dad and called him the devil! If I could have, I would have immediately removed her intravenous tubes. My dad didn't openly share his emotions at that time, but I know it really hurt him. Here was the woman who gave him birth, then gave him away for someone else to raise, and was calling him names and showing great hatred toward him. Fortunately, she was soon out of our lives.

On a brighter note, when Shirley accepted my proposal, we went to my dad and borrowed about $200 to purchase engagement and wedding rings, he did so quite happily. My oldest sister Joyce had been up from Riverside to visit the folks so my mother was seeing her off at the Fresno Bus Terminal. We were able to catch them both and announce our engagement to them. The Fresno Bus Terminal is not exactly an elegant place to be announcing an engagement!

Since my dad was the only one who drove for the eleven years we made our annual trips to Oklahoma, he wanted to just drive straight through as quickly as we could get there. We usually left home in Clovis at midnight so we could cross the Mojave Desert before the hottest part of the day hit us. I was always happy to see the forests as we approached Williams, AZ. Besides being prettier than the desert, it tended to be a little cooler.

Daddy was not much into tourism, so our trips were kept pretty much in line with the shortest route between two points. To our surprise, he did take a detour off Route 66 at Flagstaff, AZ, and drove us up to Grand Canyon National Park. We went right to Yavapai Point, jumped out of the car, and spent about fifteen minutes staring down into the canyon, then piled right back into the car and headed back to Route 66.

On another occasion, we had visited our aunt and uncle in Houston, TX, so we were driving home on I-10. We had been begging Daddy to take us to Mexico so we could say we had been there. At El Paso, TX, he drove across the Rio Grande River at Ciudad Juarez. We had to stop at the border control station on the US side of the bridge. They waved us on through with no problems. At the other end of the bridge, Daddy turned around and drove back across the bridge. We were back at the border control station before the guard got settled back into his seat inside the station. That was the extent of our "excursion" into Mexico!

While at my grandparents in Oklahoma, my dad would spend a lot of time at the OSU library doing research for his PhD. On several occasions, he would travel further east to attend poultry conferences or workshops. When I was about eleven years old he asked me if I wanted to go with him to Iowa State University in Ames. I loved to travel, so it took me all of about two seconds to say, "Yes!"

On the drive to Ames, Iowa, we were going to take a route that would allow us to see the northwest corner of Iowa. However, we were hearing warnings of possible tornadoes in that area, so we took a more direct route diagonally across the state to Ames. We did the northwest part of the state when we returned to Oklahoma. That's when we discovered large swaths of cornfields where a tornado had stripped everything to the ground.

While in Ames, Daddy was in classes all day, so I was left on my own to explore the city. I found a really neat swinging bridge across the Skunk River that flowed through town. It had a nice park associated with it, so I spent much of the day hanging out there. Other times I would just roam the streets of Ames somewhat aimlessly.

We generally had breakfast together at a diner early in the morning. For lunch, I was on my own. I found a hamburger stand in town where I could get a burger, fries, and a drink for about a buck, so that's what I did every day for lunch. On the last day of Daddy's meetings, the session organizers had a closing dinner session. That was the biggest and best-tasting food I had eaten all week. It was nice to have something besides a burger and fries. On our way back to my grandparents, we stopped to visit a cousin in Owasa, OK. Would you believe they served us barbecued hamburgers for dinner that night? I figured out I had eaten about a dozen burgers that week. I was really ready for some of my mom's and grandma's healthy, homestyle cooking by the time we got back to Perkins.

THE BLUE CREEK FLOOD OF '96

Before moving to assume my new job as Chief of Natural Resources Management in Walla Walla, WA, I thought the only place to live was in town, in the middle of a wheat field, or in an onion patch. However, when I started talking to realtors, I discovered there might be a fourth option—live in the Blue Mountains just a few miles east of town. In fact, we found an undeveloped plot of ten acres that was just begging us to move there. It had about two acres of flat ground for our home, eight acres of a steep hillside covered in brush and evergreens (mostly yellow pines), and a creek.

We ended up purchasing a new manufactured home. In preparation, we had to build a road to our site on an easement across the lot to the west of us. We drilled a 325-foot deep well, brought in power and phone lines, developed a septic system, and cleared the house site of tons of dead and downed brush and trees. The home manufacturer agreed to flip the house plan so that our main view was looking east up Blue Creek Canyon.

We have many wonderful memories of living along Blue Creek. We saw a wide variety of wildlife including deer, elk, bear, turkeys, quail, and lots of other bird species. The creek generally flowed lazily along the south side of our house. It was usually a pleasant sound that lulled us to sleep when we had our windows opened at night during the warmer months.

Our winters were quite cold with snow from November to March. February in the Blue Mountains of Washington and Oregon can unleash quite a variety of weather patterns. One February, when temperatures reached 70°F, I wheeled the barbecue out of the garage and set about producing the first barbecued Hawaiian burgers (barbecued pineapple ring on top) of the year outside on our sunny deck.

However, February would also be the coldest and wettest month in most years. The year '96, although atypical in many ways, will serve to illustrate what I mean. It actually started at the end of January when the temperature dipped to −10°F. It remained at that temperature, or very close to it, day and night for the next seven days while snow began to deepen across the Blue Mountains of southeastern Washington. The accumulation finally reached about eighteen inches of snow on the ground at our home. In the meantime, the ground beneath the snow had frozen solid.

Then, on a Tuesday morning of February 6, with the arrival of a warm Chinook wind coming down from Canada, the temperatures shot up to 67°F in just a couple of hours and it started to rain. It didn't rain just a little bit, it poured down hard and steadily for the next three days.

At first, most of the rain was absorbed by the snowpack. However, due to the warmer temperatures, the snow started to melt rather rapidly. Since the ground was frozen, all the water could do was run off into the nearest creek. Blue Creek, about a hundred feet from our house started to rise rapidly.

I was at work when I began receiving reports of potential flooding in the canyons near our home, so about noon, I went home to check on our house. Sure enough, the creek was quite muddy and running fast. To my surprise, it was rising rapidly and moving through the riparian vegetation along Blue Creek.

Our neighbor's daughter was in town and had no way of getting home, so I volunteered to go get her. I also wanted to have Shirley follow me home from her teaching job just to make sure she made it home safely. By the time we left Walla Walla, the sheriff had already established roadblocks to keep people from driving into a potentially dangerous flooded area. I had just talked to the county sheriff before heading for town and he had assured me we would be allowed to get back to our home. I explained this to the man at the roadblock and he let us through.

By the time we arrived home, the creek was completely over its banks and was gradually engulfing the meadow between our neighbor's and our house. Our neighbor, Donna, and her daughter joined us at our house since they could not easily get to their house. Blue Creek flowed straight across our property, then took a slight bend to the north and aimed directly at their house. Donna had an older station wagon that they had parked a short distance down the hill from their garage but not quite in the meadow between our houses. As the afternoon progressed and the creek kept rising, we saw the tires of the car go underwater; a short time later the hood disappeared followed soon by the disappearance of the windshield. By mid-afternoon, the entire car was underwater.

Later that same day, we noticed a large tree carried downstream by the rushing waters had become hung up in the berry vines and alders along our portion of Blue Creek just about straight south of our house. This tree soon became a dam as it collected all the other brush and debris that was being carried along by the creek. It eventually caused the water to move out of its original bed as it began creeping through our riparian zone and heading for our backyard. Normally, the creek was about fifteen feet lower than the floor of our house. But that elevation was beginning to diminish rapidly.

That night the rain continued unabated. By this time the ground was beginning to thaw allowing it to soak up some of the runoff. However, it continued to rain so hard that the runoff kept increasing. We stayed home from work on Wednesday to keep an eye on things in case we needed to evacuate.

When friends would call, we would hold the phone up to a window and let them listen. They would say it sounded like a train going by. Yes, it certainly did. It was quite eerie at night to lie in bed and hear the roar of the creek, as well as the boulders thumping as they bounced down the rocky creek bed! Our normally "quiet little creek" had become the dominant sound in the canyon.

A local reporter called that day and was asking about conditions on Blue Creek. While talking to her, I noticed four deer entering the water from our backyard. They were intent on swimming the creek and climbing the hill on the other side. I watched as each deer gradually made it across the creek, but not before they had been swept downstream at least a hundred yards.

The rains continued to come for a second night and into the third day. As we were getting up on Thursday morning, we felt and heard a noise not unlike a semi-truck driving by. Later that day, we discovered it was the first, and perhaps the largest of many landslides we would hear and feel. One small landslide came off the hill to the north of us just above our garage. Fortunately, it stopped at the road about sixty feet above us. Another one came down the hill just above the house and it too stopped at the road. We later realized that after the snow had melted and the ground had thawed, the waters seeping into the ground would eventually hit a rock base that enabled the slippery mud on top to slide off into the canyon below. Many of those landslide scars are still visible today.

Thursday night, the rains seemed to intensify. After dark, we began to hear and feel more landslides, but we were unable to determine where the sounds were coming from. At the same time, the waters that had moved across our backyard had finally reached the corner of the foundation of our house and the garage. Luckily we had moved our dogs into the garage before their chain-link kennel was totally swept away by the rising waters.

At about 3:30 Friday morning, I awakened Thomas, our high school-aged son, and Shirley (I have no idea how they could sleep given the circumstances—it must have been sheer exhaustion!) and told them we were going to have to leave since the waters were getting so close to the house and we couldn't predict if the next landslide would hit us or not. We made some quick arrangements with friends in town, loaded the dogs in the back of our faithful '69 Chevy pickup, and headed for town. As we got to the top of our driveway, we encountered a landslide that had just come down across the road. I said, "We're either going to drive right through this, or we're walking to town!" Somehow that old Chevy got us through the foot-deep mud! We dropped Thomas and the dogs off at some friends and Shirley and I headed to another friend's house for the rest of the night.

On Friday morning, the rains ceased and the waters immediately began to recede toward their original creek beds, or to new channels that had been carved during the high flows. I returned to work that day and Shirley was able to return to the house. My office sits right next to Mill Creek, the channel Blue Creek flows into a couple of miles downstream of our house. As I walked by its concrete-lined channel, it smelled like freshly turned soil in a farm field. The silt load of the many creeks eventually pouring into the Walla Walla River was so high, forty acres of new land was added at the mouth of the Walla Walla River where it flowed into the Columbia River.

We discovered a very different look of the canyon upon our return home. Blue Creek had changed its course in some places and the steep sides of the canyon were scarred where landslides had dropped into the canyon. We now had about one and a half feet of silt piled up in a large crescent shape in our backyard. Our riparian zone was devoid of blackberries and willows and many of the cottonwoods and alders were down. Over the next two years, we would lose over thirty-six alders due to the subsoil structure having changed (this kept them from getting the amount of moisture they needed). We had large boulders all through the riparian area. Just off the south end of our house, the fast-flowing waters had cut a large "V" in the ground about ten feet deep and extending to thirty feet wide at the downstream end.

When we constructed our home, we had surveyed to make sure it would always be high and dry. The floor of our house is fifteen feet above the normal flow of Blue Creek and we were across the canyon a hundred feet. Even at that, the creek still reached the southeast corner of the house foundation. Fortunately, it did not get into the house. We only ended up with about a foot of water under the house in our four-foot crawl space.

A couple of neighbors who grew up in Blue Creek Canyon said this was the worst they had ever seen. The previous high flows had been recorded during the flood of '64. A prior flood in '31 prompted the City of Walla Walla to ask the Corps of Engineers to build an off-stream storage dam on Mill Creek to protect the city from future flooding. That structure did its job of keeping Walla Walla safe in '96.

While some of our kennel chain-link panels were found downstream and salvageable, some were never seen again. The doghouse was damaged beyond repair. Our only other casualty was our canoe that we stored next to the house; it was gone.

We hired our friend, Larry, to come out with his road grader to begin restoring the riparian zone so that it would again provide a good buffer between the creek and our house. I used my little garden tractor with a scraper attachment to start removing the tons of silt from the backyard. This was a long process as I could only work the soil after it had dried on the surface for a few days. If I got below the dried zone, the little tractor immediately sank into the still muddy silt below. After a couple of weeks, I was able to get most of the silt off the backyard.

A few days after the flood waters receded, our neighbor to the west of us informed me that our canoe was over at their place. Her husband had built a small walk bridge across the creek when they built their home. The floodwaters caused that bridge to collapse and it managed to snare our canoe beneath it.

After the flood, we found sports equipment in the creek bed and soon discovered it belonged to an upstream neighbor who had stored his family's sports equipment in a small shed next to the creek. The shed and equipment were no longer there. A few weeks later, while walking along the creek, I spied an especially shiny, smooth, round black rock in the water. A closer study of this rock revealed its true identity: it was a bowling ball from the neighbor's equipment shed.

We were also the recipients of an upstream neighbor's bridge support logs. They're still out by the creek. Due to the large nails in them, we chose not to try to saw them up with a chainsaw.

The large tree that originally started the dam on our portion of the creek turned out to be a sixty-foot-long red fir complete with its root wad still attached. We managed to sell the tree for $200. We kept the root wad and used it for our streamside campfire backdrop.

We heard FEMA was in the area to assess damages and see what they could do to help. We filled out the requisite forms and were soon reimbursed for our costs to clean up the riparian zone.

A week or so after the flood, I was using a garden hose to clean up the outside of the house foundation. All of a sudden I had no water flow. I crawled under the house and discovered that mud from the water that had seeped under the house had clogged our water pump toggle switch so that it could no longer fill our water tanks. The money we got from the sale of the red fir just about took care of the cost of replacing the damaged switch.

Eleven years after the flood in 2007, the blackberries and willows had come back with a vengeance. We had the biggest crop of blackberries and the largest berries we had seen in years—perfect for making berry cobblers. The alders had also returned along the creek bank. Some were already approaching twenty feet in height.

The ponds our neighbor had built prior to the flood had attracted ducks to the area, but after the flood the ponds were gone, having been filled in with river rocks and silt. The neighbors' deck was spared by only four inches of soil that didn't erode away from supporting posts. The creek now flows straight across her property instead of meandering across it.

The Confederated Tribes of the Umatilla Indian Reservations (CTUIR) and the state Natural Resources Conservation Service (NRCS) approached our two nearest downstream neighbors with the idea of granting a conservation easement so they could "restore" the creek. I decided to ask them what they would do on our stretch of the creek. When they described how they would create some bends in the creek bed and plant vegetation, I decided I didn't want a meander like the one next door that had aimed the creek directly at the neighbors' house. Being a biologist and a natural resources manager, I also explained to them that restoring a stream in the middle of the length of the creek was a bad idea. You have to restore the upper reaches first in hopes of holding back more water and slowing the flow before it reaches our elevation. Then you can gradually continue to restore the area downstream.

The CTUIR and NRCS proceeded with their restoration projects. They dug some pools in the creek and placed logs across the creek to keep boulders from filling them in. They also planted a number of riparian trees and shrubs along the creek. They actually came out to water these plants periodically. Unfortunately, the floodwaters had washed most of the fine soils out of the river gravels, so most of the vegetation did not survive. It only took a few high-flow episodes in the spring for the pools to fill in with silt.

In the meantime, our riparian zone had pretty much returned to its pre-flood conditions. The alders are younger and there are more of them, but they'll thin out as they age. The willows are thriving right alongside the blackberries. It would be so easy to forget what the flood of '96 did to the land. That's why it is important to pass this kind of information on to the next generation of people living here so they can be prepared for such an event in the future as history shows there are likely to be more floods in the years to come.

THE PIZZA CHRONICLES AND VERMONT'S PIZZA-EATIN' MOUNTAIN MAN

To my best recollection, pizza parlors were just taking off in California when I was in high school. I ate my first pizza at Me-n-Ed's Pizza Parlor in Sunnyside, one of the ritzy areas of northeast Fresno. While it was a pleasant experience, I was definitely not hooked on pizza during that first encounter.

While in college, some of my friends and I would occasionally, but not frequently, visit a pizza parlor in Riverside, CA. What I remember most about those pizza encounters was saving a cold slice or two for breakfast in my dorm room the next morning.

When Shirley and I married, we were poor college students who could seldom afford to eat out. On rare occasions, we would splurge by eating at a Happy Steak. Pizzas were seldom part of our diet at that time.

While working at Lava Beds National Monument during the summers of 1970–1973, we would make weekly treks to Klamath Falls, OR, to do our grocery shopping. It was there we encountered our first Abbey's Pizza Parlor. Several times each summer we would indulge in a pizza while in town.

It really wasn't until we had our two boys, Matthew and Thomas, that we started frequenting a local Abbey's Pizza Parlor in Clarkston, WA. This was where we finally got "hooked" on pizza. Still, we only hit Abbey's about once every couple of months. Eventually, the Fazzari brothers from Walla Walla purchased Abbey's and aptly named it Fazzari's Pizza. They made the best pizzas in the Lewiston/Clarkston Valley.

Shirley decided to surprise me on one of my birthdays by making my absolutely favorite food: a cherry cream cheese pie. But first, we were going to take the boys out for pizza at a parlor we had only heard about but had never visited. Village Inn Pizza in Lewiston, ID, was just across the Snake River from Clarkston, WA. We heard they showed cartoons and old-time Laurel and Hardy movies for the kids. They also had a little merry-go-round for the kids. These things sounded like a good diversion for the boys while waiting for our pizza. However, the wait became more of a distraction than anything else.

The boys were about three and six at that time, so the diversions were a good thing for them. I ordered our pizza and we began a forty-minute wait. Each customer is given a number for their order, so all you have to do is let the kids play while you wait for the cooks to call your number. I noticed that they kept calling numbers well beyond our number "42." When I went back up to the order counter to inquire about our pizza, I was told they forgot to make it! So, they would get right on it.

About a half hour later, they started calling for customer "43." They called that number several times, so I thought I had better check and see if they really meant number "42." No, they really had made a number "43," not a number "42." We had left home at about 5:00 p.m. with two hungry little boys and two adults who were getting hungrier by the minute. I calmly explained to the cook that they had made the wrong pizza and since it was getting later and later, I asked to have our money back so we could go somewhere else to eat that night. The person behind the counter never apologized; he just gave us our money and sent us on our way.

So, why not go to our old favorite Fazzari's over in Clarkston? We knew the service there was good, so we could feed the boys, go home and have a piece of cherry cream cheese pie, and put them in bed. We ordered our pizza and sat down to wait. The boys liked to climb up on the little stairway that afforded them a view into the kitchen where the cooks were building pizzas then sliding them into and out of the oven on one of those long wooden spatulas.

After a while, we noticed people coming in behind us already getting their pizzas and sitting down to devour them. Finally, after a much longer than normal wait and long after the boys were becoming restless, I approached the order counter and inquired about our pizza. The person let out a gasp and told me they had accidentally burned our pizza and had forgotten to remake it! I could not believe what was happening. We were obviously destined to NOT eat pizza that night. I explained to the order person what had happened previously that evening and again asked for my money back so we could take the boys home to get them something to eat. They profusely apologized and gave our money back along with a coupon for a free pizza on a future visit.

Three hours after leaving home, we returned, got the boys something to eat along with a piece of that cherry cream cheese pie, and ushered them off to bed. To this day, I've never needed to ask for my money back at any restaurant again, and yet, I had to do it twice in one night!

There was also a "take it home and cook it yourself" pizza place in town (also owned by the Fazzari brothers) that made an apple and cheese pizza. That became a special pizza we would purchase occasionally as a dessert entre. It soon became one of our favorites.

We moved to Walla Walla, WA, in 1992 and discovered a local Pizza Hut that seemed to be fairly popular. By this time, Matthew was attending Walla Walla Community College and Thomas was attending WA-HI. So every once in a while, Shirley and I would visit Pizza Hut after work. It was not "cool" for a high schooler to be seen eating out with his parents, so it was usually just the two of us. We usually had some leftover pizza to take home with us, however Shirley and I seldom ever saw it again.

The Walla Walla Pizza Hut is where our real pizza saga begins. We discovered the "Meat Lovers' Pizza" which we liked to top with black olives, bell peppers, and mushrooms, but no onions. We usually ordered a large pizza so we would have some leftovers to take home. Well, it seems that restaurant had problems making the exact pizza we ordered. We've now lost track of all the "free" pizzas we've received there due to their inability to deliver what we asked for. We didn't try to make things difficult; in fact, we generally ordered the same thing every time.

Over the years, we have been presented with pizzas that had onions (that we did not want) on them. Another time they forgot the black olives. When I pointed this out to our waitress, she offered to bring us some olives that we could sprinkle on our pizza. I pointed out that cold olives on a hot pizza really wasn't the same, so she had them bake another one for us.

One classic incident involved our "Meat Lovers" order. It arrived and we attacked it. However, after a couple of bites, Shirley said she wasn't tasting any meat. Sure enough, there was no meat on this "Meat Lovers" pizza! The veggies we ordered were all there, but nothing else! Yes, we got another free pizza that night and they included the meat.

We estimate we've received about a dozen free pizzas at that same restaurant due to their inability to prepare what we requested which was almost always the "Meat Lovers' Pizza" topped with black olives, bell peppers, and mushrooms. It has now become a joke with us when we go to a Pizza Hut anywhere to satisfy our pizza appetite. One of us always asks what we can do to get a free pizza this time, not that we have ever done anything ourselves to get one free. We're usually not surprised to find they've done something wrong, and many times we don't even have to point it out. More often than not, they would send us home with the first pizza that was made incorrectly. That always delighted our boys as they were less picky about what was on their pizzas.

One Tuesday at lunchtime was a classic example of what can happen totally unexpectedly. This particular restaurant has a pizza buffet at lunchtime each day. However, with my Type II diabetes, we decided to order our old standby and forego the "all you can eat" buffet. From where I was seated, I could see the place where the cooks placed the pizzas under heat lamps while they were awaiting delivery by the waitresses. One waitress would pick up the pizzas made for the buffet and take them to the heated serving table. I finally saw a pizza that looked about like what we had ordered, but the serving table waitress snatched it up and quickly delivered it to the buffet.

A couple of minutes later, I observed our waitress in a confused exchange with the cooks who insisted they had already made our pizza and had set it out for her to deliver. It took them a minute or so to discover the buffet waitress had "confiscated" it and served it up to the buffet customers. Well, this time we didn't get a free pizza, but since it was going to be a while before they could make us a new pizza, they let us hit the salad bar for free. We really thought we had encountered all the goof-ups they could perform, but here was one we had never even dreamed possible. Now we're wondering how they can creatively come up with a new way to mess up our order on our next visit.

In February, March, and April of 2015, we took a road trip through several of Utah's Red Rock National Parks and Arizona's Grand Canyon National Park. While in Flagstaff, AZ, we arrived at our motel rather late in the evening so we thought we would have a light dinner that night. We decided to hunt up the nearest Pizza Hut and order a small pizza. We placed our order and began a lengthy wait. Finally, our waitress came to our table and explained that the cook had not put enough oil on the pan, so our pizza was stuck to the pan. They soon brought us the pizza we had ordered. Yup, it was a new way to get a free pizza and an apology!

A couple of months later, we were taking another road trip to the East Coast to attend a Timeshare Board Members Association (TBMA) meeting in Providence, Rhode Island. We took Highway 2 from Newport, WA, all the way to Sault Saint Marie, MI, then drove the northern route through Ontario, Canada, before dropping back down into the States. Our first night out we made it to Cut Bank, Montana. Since there was a Pizza Hut just across the parking lot from our motel, we decided to amble over there for dinner. You aren't going to believe this. They forgot to put some of the meat on our pizza, so while they let us munch away on the first one they were already cooking one that had all the correct ingredients. We paid for one, but the other was free. At least we had a meal already prepared for the next day.

We occasionally stopped at the Walla Walla Pizza Hut on the way home from work. We were surprised on one such stop when one of Shirley's former students from her days as a home ec teacher at Garrison Middle School in Walla Walla was our waitress. The young lady took our order and headed toward the kitchen. A short while later, she returned to our table and asked if Shirley was her former home ec teacher. Shirley replied that she was. The young lady then began to apologize for her behavior in the classroom years before. The young waitress said she was probably the "horriblest" student Shirley ever had. Shirley graciously accepted the apology and later told me she probably was the "horriblest" student she ever had. It turns out this young lady had matured considerably and was now a student at Walla Walla Community College where she was studying to become a radiologist!

While traveling from Maine to Vermont, we stopped at a little Italian restaurant for lunch. They offered the typical fare of pizza, calzone, stromboli, and spaghetti. We ordered our food and awaited its arrival.

In the meantime, a forty-something guy with a young boy about five years old came in and sat down near us. The guy was wearing a camo t-shirt, khaki shorts, high-top lace-up hiking boots, and a rather long-bladed hunting knife in a sheath at his waist.

When their food arrived, the "forty-something guy" drew out his hunting knife, gave it a few spins in his hand before stopping to admire his knife-spinning skill, as well as the wolf's head on the end of the handle. He then proceeded to cut up his and the kid's food with the knife. Next, he began eating his food with the knife! So, what do you do with a pasta and tomato sauce-covered knife when you're through eating; you certainly wouldn't put it back in its sheath that way. Nope, you stick the knife in your beer and stir it gingerly then wipe it on your napkin. Another spin or two to admire his knife-handling skills, and perhaps help dry off the remaining beer, then sheath the knife with a grand show of dexterity!

Don't think I've ever seen anything quite like that before in a restaurant. Perhaps he was trying to be a Vermont "mountain man," but he looked more like he could have been a clerk at Home Depot!

THE GENERAL HIXSON TREE

The question came from a visitor who had just arrived at the entrance station at Kings Canyon National Park (KCNP). This individual was probably already well aware that most of the larger Sequoia trees in the park had names. Some trees were named after famous generals while others were named after various states. So he asked me the name of the Sequoia just across the street from the entrance station booth where I was on duty as a National Park Service Ranger. I told him I didn't know if it had a name or not. He looked at my name tag and told me the name of that tree was the General Hixson Tree! It turns out he used to work in that same entrance station and when asked that question, he always told them it was the General Kubota Tree as his last name was Kubota. Apparently, rangers had been attaching their names to that tree for many years.

So, on future trips when I visited the park, I always asked the park ranger on duty at the entrance booth the name of that Sequoia across the street. When they said they didn't know it had a name, I would tell them it was the General "whatever name was on his/her name tag" Tree. They would smile out of curiosity; then I would explain the tradition.

On a trip to KCNP in October 2008, I noticed that the entrance station was no longer at its former location. When I asked a ranger about the station's new location, she informed me that they had moved it as there was some danger that my beloved "General Hixson Tree" could someday fall on top of the station.

There is some validity to that belief. Sequoia trees are very shallow-rooted. They also grow in areas where the soil tends to stay fairly damp. The trees grow to be over two hundred feet tall and accumulate a very weighty mass. Sequoias are very resistant to fires, but occasionally a very hot fire will burn a chunk of the trunk from the ground level up to twenty to thirty feet on one side of the trunk. This can weaken the base of the tree where it connects to its shallow root system. During a strong wind, these trees are susceptible to being blown down. In some large groves, a single tree toppled by the wind can cause a domino effect taking out several of these monstrous trees at one time. The "General Hixson Tree" is one Sequoia that not only has a huge burn scar at its base, but it also has the disadvantage of having the road pass directly over part of its root system. The road also creates an opening in the forest where the wind can move less impeded, thus leaving the beautiful Sequoia a wide-open target for a strong wind.

In the 1960s and 1970s, it was becoming apparent that Douglas firs were becoming the most populous young trees in the Sequoia groves. The Park Service, in an effort to protect the ancient Sequoias had been putting out all fires in the groves for many years. Their scientists finally discovered that Sequoia cones had to be opened by fire before their seeds could germinate on bare soil. In the meantime, fir trees were the only young trees in the groves. The Sequoia cones actually have a purple powdery substance in them that serves as a fire retardant to help the seeds survive a fire.

My NPS mentor, Rob Zink, was the Chief of Interpretation at Kings Canyon NP for many years. He helped encourage the NPS to start introducing controlled burns in the Sequoia groves. Today you will see many new young Sequoias growing along with other species.

The "General Hixson Tree" has been there for perhaps twenty to thirty centuries. It may be there many more centuries after we are all gone; only time will tell. I hope our grandchildren and many of their future offspring will get to see this Sequoia far into the future.

FOND MEMORIES OF HUME LAKE

Dr. Ball was my dad's office partner in the Agriculture Department at FSC about the time I was in junior high and high school. He and his wife had bought a small cabin at Hume Lake in California's Kings Canyon, about five thousand feet up in the Sierra Nevadas east of Fresno. As a teenager, I was invited to spend a weekend with the Ball family at their cabin. It was a fantastic weekend of hiking, eating food cooked on a wood stove, row boating on the lake, and exchanging stories while sitting in front of a cozy fireplace in the evening.

Hume Lake was created in 1908 when a small dam was built across Ten Mile Creek. The lake is only about half a mile long, but it is in a beautiful valley surrounded by black oaks, incense cedars, yellow pines, and one of my very favorites, sugar pines (these tall pines often have cones eighteen inches long hanging from the ends of their graceful branches).

During my freshman year of college, I was fortunate to attend a Baptist Student Union weekend retreat at the Christian Conference grounds which dominate the west end of Hume Lake. I still remember the text the preacher used on Sunday morning as it came from the cartoon strip "Peanuts" in that morning's edition of the Fresno Bee.

The cartoon started with Charlie Brown on the pitcher's mound. In the second panel, his catcher had joined him on the mound. As the panels progressed, more of his team joined him on the mound and they began discussing things totally irrelevant to the game at hand. Eventually, the entire team was there and the discussion finally wound down and everyone went back to their assigned positions on the field. As Charlie Brown stood there on the mound, he said to himself (for our benefit, undoubtedly), "We may never win any games, but we sure do have some interesting discussions!" Now if that wasn't one of the best sermon "texts" I've ever heard, I don't know what is!

Choosing a place to spend one's honeymoon is a daunting task, especially when both newlyweds are "poor" college students and no one had stepped forward to offer to pay for us to go to an exotic tropical island for a week or two. Working at Sears as a salesperson part-time making only $2 an hour for about twenty-eight hours a week isn't quite enough to support a young couple, let alone, pay for an extravagant honeymoon. Neither is the paltry amount my wife-to-be was making working as a telephone operator (ask your parents, they'll know what an operator was) employed by Pacific Bell. So, what to do for a honeymoon. Fortunately, Dr. and Mrs. Ball still had their cabin at Hume Lake. They were gracious enough to let us occupy it for free for the weekend (we had to be back for classes and work the following Monday). Wow, were we ever grateful for that opportunity.

We drove up to the cabin in the dead of night following our wedding in Clovis, California on a Friday night. We drove east on Highway 180, passed through Grant Grove in KCNP, then dropped two thousand feet into Kings Canyon over the next ten miles. We arrived at the cabin to find a couple of deer standing on the back porch. After shooing them off the porch, we got inside and decided the November evening temperature inside the cabin (probably below freezing) warranted having a fire in the fireplace. I also had to find the shutoff valve for the water as the system had been shut down for the winter already. As they say, the rest of the night was history!

We cooked our breakfast the next morning on the wood-burning cook stove in the kitchen. We spent most of that morning hiking up

Ten Mile Creek above Hume Lake. The rest of the day, as they say, was history.

I was to have a Chemistry midterm exam the following Monday, so we decided to head home Sunday morning so I could study for it. We arose very early and drove all the way to Clovis so we could attend the Sunday morning worship service at our church where we had been married just two days previously. My dad was a deacon at that church. As it happened, he was at the pulpit making the announcements when we walked in. His comment to the congregation was, "Well look who just drug in!" Incidentally, I did get a passing grade on the exam Monday morning.

We continued to make trips to Hume Lake whenever we could. We had our faithful little bright red 1965 Datsun pickup that would get us there and back safely.

When I graduated from college, I started teaching school at Great Western Elementary School north of Reedley, CA. My classroom had a nice view of the Sierra Nevadas. I had a good view of the mountains coming to work every day when it wasn't foggy. My school district was Kings Canyon Unified. The teacher in the room to the west of mine was Don Enns. He had a small plane at the rural airport across the street from the school. On several occasions, he would come to my room after school and invite me to go for a ride with him. My favorite flights were those that took us up over the mountains of Kings Canyon and Sequoia National Parks.

After two years of teaching fifth grade, I landed a job at Alta Elementary School in the same district. This one was about three miles east of Reedley in a rural setting surrounded by peach and almond orchards, an orange grove, and a grape vineyard. Again I had a nice view of the mountains from the schoolyard.

I started working for the National Park Service as a seasonal park ranger the summer after my first year of teaching. In my second year of teaching, I worked as a park ranger at Grant Grove in KCNP on weekends. Yes, that meant seven days a week of work, although I really looked on the park service job as my potential "open door" to becoming a full-time park ranger.

As a teacher, I was "rich" enough to afford a new Chevy pickup ($2,600) to replace our little Datsun. After all, I signed my first contract for $6,000 a year in 1969! My teaching partner and I shared about forty to fifty students each year. I put that pickup to good use by taking small groups of sixth graders up to Hume Lake on Saturdays in the spring. It took about ten weeks to take all of the students there in groups of three to ten. This was well before teacher transportation liability was any kind of an issue. The students rode in the back of my pickup. Shirley always went along and took goodies she had prepared for the students. Occasionally, my former teaching partner, Laraine Miyake-Combs went with us.

In order to make sure the kids were paying attention from the outset of our hike, I would immediately take them to a small rock wall and have them climb over it. No, it was not a "manufactured" wall kids climb today, nor did we provide safety ropes; we just climbed the rock. It wasn't like climbing El Capitan, but it was enough to get them listening to simple instructions. It even took some teamwork to get everybody safely up and over it. We then proceeded to hike down Ten Mile Creek below the Hume Lake Dam. Along the way, we would stop to study plants, observe animals, and enjoy the creek's meanderings and waterfalls. On our first trip, we found a pair of dippers (water ouzels) building a nest of moss beside a small waterfall. There would always be enough moisture in the air to keep the moss nice and green through the nesting season.

Each successive week as I took other students to the area, we would take pictures of the progress of the nest building. The last group to visit the site got to see the young emerging from the nest. After all the students had been to the site, back in the classroom I was able to show them the pictures of the nest building, the parents, and the young fledglings as they left the nest.

We had a tradition on these trips that was played out after everyone had devoured their sack lunches. Shirley used to make German chocolate cheesecake brownies to share with the kids (don't worry, we got our share too!). The brownies were always one of the highlights of the day. Unfortunately, the company that used to sell that package mix quit making them many years ago. I still long for one of those brownies.

After eating our lunch, we would head to one of my favorite spots along the shore of Hume Lake to introduce the students to the Pacific tree frog. These little guys, only about an inch long, were everywhere in the water, on the muddy shore, on nearby trees, on the pine needles that covered the ground, and in the nearby grasses. One special characteristic these tree frogs have is the ability to camouflage themselves so that they blend in with the color of whatever they are on. While on green grasses, they were green; on the bark of trees, they would be the color of the bark; on pine needles on the ground, they would be the tannish red of the needles! The kids would get all excited as I challenged them to find two frogs that were exactly the same color. Never happened!

After a brief rest, we would drive around to the other side of the lake and hike up Ten Mile Creek. Here we focused more on the water and how it affected the geology and flora of the area. One last challenging experience for the day was walking across a log that straddled the creek. This was a confidence builder even though the log was big enough not to be much of a problem to walk on. It wasn't exactly a gymnast's balancing beam. However, the kids got a kick out of Mrs. Miyake-Combs when she would sit down on the log and scoot herself the twenty to thirty feet across it. This log was a good ten to fifteen feet above the creek. As I said earlier, this was before "liability" became such a big issue! A teacher would never be allowed to take kids to the mountains in the back of a pickup today no matter what the good intentions were.

The neat thing about these trips (other than not worrying about liability issues) was that I was teaching the SciCon Program (environmental education) the entire day while the kids thought they were just on a fun hike in the mountains with a few of their classmates and their teachers. Plus, although all of these kids lived only sixty miles from Hume Lake and only fifty miles from Grant Grove in Kings Canyon National Park, it was the first time most of them had ever visited either place.

We have visited Hume Lake many times over the years, but since living in Washington, we've not had the opportunity to visit as much as we would have liked. One week before our forty-second wedding anniversary, we were visiting relatives in Fresno when we decided to play hooky for the day and take a drive up to Grant Grove and Hume Lake.

We drove down to Hume Lake and looked for Balls' family cabin where we had spent our honeymoon. It is still there among some much newer and more expensive cabins, but it is still in excellent "rustic" shape. While hiking around the lake, we observed some larger frogs near or in the water, but we didn't find any of our smaller Pacific tree frogs—I imagine they were already nestled in for the winter. There were a few mallards and coots on the lake, but they would be taking off for warmer environments soon. The surprise was finding a set of fairly fresh bear tracks right at the water's edge possibly made just minutes before we discovered them.

It was a beautiful late fall day at Hume Lake with temperatures soaring clear into the 70s. The black oaks, dogwoods, and other deciduous trees were about maxed out on fall colors. Mountain misery made itself evident in several places as its aroma filled the air (they smell a little bit like dirty socks). Chipmunks and squirrels made themselves known with their distinctive high-pitched barks, as they skittered across the trail ahead of us, or while sitting on a branch stripping a fir cone to eat the seeds inside it. And the lake was as blue as it could possibly be.

I shared this chapter (via email) with Tim Goodrich, one of my former sixth grade students I still correspond with. Here is his response:

"Hi, Phil!

Wow! Your message took me right back to that Saturday trip we made up to the lake! I'm a little fuzzy on some of the details, but I remember on the way back home, some sort of turtle or tortoise was attempting to cross the road. You maneuvered to avoid hitting it, but the guy behind (or was it in front) of us deliberately swerved to run it over! We stopped and went back to check on the poor reptile's condition. I remember you took it to the side of the road and put it back into the forest, so it could either recover, or—more likely—let nature "take its course." I think that was one of the first times in my life I witnessed deliberate meanness and cruelty on the part of an adult! The memory of that injured turtle/tortoise has stayed with me my whole life. I still can't see one without flashing back to that day!

Thanks for the beautiful pictures, and the great memories! I have had a greater appreciation of the beauty of God's creation because of what you taught us in that classroom at Alta Elementary School, and in the hills and mountains above the Valley floor! Thanks for that, too!

God Bless!—Tim Goodrich"

NEVER, NEVER, EVER PICK UP AN INJURED BOBCAT!

The entire time I taught school in Reedley, I still wanted to be a full-time park ranger with the National Park Service (NPS). To further that cause, I managed to work weekends at KCNP about an hour's drive up in the Sierra Nevadas of Central California. After a full week in the classroom with twenty-five or so students, I would drive up to Kings Canyon early on a Saturday morning and work that day and Sunday at the entrance station collecting fees. It wasn't very exciting, but it kept my foot in the door with the NPS.

Three years later, I worked as a volunteer in parks also at KCNP. Again, I was trying to keep my foot in the NPS door. This time I chose to work as an interpreter at the Visitor Center in Grant Grove. I gave guided snowshoe walks on both days if a sufficient number of people signed up. Chief Interpretive Ranger Rob Zink was my immediate supervisor; he turned out to be the best interpretive ranger I ever met. After his retirement, he became known to our kids as "Uncle Rob." My family spent many of our vacations and holidays together with Uncle Rob over the next twenty-plus years.

Never, Never, Ever Pick Up an Injured Bobcat!

The drive up to KCNP was usually uneventful unless it had been snowing. My two-wheel drive, six-cylinder '69 Chevy pickup didn't care much for snow travel. On more than one occasion I actually arrived at the park only to find the snowplow was making its first run up the mountain right behind me!

On one of those early Saturday morning trips up to the park, as I was passing an area where the road skirted a steep granite cliff on the left, I encountered a bobcat sitting in my lane of traffic and not moving. I proceeded around it slowly and noticed it still had not moved.

Being curious, I parked my pickup, got out, and slowly (and ever so cautiously) approached it. Other than turning its head in my direction, there was no other sign that it was alive. When I approached within about four feet of that wild bobcat, it sprang to life as it lunged at me! Unfortunately, it became clear at that moment that the bobcat was severely injured and unable to control its hind legs. It appeared to have been hit by a car or suffered a fall from the adjacent cliff.

This was one of those handsome male bobcats with the long tufted ears. Amazingly, even though it had been injured, there was no sign of an open wound or blood on the ground where he had been sitting like a statue. Obviously, due to the severity of his injury, he would not be able to survive on his own.

When a car came by heading toward the park, I gave them a note and asked them to take it to the Interpretive Center at Grant Grove and give it to a park ranger. I had asked that a ranger bring a gun so we could put the bobcat out of its misery. Also, having recently graduated as a biologist, I knew the college (FSC) would like to have this specimen for its mammals study lab as it was in perfect condition externally.

During the time I awaited the arrival of a ranger, the bobcat had dragged himself to the side of the road using just his front legs. He had tumbled about forty feet down a rip-rapped embankment finally coming to rest on a rock shelf about the size of a bathtub.

When the park ranger arrived, he informed me he had brought only one bullet! Okay, that should do the trick. However, I had to caution him not to shoot the poor guy in the head as the skull is a very important part of a study skin—it helps identify its subspecies. So, he shot the bobcat in the chest. Having done so, we waited until it did not appear there were any signs of life left in him.

I've always known that mother cats, and most people, usually carried kittens by the backs of their necks. So I cautiously reached down and picked the "dead" thirty-five-pound bobcat up by the back of his neck with my right hand. I used my left hand to help stabilize myself while climbing back up the riprap to the road. About halfway up the embankment, I felt the "dead" bobcat come very much alive in my right hand. There was growling, hissing, gnashing of teeth, nasty snarling, and front paws flailing perilously close to my shirt sleeve as I felt I was about to have a heart attack! My arm went straight out as far as I could reach away from my body. I wasn't about to drop him for fear of what he might do to me. With much commotion going on at the end of my right arm, I hurried up the embankment as rapidly as possible (probably a lot faster than I had previously thought possible!) and deposited him in the back of my pickup.

The park ranger and I drove on up to the park where another bullet was retrieved and a second shot was fired into the bobcat's chest. I was feeling so sorry for the cat now that it almost made me sick. Unfortunately, the second bullet did not complete the job. It was suggested that I cut off his air at his throat—not a pleasant thought, but something had to be done to stop his misery. As I did so, we realized he had a flailed chest and was actually breathing through one of his wounds that had apparently also pierced a lung. A third bullet ended his life.

Through all of this, we never saw a drop of blood. I assume he had lost so much blood internally at the site of his original wounds that there just wasn't any left for him to give up.

That night I had been invited to dinner with one of the permanent rangers and his family. He was telling me that earlier that morning they were taking his mother to the Fresno airport for her to fly home. While passing a granite cliff along the highway, a bobcat had launched from the granite and his car had hit it! I then shared with them (as Paul Harvey would have said) "the rest of the story."

While taking a mammology course from Dr. Hawbecker at FSC, we had to prepare five study skins for the college's collection. These are used to identify mammal species and in some cases varieties of a species. This bobcat was a beautiful animal and in very good shape. It would become a very valuable addition to the collection. So I had placed it in a plastic bag and buried it in the snow overnight. When I got home the next night, I called Dr. Hawbecker and he drove out to our place in the country to retrieve this specimen for use at the college.

My recommendation: Don't ever pick up a "dead" bobcat until you know for certain it isn't about to spring back to life!

A "BUCKET LIST" EVENT

Shirley and I have an unwritten "Bucket List" which we call into play from time to time. March 17, 2012 turned out to be a "Bucket List" day for us. On a partly overcast day in Phoenix, AZ, we finally attended a Cactus League spring training professional baseball game. We saw the White Sox skunk the Mariners 5–0. When we first arrived, we were in Row 2 halfway between first base and the right field wall. All the autograph seekers preferred to line up right in front of our seats until just before game time, so all we saw for the first forty-five minutes we were seated awaiting the start of the game was autograph seekers' backsides standing in front of us. Since the stands were almost empty after the second inning we moved to seats just behind home plate.

What makes this game so memorable was the spectacular play I made in the bottom of the third inning when Eduardo Escobar of the White Sox hit a foul ball around the backstop screen. A guy way up behind us, and about ten seats to my left made a valiant effort to catch it, but all he managed to do was knock it down. The ball began rolling down the row immediately behind me where no one was seated.

So, I "dove" over the back of our seats and snagged it with one hand. However, in the process, I pulled a muscle in my upper left thigh (the hamstring) and could barely walk afterward. It was extremely painful. I knew I had to keep moving, so after each half-inning, I would get up and take a short walk. Shirley only had one Tylenol so I took that and it did help relieve some of the pain. Two more Tylenols before bed helped me sleep a little bit that night. My nephew's wife, Krista, who was a sports medicine graduate suggested alternating hot and cold treatments, wrapping with an Ace bandage, and using a heating pad. So, I went right out and purchased the bandage and heating pad (we don't usually travel with those items in our fifth wheel), and on a couple of occasions, I would sit in a cold swimming pool for a while followed by a soak in a hot tub.

We continued to do quite a bit of walking and hiking over the course of the next month. I kept the leg wrapped and occasionally resorted to the heating pad. Slowly it became better. Two months later, I hardly even noticed it.

What I did notice one night later that year was that the White Sox were playing the Mariners in Seattle, when once again they walloped the Mariners. This time the score was 4–0 and White Sox pitcher Phil Humber pitched a perfect game! Since the Mariners were doing so poorly, I thought I might have to change my allegiance at least for that year.

The baseball I dove over the seats to retrieve is now displayed on my desk in a small plastic memento case where it reminds me every day not to chase foul balls.

That just reminded me of the time two of my college friends and I went to Chavez Ravine Stadium to see the Dodgers play the Yankees. The three of us sat out in the center field bleachers so we could have a chance of snagging a home run ball. There did not seem to be anyone near us, so we should have had a good shot at being first to grab a home run ball. However, when Yogi Berra finally hit a home run in our direction, kids came pouring into the area where we were seated. We never even had a chance with all those speedy little guys running for their souvenir home run ball!

SNAKES IN MY LIFE

While reading John Muir's account of his having killed two snakes in his lifetime, I got to thinking about my encounters with snakes. Muir relates that he once killed a rattlesnake just because he always thought they were a menace that needed to be eliminated. He later developed a more realistic approach to snakes that led him to believe that they have an important role to play in the environment. The only other time he killed a rattlesnake was when it invaded his cabin in Yosemite Valley. He decided he had to be rid of it because of the large number of visitors, including a number of children, who visited his cabin frequently.

I have never purposely killed a snake, but I did accidentally kill one once in the course of my duties as a park ranger for the Corps of Engineers. An entrance road to a marina at Pine Flat Lake on the Kings River passed through a mobile home park where a number of elderly people lived. Many of them had beautiful flowerbeds and small gardens that they developed and cared for throughout the summer. While patrolling in that area one night, I saw a rattlesnake crossing the road headed in the direction of those flowerbeds and gardens.

I decided I couldn't just let it move into that area where someone might stumble across it in the process of tending their plants. So I quickly stopped the truck, jumped out, and grabbed a shovel with which I intended to move the snake elsewhere. However, after searching for it all around the truck I was unable to find it. I did not believe it could have disappeared that quickly, so on a hunch I got back in the truck and moved it forward a few yards. What I found was a very flat coiled-up rattler that had the misfortune of stopping and coiling at precisely the same place the left rear tire of the truck had stopped! I scooped it up, set it in the bed of the pickup, and drove to a more remote site where I buried it. Later that night, I wrote in the ranger log that after burying the poor dead snake I had sung a couple of verses of a popular song of that era as I laid it to rest. The song: "Sneaky Snake" by Tom T. Hall.

My earliest recollections of snakes are from visits to my grandparents near Stillwater, OK. They believed snakes were to be feared and killed immediately. Occasionally, a large king snake would find its way into their cellar where they kept canned fruits and vegetables and where people would seek shelter during tornado warnings. The long black and yellow king snakes were always dispatched as quickly as possible. Snakes obviously found the cellar to be a cool respite from the hot, sunny summer days in Oklahoma.

Since I grew up in town, I didn't have much interaction with snakes in my younger years. In college, Dr. Hadsall, my ornithology professor, also taught herpetology. He kept a rather formidable Pacific rattler in a cage in our classroom. Three other classmates and myself sat at a table immediately in front of this seemingly docile critter. One day during class, it decided to make itself known to everyone within hearing range. I had never heard a live rattlesnake rattle before, but within seconds all four of us removed ourselves from that table and were across the room looking to see if it was still in its cage! I will never forget that first rattler I ever heard. We never did figure out why it chose that moment to make itself known; it probably derived great pleasure watching four college students panic as we ran from our seats.

The students I taught in fifth and sixth grades were country kids. They were constantly bringing in critters they found while playing outside. I kept a cage in my classroom for teaching opportunities when they brought some of these critters to school. Teaching in a rural community meant I never knew what my students would bring to school. Twins Wayne and Dwayne Tincup were constantly bringing in animals they had found around their family farm. They brought a sparrow hawk they had rescued after it dove into tall grasses in hopes of snagging a meal. It had become stuck and could not escape the grasses. We kept it in a cage in the back of our classroom for a couple of days where it accepted our offers of fresh hamburger meat. We finally released it in the schoolyard and watched it fly straight up before heading to one of the nearby orchards.

Another time they brought a baby opossum to class. Sometimes I would let the students handle the animals, but I decided I needed to test this one before I let them touch it. I went to my pickup and got my leather work gloves so I could safely handle the little guy. I teased it a little to see if it was likely to bite. Since it did not bite me, I took the gloves off. Almost immediately, it bit my left thumb next to my fingernail and would not let go. I finally had to pull it off with its teeth still stuck in my skin. Later that day while doing a little research, I discovered that opossums have more teeth than any other North American mammal. Not only that, but all fifty-four teeth are cone-shaped, sharply pointed, and quite capable of inflicting a very painful bite!

One day the twins brought us a three-and-a-half-foot-long gopher snake. We put it in the cage so we could observe it. The following day, our kindergarten teacher, Mrs. Smith, approached me and asked if I would bring the snake to her class and share some information about it with her kindergartners. I agreed to do so. Not wanting to haul the cage to her classroom, I decided to just carry it there. I managed to hold the snake's head down with a ruler while I gently picked it up right in the back of its head. I then wrapped its body around my forearm several times.

Now kindergarten kids are not going to want to sit and hear a long herpetological lecture, so I decided to engage them in a way that might pique their interest. I asked them if they wanted to touch the snake. Most agreed that would be okay as long as I kept a good grip on it. First I had them rub their thumbnails. I explained that their thumbnails were made of the same material as the snake's scales that covered its body. I asked them if their thumbnail was wet and slimy. When they responded that it wasn't, I asked them if the snake would feel wet and slimy if it hadn't been in any water. They didn't think it would be.

So as I started around their tables, they were allowed the opportunity to touch the snake if they chose to do so. After the first five or six students reached out for their opportunity to feel it, I began noticing a pattern of behavior from the snake. When a student reached out to touch it with no hesitation and just patted it lightly, the snake did nothing. However, if a student reached out tentatively and hesitated before touching it, the snake would tighten up on my arm as though it sensed danger. The rest of the way around the room I was able to identify each student as being "afraid" of the snake, or not being "afraid." This led me to believe that this snake had an innate ability to detect "fear" in the students who showed hesitation to touch it. Thus, I learned something about snakes in kindergarten that day that I had never known before.

Shirley and I loved to take hikes in the Sierra Nevadas. While hiking in the Sierras east of Porterville, CA, we came across a beautiful green and orange western ringneck snake. At once I thought this would be a good snake to show my class because it was so colorful and didn't look very dangerous. So I picked it up and carried it to our pickup. It was only about ten inches long, so I searched for something to put it in until I could take it to school and put it in our cage.

Because it was so colorful with its green upper body and head and the bright orange ring around its neck and on its underside, we decided to give it a "colorful" name. So we named it Robespierre (don't know where that came from—just knew it was French). The only thing I found in our pickup to put it in was a two-quart camp cooking pot. It was about eight inches deep, so I wasn't afraid it would escape. When we got home, I set the pot on the kitchen floor where we watched it try to escape to no avail. However, upon returning to check on it later that evening, it had disappeared! We never saw Robespierre again. I always wondered if Robespierre had shown up in one of the adjacent apartments!

It would be over forty years before we would find another ringneck snake. This time it was while we were on a hike around Beaver Lake in

Virginia's Pocahontas State Park. This one was only about four inches long and not much bigger around than an ink pen refill. The orange ring around the neck was prominent, but its topside was black. Less than a hundred yards away was a nice big garter snake sunning itself on a warm rock. I'm sure the garter snake would have made a meal of the smaller ringneck if they had crossed paths.

While a seasonal park ranger at Lava Beds National Monument (LBNM) about thirty-five miles northeast of Mount Shasta in CA, I had the opportunity to come across several species of snakes on many occasions. Rattlesnakes were quite common in the area. At least once or twice a summer I would have to remove one from the campground. I did so with a long stick with a rope on it that could be used to slip over the snake's head and hold it firmly. Then, placing the stick and snake in a large garbage bag, which I held outside the car window, I would drive the patrol vehicle a couple of miles away from the campground and release the rattler into the wild a safe distance from people, trails, and the road.

Lava Beds also had other non-venomous snakes throughout the park. One of the more commonly seen species was the western yellow-bellied racer. While clay gray above, they indeed had a yellow belly. They were very fast as far as snakes are concerned. Their young looked more like a baby gopher snake than like the adults of their species.

One sunny summer day as I was preparing to give a guided walk through the Stronghold, the site of the most important battles of the Modoc Indian War, I came upon a young yellow-bellied racer that was slower than I was that day. It was only about eight inches long, so when I captured it I put it in my uniform shirt pocket just below my ranger badge for safekeeping. Daytime temperatures during the summer at Lava Beds are quite warm. So, I would give most of the Stronghold "guided tour" talk about the war in Captain Jack's cave (a collapsed lave tube) where it was shaded and considerably more comfortable than out in the sun. The little snake in my pocket remained motionless during the entire time we were in the cave.

As we later continued walking through the Stronghold, we came to a junction in the trail where I ended the formal part of the walk. Part of the group would return directly to the parking lot while others chose to take a longer trail back. While we were still together, I asked if anyone was interested in snakes. Several indicated they were, so I unbuttoned my shirt pocket and pulled out my little friend who had become quite cozy. They were shocked to see that I had had it in my pocket the entire hour we had been together. After we studied it for a bit and people got to touch it, we turned it loose along the trail.

One of my favorite Lava Beds snakes was most often encountered in the many lava tubes where people were able to explore on their own. The rubber boa is a brownish, docile snake. I've never known one to be aggressive toward humans. They have a habit of coiling up with their head near the ground while sticking their tail in the air. This would tempt a predator to grab the snake by the tail rather than by the head. While the predator would be thinking about its upcoming meal, the tail would break off the rubber boa and continue to wiggle so the predator thought it had a nice clean catch. However, the rubber boa would slither away with no more damage than having lost the end of its tail! If we found a rubber boa in one of the lava tubes, we could always tell if it had lost its tail previously by the white scar it left at the blunt point where the tail broke off. It was always easy to pick up a rubber boa to get a better look at it, but it gives off a putrid-smelling liquid that makes you want to wash your hands right away.

We invited sisters who had been in my sixth grade classes to come to Lava Beds for a week-long visit. Since I had to work most of the days they would be with us, Shirley was their primary tour guide for the week. It was an exciting week for the girls that included seeing a bobcat stalking a jackrabbit in the middle of the road after dark, a lightning-caused fire that surrounded our housing and caused Shirley and the girls to retreat to a motel outside the park, and an encounter with a rattlesnake.

Spelunking is one of the most popular activities at Lava Beds. The caves (actually lava tubes) stay at a nice cool temperature (about 54°F) throughout the summer. So Shirley decided to take them spelunking one afternoon to escape the heat of the day. While one of the girls was descending a ladder at the cave entrance, Shirley happened to notice a rattlesnake coiled up on a shelf in the wall of the cave. She told the girl to stop, then had her slowly climb back up the ladder to safety.

When the girls were safely on the bus headed home at the end of their week-long visit, Shirley called their mother to let her know they were on their way home. She also told her it had been an exciting week for the girls and no matter what tall tales they told her, it all really happened!

While I'm still not a herpetologist, I have learned to have a healthy respect for snakes and their vital role in the environment. Just think how many mice, rats, and other disease-carrying critters they eat!

HORSES IN MY LIFE

Horses have always been of interest to me. Remember one of my first two words was "horse." My first recollection of being around a horse occurred on one of our summer trips to Oklahoma. My cousin, Arlis, had a black and white Paint horse. Arlis was showing off by riding it bareback. Whether on command or on its own, the horse reared up and Arlis nonchalantly slid off the back of the horse over its rump as if this was the way he always dismounted.

A couple of years later, one of the ag professors at Fresno State (a colleague of my dad) was hosting a barbecue at his ranch in the Sierra Nevada foothills northeast of Fresno. One of his teenage boys had rounded up some of their horses and saddled them so guests could go for a ride. That is the first time I ever remember riding a horse. Of course, someone was leading it, so I wasn't in control.

Mr. Golden was the man who had hired me on several occasions to help him with a variety of building projects. He called me one day to ask if I could help him with a horse. His wife's uncle was president of the Appaloosa Horse Association up in Moscow, ID. He owned Double Patch, a beautiful stallion just three years old. Double Patch was very large and muscular with perfect Appaloosa markings.

Double Patch had been shipped down to Clovis where the winter would be much less severe than it would have been up in Idaho. This was about the time that Appaloosas were starting to be used for racing. It was January and the racing season was several months away. The owner of Double Patch, George Hatley, wanted Mr. Golden to find someone to begin exercising the horse every day. Since I only weighed about 125 pounds (jockey-sized) at that time, Mr. Golden thought I would be an ideal candidate to take on the job of exercising Double Patch. Although a little apprehensive about taking on this project, I was eager to get to ride a horse every day. Double Patch was a highly spirited horse with lots of energy. I really didn't know what I was getting into.

Mr. Golden took me under his wings and taught me what he felt I needed to know about the horse: how to saddle up, and how to control him. It was a one-time lesson that taught me some of what I needed to know, but certainly not everything.

I started the horse exercise program immediately. Double Patch wasn't used to being caught, bridled, saddled, and ridden a lot, although he was definitely broken for riding. He made it fairly difficult for me to catch him each day, but once the bridle was in place he was resigned to going through the rest of the process. Mr. Golden lived out in the country in an area with vineyards and orchards and lots of dirt roads. I would mount Double Patch and head for the dirt roads around the farms. There was one dirt road that passed a vineyard that I usually saved for our last stretch before heading back to the corral.

It was that last road that always gave me the biggest "thrill" of the day. A local farm dog (looked like Lassie, but not nearly as nice) would lay in wait for us hidden somewhere in that vineyard. As soon as we passed its hiding place, that dog would fly out of the vineyard at full speed and try to nip Double Patch's hind legs. I never knew when to expect the dog to show itself, but invariably it would shoot out of the vineyard and head straight for Double Patch. That's when I learned how fast Double Patch could go from zero to top speed in a split second. It always amazed me how far he could leap as he shot forward. All I had to do was hang on and enjoy the ride. From that experience, I learned that the smoothest ride on a horse was when it was running full out. Once we outran that obnoxious dog, it was time to head back to the corral and call it a day.

Double Patch went on to set several Appaloosa racing records for his breed. I believe one record still stands merely because they quit racing that particular distance (770 yards). I secretly wished I could have been his jockey in one of those record-setting races.

About a dozen years later when I began working for the Corps of Engineers in Clarkston, WA, I noticed the Alpowa Ranch west of Clarkston along Highway 12. On a sign at the entrance to the ranch, it read: "Home of Double Patch". Seems my old friend was now retired and had become a very sought-after Appaloosa stud! Driving past the ranch one day as I was heading west out of Clarkston, I noticed several people standing around the Alpowa Ranch corral. I was in a Corps of Engineers vehicle and a lot of people in that area would dearly love to have harassed me and sent me on my way. However, as I approached the man who seemed to be in charge, he looked at my name tag on my Corps park ranger uniform, and merely said, "I know who you are. Lyle Golden has told me all about you." I was much relieved at his reception. Although he told me I could stop in anytime and visit Double Patch, I never did stop again. It was enough just to see him in his new home every time I went by. He lived to the ripe old age of twenty-seven.

When Shirley and I married, we were fortunate to live in a tiny house on a small ranch east of Clovis. The owners, the Watsons, had a 1940s vintage one-bedroom house in the back of their older farmhouse. We paid $25 rent per month and I was responsible for keeping the lawn between our houses mowed. After a couple of months, Mr. Watson told us our rent would only be $20 per month as that was all they had been charging their daughter and son-in-law while they lived there.

Mr. Watson had several horses and a few steers. Most of the ranch was across the street where the Watsons had constructed a rodeo-type arena. He told me he had too many horses to keep them all in shape, so he wanted me to be responsible for riding Sandy, a palomino, to keep her in shape. I had classes on the college campus most days and I was working evenings at Sears Roebuck & Company in Fresno. If I had a short day at school, I would head for home, saddle up Sandy and we would travel the country roads and along the irrigation canals for an hour or so. Sandy was growing quite a bit during that time. One day as I drove in from school, she was in a small pasture near the houses just giving birth to a foal.

Occasionally, Mr. Watson would want to do some work with his horses in the arena. After saddling up, we rounded up about a dozen young steers and herded them into the arena. The steers would all bunch up like they were looking for support from each other. What we were to do was single out a steer and separate it from the rest of the herd. I soon realized that once Sandy knew which steer to focus on, all I needed to do was hang on for dear life! She would stay right with the targeted steer until it had been separated from the others. It was almost magical the way she would take over once she knew which steer I was after.

One of the privileges I had as a park ranger was having horse patrol duty at Crater Lake once or twice a week during the summers of the '75 and '76 seasons. That was the most enjoyable job I ever had!

Our seasonal park ranger supervisor, Marion Jack, owned a pair of fairly well-matched Appaloosa geldings, Duke and Dale, which were used for horse patrols and interpretive programs in the park. We focused most of our patrols around Rim Village and Crater Lake Lodge, areas where people tended to congregate. Duke was my favorite due to his gentleness when surrounded by people. Duke and my NPS uniform attracted a lot of people. They had lots of questions, took lots of pictures, and loved to pet the horse.

While getting ready to go on duty, I received a radio call that went as follows: "Phil, we've had an incident out along the north entrance road. You need to get the horses and one of the other patrol rangers and head up this way. I'll fill you in when you get here." That was our supervisor, Marion Jack. While hooking up the horse trailer to a pickup, I was able to contact a fellow park ranger, Pat Toops. We quickly rounded up Dale and Duke, saddled them, and loaded them for the drive to the north side of the park. When we arrived, we were told that one of the female YCC crew had been accosted by a male carrying a knife. She managed to get away and ran back to report the incident to the crew leader.

Pat's and my job was to ride in opposite directions along a newly constructed section of the Pacific Crest Trail northwest of the lake looking for any signs of the possible assailant. While I headed north about five miles, Pat headed toward the rim of Crater Lake. Finding nothing, we returned to the trailer. That's when we learned "the rest of the story."

The YCC crew, made up mostly of older teenagers, had been developing the portion of the Pacific Crest Trail that would traverse Crater Lake National Park. Each day they would drive to the work site, work till their noon break, then continue with trail building until time to call it a day. It made for a long laborious workday for the crew. On that particular day, one of the crew noticed that their crew leader had failed to take a radio with them out to the work site. So, after stepping off the trail some distance to relieve herself, she came running back to her crew leader telling him of her horrible encounter with a knife-wielding man with obvious evil intentions.

She had given us a description of a bearded man in a blue work shirt, and wearing blue jeans. He was probably in his thirties or forties. While Pat and I searched the trail, other rangers had stopped a few vehicles carrying persons who vaguely met her description. None of them seemed to have any knowledge of the incident, especially since most had just recently entered the park.

By the time we got the horses back to the corral, the story had unfolded. The young lady knew they would have to drive to park headquarters to report the incident due to failing to have a radio on-site. That would take almost an hour by the time they gathered up their equipment and headed in. By the time she was through reporting what had happened, it would definitely be too late to return to the work site that afternoon. So, while it got a lot of action from us rangers, it kept the young lady and the entire crew from having to return to work the rest of the day.

For Pat and me, the positive thing that came out of this incident was that each of us got to ride horseback on several miles of the Pacific Crest Trail before anyone else ever had a chance to do so.

Each person on the YCC crew was encouraged to go on patrol with a park ranger once during the summer. Wouldn't you know it, I was the "lucky one" who got to take this young lady for half a day. Neither one of us felt it necessary to relive her little shenanigan a few weeks earlier.

Patrolling on horseback in Rim Village allowed one to see a lot more than when you were in a car or on foot. One day, I noticed a two-seater sports convertible heading toward Crater Lake Lodge with a young lady sitting on the back of the car above the two seats. The road only went as far as the lodge, then it came back to where I was then sitting on Duke in the middle of their lane. Duke probably weighed almost as much as the tiny car so I was able to persuade the driver to stop. I advised the driver that the female passenger would have to sit inside the car, not on the trunk. He wasn't too happy and informed me the only place for her to sit was on his male passenger's lap. The passenger broke out into a broad grin and was obviously only too happy to accommodate the young lady.

On a slow day at Rim Village, I rode Duke all the way to the top of Garfield Peak which forms part of the rim around the lake. I was a little nervous at one point where the trail was no more than eight feet wide and right on top of a ridge; it was over a thousand feet to the lake on the left side and at least six hundred feet to the rim road on the right. I needn't have worried as Duke went forward seemingly oblivious to the danger!

Marion knew how much I enjoyed working with the horses, so when it was time for the US Bi-Centennial Independence Day Parade in Klamath Falls, OR, in 1976 he invited me to participate with him. I was extremely happy and honored to do so. Marion rode Dale while carrying the Department of Interior flag and I rode Duke carrying Old Glory. Both our horses were adorned with a National Park Service saddle blanket and Marion and I were in our park ranger dress uniforms. I must say that we, and the horses, really looked sharp that day. It just happens that I wrote this chapter forty years to the day after that Bi-Centennial Fourth of July Parade! My "random access memory" must have been working overtime that day!

As we rode through the parade route in Klamath Falls, we discovered there were manhole covers in the middle of every intersection on Main Street. That presented a new issue for Duke to deal with as he had never before encountered such a thing. At each intersection, he would keep his eyes on the manhole cover and walk sideways around it until he felt he was safely past it. No amount of encouragement from me could distract him and keep him walking straight. Dale, on the other hand just kept walking straight.

Shirley and our year-and-a-half-old son, Matthew, were watching the parade go by. When Marion and I rode past, Matthew pointed his finger at me and yelled out, "Dad-DY!" (emphasis on the second syllable), loud enough that it attracted the attention of the other parade watchers along the street. The crowd then applauded him as we rode on!

A few weeks later, Marion and I rode in the Chiloquin, OR, annual parade. Since their grand marshall didn't arrive in time for the start of the parade, we were asked to move up and lead the parade. A lady from Chiloquin was impressed with our snappy-looking horses, our NPS saddle blankets, and park ranger uniforms (not to mention the handsome rangers!). She approached us at the end of the parade and asked if we would like to be the flag bearers for the grand entry to the Chiloquin Rodeo which was scheduled a few days after the parade. We said we would be honored to do so. We asked her to make her request in writing to the park superintendent at Crater Lake to make everything official.

In the meantime, Marion and I decided we needed to practice our "grand entry." Normally the flag bearers would enter the arena with their horses running at full speed as they approached the grandstands. Then they would bring the horses to a sliding stop just short of crashing into the crowded grandstand. We thought it would be a good idea to practice this maneuver since neither of us had ever tried this before.

We waited until the park superintendent was out of his office then snuck in and unofficially "borrowed" his office flags (Department of the Interior and US). We made some holders out of pieces of fire hose and attached them to our saddles. We loaded up the horses and headed down to a softball field at the park's gravel pit. In order to be assured the horses would make a quick sliding stop, we decided to start them running from centerfield, across second base and the pitcher's mound, then slam on the brakes right when we hit home plate. There was a chain-link backstop about fifteen feet behind home plate, so we were fairly certain the horses would accommodate our order to "WHOA"!

Our adrenalin was running pretty high as we ran past second base and the pitcher's mound on our way to a skidding stop at home plate. I'm sure it was a sight to behold. Everything was going as planned until the skidding stop began. It was then that it became obvious we did not anticipate the need to hold the flagpoles against our shoulders as we came to a quick skidding stop. Therefore, the two flagpoles left our hands and went flying right into the backstop! If anyone had been standing there we would have impaled them! Fortunately, the gold eagles on top of the flagpoles were not sufficiently damaged for anyone to notice. So, our next move was to discretely return the flags to the superintendent's office without anyone knowing what had happened.

Unfortunately for us, either the lady from Chiloquin didn't contact the superintendent or the superintendent chose not to sanction our participation in the rodeo grand entry. At any rate, Marion and I had fun preparing for it and we learned how important holding onto the flagpole would have been as we skidded to a halt in front of the crowd in the grandstand!

About ten years later, while visiting Crater Lake National Park, we were given a newspaper and brochure at the park entrance station that contained maps and interpretive materials. Since Shirley and I were familiar with the park, it wasn't until a day or so later that I opened the newspaper and discovered the "centerfold" was a black and white picture of Duke and me with a few kids whose mother was taking their picture.

Our horses were magnets for park visitors. They loved seeing a ranger on a horse. You could drive through the Rim Village parking lot all day in a patrol vehicle and only a handful of people would flag you down to ask directions or discuss some of the park's features with you. But get on the horse and you couldn't ride across the parking lot without attracting a crowd. I enjoyed horse patrol so much that I seldom even got off the horse for a lunch break.

Marion told me about the time one of the employees at Rim Village Store came running out and yelled at him (while he was on horse patrol) that a person had just stolen something from the store.

Marion saw the guy running and took off in hot pursuit. The thief wove through parked cars and road traffic with Marion and Duke following his zigzagging trail. The thief finally made it to the front of Crater Lake Lodge, ran up the steps, and disappeared inside.

As Marion arrived at the front of the Crater Lake Lodge, someone he knew came strolling out. Jumping off his horse, Marion told his friend coming down the steps to hang on to his horse while he proceeded to continue the chase inside the lodge. The thief ran to the back of the lodge and jumped over a short wall down to a walkway just below. He was about to jump over the next wall when he realized he was several hundred feet above the lake and it was going to be a rough ride all the way down. Marion nabbed his man and took him back to the store. That's when he learned the guy had stolen a tube of toothpaste! I don't remember if he even wrote the guy a citation or not, but at least it made for an exciting day at the Rim Village.

It was about a half-hour ride to Rim Village from the Sleepy Hollow housing area where the horses were corralled. One day I let Matthew (then about a year and a half old), ride up the trail with me to the main road near Rim Village. Shirley would meet us there and take him home and I would continue on with my horse patrol. It was Matthew's first-ever horseback ride. He sat very still and wasn't saying anything, but he seemed to be enjoying the ride. He was even wearing his little blue suede cowboy boots. When we arrived at the meeting point, Shirley asked where his other boot was since he only had one on. He hadn't bothered to let me know he had lost the boot while coming up the trail. So, I headed back down the trail and retrieved the boot. Fortunately, he had lost it near the top of the trail.

Park visitors were frequently wanting to have their kids, wives, or girlfriends photographed with the park ranger on the horse. The best we could offer was to have them stand near Duke's head for the family vacation photo opportunity with a mounted park ranger. I had to turn down a number of requests to have photographers' girlfriends sit on the horse with me!

A mother had her two young boys with her and she was trying to get them to get closer to the horse for a good photo shot. I was conversing with someone beside me at the time and wasn't really paying close attention to the photographer and her boys. Duke would stand absolutely still all day with people milling all around him so he didn't alert me to anything unusual happening. I did hear the mother tell the boys a couple of times, "Get closer. Get closer." The next thing she said was, "Get your hand out of there!" in a rather excited voice. That got my attention promptly! The boy had inadvertently stuck his hand in Duke's mouth while trying to reach up and touch him. Duke delivered a subtle message to have the boy remove the hand from his mouth by merely biting down gently. The hand was extracted immediately. The mother identified herself as a nurse. She and I (an EMT at the time) checked her son's hand and discovered Duke had not even broken the boy's skin. It just happened that some of the Park Service maintenance crew observed the incident and word got around to other park employees that day that, "Hixson let his horse bite a kid today!"

I was on horse patrol at Rim Village when a thunderstorm moved in. I'm not particularly fond of being one of the highest things around when lightning is popping everywhere, so I thought it was best to head Duke down to his corral. Just as we entered the meadow behind Rim Village, lightning struck a tree close behind us. Duke suddenly decided, all on his own, that we might ought to expedite our trip to the corral. Since I was equally ready to hightail it out of there, I gave him his head and went for a lickety-split rapid trip across the meadow.

Just before we got to the road, there was a bit of a ditch we had to cross. I was ready for Duke to run down through the ditch and then up onto the road. Duke once again had a "better idea" that was a little faster; he decided to jump the ditch! I hung on for dear life since I wasn't used to riding a jumping horse. By then the road surface was wet from the rain. When Duke hit the wet pavement, he skidded a bit before he could get all four hooves back under himself. Still in a hurry, he decided to jump the ditch on the other side of the road also. We had only another hundred yards or so before we got to the trail. I let him continue his fast pace until we got to the trees. Not being the tallest thing around any longer, I brought him down to a rapid walk the rest of the way to the corral. I'm not sure if Duke was more afraid of the lightning than I was of jumping the ditches, but we both survived to serve another day.

Many years later while visiting Marion and Betty Jack at their retirement home in Talent, OR, I got to see Duke for the last time. He was no longer the traditional Appaloosa with a big white rump patch. Like most of us old guys, he had turned almost pure white from head to tail!

After we married, we occasionally went up into the Sierra Nevadas and would rent horses for a couple of hours near Wishon Reservoir. As I recall we had to pay about $3 an hour in those days. One time we took my middle sister, Mary, along with us. She was riding behind us on the trail. Unfortunately, her horse was a hundred percent "barn sour." That's a horse that can only stay focused on getting back to the barn where its feed was located. It had already turned around as if we were ready to head back to the barn. Although we were on a fairly narrow trail, I had Mary toss me the horse's lead rope over its rump. Riding forward on the trail, I pulled on that rope until the horse was forced to turn around and follow us. I had to "drag" it along behind me the rest of the ride until we headed back to the barn. Then all I had to do was keep him from passing me and running to the barn. I don't think Mary enjoyed that ride at all.

While we lived in Clarkston, we often took camping trips with our boys into central Idaho along the Selway and Lochsa Rivers. When the boys were about four and seven years old, we thought they were old enough to take them on a trail ride for an hour or so. The "wrangler" assigned them each an old "plug" (very gentle older horse). These horses were at their best when walking slowly in a line of other horses. It turned out this wasn't the best day for the boys to make their first ride as it started to rain lightly. The trail became slippery and the horses were having a little trouble trying not to slide coming down the mountain trail. When we arrived at the corral, we were surprised to see that the boys' feet were all the way through the stirrups. I'm not sure if either of them has ever ridden a horse again.

An optometrist friend of mine, Dean Hattan, lived a couple of blocks from us in the Clarkston Heights area. He would call occasionally and ask if I wanted to go for a ride with him. He had a nice little Appaloosa that I could ride alongside his taller and bulkier horse more suited to his size and weight. We would ride all over the hills west of town.

There were some cliffs above Highway 12 leading into Clarkston that we would occasionally ride along. One day we stopped facing the road and the Snake River a couple of hundred feet below us. I thought of all those cowboy movies where the hero was trying to evade the bad guys so he would have his horse jump off a cliff into a river. I decided I didn't like looking over the cliff at that moment in case something spooked the horses from behind.

On a rainy Sunday afternoon, Dean called and asked if I wanted to go over to Lewiston and participate in a game of "cowboy polo." I told him I didn't know what that was. After he explained it to me, I agreed to go along. We loaded up his horses and headed over to an indoor arena south of town. I still didn't quite understand what I was getting myself into. Some of the participants had played this game a number of times before. Several others, including Dean and me, didn't have a clue what we were supposed to do, nor how to do it. Not only that, our horses didn't know what was going on either.

The game was played with an inflated rubber ball like the ones we used to play kickball with in elementary school. Since this was a variation of polo, we had to have a mallet. Someone had made mallets using a long piece of rebar with a block of wood encircled by one end of the rebar. The players hung onto the straight end of the rebar and used the wood plug to hit the rubber ball. They had some traffic cones set up at each end of the arena to serve as the goals.

The game was pretty much a "free-for-all," meaning anywhere the ball went you and your horse could pursue it. Since these horses weren't trained for this activity, there were frequent collisions as horses were guided from different directions to place their riders in position to hit the ball. We riders were not necessarily "skilled" for hitting the ball with the cumbersome mallets, so we might hit our own horse, or an opponent's horse, the ball, or nothing but air. As often as not, when I swung my mallet at the ball, I would miss it entirely and the weight of the mallet would cause it to swing in front of the horse—this usually caused a negative reaction from the horse. I shot across the arena toward the ball at the same time one of the opponents headed for it. My horse decided it did not want to have a collision with the other horse, so it slammed on the brakes and reared its head right straight back into my face. My glasses went flying off and landed on the dirt floor of the arena. Things slowed down long enough for me to retrieve my "flattened" glasses. At least the lenses were still in place. I walked over to Dean, reminded him he was my optometrist and asked him to fix my glasses. Since I couldn't see without them, that pretty much ended my one and only attempt to play "cowboy polo," and I don't remember Dean ever doing so again either.

PAT AND BABE, THE COVERED HAYWAGON, AND THE PARTY BARN

Afriend of ours in Clarkston introduced us to her mother, Ev Snedden, who lived on the shore of Pend Oreille Lake near Sandpoint, ID. During the years we lived in Clarkston and Walla Walla, we made many trips to visit Ev. Matthew and Thomas grew up knowing her as "Grandma Ev." The boys loved to play near the shore and occasionally used her paddle boat to putter around on the lake. When the boys were grown and gone, Shirley and I still ventured north to visit Ev frequently. On one of those trips in the fall of 1992, Ev said there was something happening in Sandpoint that she wanted to take us to see. Turns out it was the annual North Idaho Draft Horse and Mule Show at the Bonner County Fairgrounds.

The show really piqued our interest, so each year we would return to see the draft horse and mule show. It never dawned on me what kind of impact that show would have on us. In 1995, as I was driving home from work to begin our Christmas vacation, I said out loud to myself, "That's what I want, a couple of Belgian draft horses!" That really surprised me as I had not really thought of ever doing something like that until that very moment.

We were living in the Blue Mountains about ten miles east of Walla Walla in Blue Creek Canyon. While most of our ten acres was steep timbered land, we had about two acres of fairly flat land north of the creek that bisected our property. There was plenty of room to build a barn and a corral in back of our house. I began looking for barn specifications and drawings and soon enlisted our friend, Larry Bayman, to begin building the barn. It would actually be a two-story earth-sheltered barn with a dirt road running up the north side giving us easy vehicular access for stacking hay upstairs in the loft. Eventually, we added a four-rail white vinyl fence to establish a corral.

At that time, Shirley and I taught a young married couple's Sunday School class at the Nazarene Church in Walla Walla. One young couple, Craig and Tami, were involved in cattle ranching. Craig and his father also owned and operated a stockyard west of Walla Walla where they held livestock auctions weekly. I thought when I was ready to buy the horses, since I wanted Belgians, I should go to the mid-west where they were more abundant especially near the Amish communities. I had mentioned to Craig that it would be good if he could go with me to pick out a pair and help me transport them to Walla Walla.

I thought taking horse driving lessons would probably be a smart thing to do before buying the horses. Someone tipped me off about a man in southwest Oregon who gave private driving lessons. I contacted him and made arrangements to visit his ranch where he had several Percheron draft horses we could work with. I learned three very important lessons that day. The first involved keeping track of where my feet were in relation to where the horse's hooves were. One of the horses taught me that by stepping on the toe of my boot; it barely caught one toe before I was able to step back.

My trainer was very particular about how to harness the horses, so he had me practice that many times throughout the day. That was the second thing I learned. If the harnessing is not done properly, it can irritate the horses or it can cause them to do something you didn't want them to do.

That afternoon we had two Percherons hitched to a small cart when we went out to a pasture to practice various maneuvers. There was an irrigation ditch that split the pasture in half. My trainer said he had never tried driving his horses over a small bridge that crossed the ditch, but he had always wanted to do so. One of the horses was quite tall and the other was fairly short. As we crossed the bridge, the taller horse almost pushed the small one off the bridge. On our return trip across the bridge, the shorter horse put its shoulder under the taller horse's shoulder which made it impossible for the taller horse to push the shorter one to the side. This was the third lesson I learned that day—these horses are smart and they learn quickly.

While all the barn construction was going on, the Corps sent me to Kansas City, MO, to attend a class entitled Organizational Leadership for Executives (most often referred to as OLE). I was there for two weeks and our instructors had us write in a journal every day discussing what we were thinking about in our private lives. The instructors would read the journals and return them with comments each day. I happened to mention that I wanted to buy some Belgian horses but I still had other things to do first to get ready to buy them. The next day I received a comment from one of the instructors that was simply: "Sometimes better is the enemy of good enough!" That has stuck with me for the rest of my life.

Shortly after I returned home from that class, Tami called me from the stockyard after an evening auction at about 9:00 p.m. and she seemed to be somewhat afraid to tell me something as she was slowly trying to get to the point of the call. It went something like this: "Craig, uh, has bought, uh, you, uh, a pair of Belgian mares!" Boy was I ever shocked! She went on to explain that a man was moving from northern Washington to the Walla Walla area and he had two well-trained mares that he had used for logging, pulling wagons in parades, and hayrides, but he had nowhere to keep them now. Reluctantly, he brought them to the auction in hopes someone would buy them. Craig realized they were "dead broke" and would be great for someone like me who was just starting out in the business and not yet even "green broke." Those are two terms well-defined in the horse business. "Dead broke" means they really know what to do and when to do it. "Green broke" means the horses or the person trying to control them hasn't a clue what to do. So, Craig saw the value of these two Belgian mares and bought them in case I wanted them.

Craig wasn't too concerned if I chose not to take them. He could easily sell them at the stockyard within a couple of weeks. Trusting Craig's judgment, I drove out to the stockyard after work the next day and got acquainted with the "girls." The horses came with bridles, leather harnesses, and a yoke. With Craig's help and gentle guidance, we harnessed them up and I drove them around the dirt parking lot long enough to believe they were truly dead broke. They not only responded to the reins, but they also responded to "gee" (turn right) and "haw" (turn left) and "whoa" verbal commands.

We paid the $800 that was being asked for each girl and they were suddenly ours. Their names were Pat and Babe, ages fifteen and fourteen respectively. Although Babe was the younger, in their relationship Babe was definitely in charge. We still weren't quite ready to bring the girls to our place, so I rushed around and bought some metal panels to make a small enclosure inside the corral. I still remembered the quote about better being the enemy of good enough. We weren't quite where we wanted to be, but we plunged ahead. I had to get a water tank and a heater to keep the water from freezing in the winter. We purchased some hay from another young couple from our Sunday School class and got it stored away in the barn loft.

In order to learn how to "drive" my horses and develop some good driving skills, I purchased a two-wheel farm implement pulling cart for practicing. The bad thing about that cart was that the driver sat so low that the view ahead of me never changed! I couldn't see where I wanted to go, what I needed to maneuver around, or when to start having them turn as all I could see was the horses' rumps.

The girls each weighed about 1,800 pounds. In order to maintain a healthy weight, we fed each about one-third of a hundred-pound bale of hay each morning. They would supplement that with about ten gallons of water daily. To let them know I was heading out to feed them, each morning I would ring an old ranch triangle as I left the house. They would come running across the corral toward me. Just when it looked like they would crash through the fence, they would come to a sliding halt—they never ran into the fence.

One snowy morning as I was heading toward the corral, I noticed that it looked like they had been chewing chunks off the top rail of their white vinyl fence. Upon closer examination, I realized the missing "chunks of fence" were merely places where they had stuck their heads across the fence knocking accumulated snow away.

We were surprised a couple of times to look out the front of our house to see the girls grazing in the neighbor's yard to the west. Their corral was on the east side of the house. Sure enough, on both occasions, I had failed to latch the corral gate correctly.

Soon after we got the girls, I was attending a fish and wildlife conference in Portland. We were staying at the Red Lion at the Lloyd Center in Portland. The morning we were to head home, I received a call at 6:00 a.m. from Shirley. She called to tell me, "The horses are gone!" She had gone out to feed them and discovered a couple of rails of the fence had been knocked down at the only diagonal corner. The girls apparently discovered if they leaned against those rails, they would pop out of the supporting posts. With the top two rails down, it was easy for them to just step over the bottom two rails.

Shirley had no idea where the girls were, so she got several neighbors and friends looking both upstream and downstream. After an hour or so of searching, she found them in a corral at a ranch on Mill Creek, seven miles from our home! When she approached the house a man came out. She told him, "You have my horses in your corral!" He explained that his dogs had been barking at something before sunup. When he went outside to see what the trouble was, he found Pat and Babe grazing on the grass along his driveway. He went to his barn, got a coffee can full of oats, and managed to bribe them into entering his corral.

Shirley was able to call me on my cell phone about the time we reached The Dalles, OR. I did manage to slow down to near the speed limit the rest of the way home. A neighbor volunteered to haul the "runaways" home once I got back. First, we placed one of the heavy metal corral panels across the broken fence opening and secured it in place. The next day, I purchased an electric fence kit. I drilled holes through the tops of all the vinyl fence posts. Then I secured one end of the wire to a kabob skewer with duct tape and proceeded to thread the wire through every post, and pulled the wire completely around the corral.

Once the "hot wire" was in place and working, the girls decided to go investigate this addition to the top of the fence. Since they always stood close to each other, we watched as Babe walked up to inspect the wire. She definitely got more than she was anticipating. She turned around so fast she almost knocked Pat off her hooves. I never saw either one of them ever approach the hot wire again.

We attended a draft horse show and auction in Redmond, OR, the following spring. While there, we came across a "mountain hack," a four-wheeled, two-seat wagon that we purchased. The owner delivered it to us in Walla Walla a few days later. This wagon was quite an upgrade from a buckboard that had no springs. This wagon had springs front to back and above each axle from side to side. It made for a much smoother ride. The first time we harnessed up the girls and took it for a drive, we realized the front wheels could only turn a short distance before they would dig into the side of the wagon.

At the draft horse shows we usually ran into Jim Jensen, owner of Ox Bow Trading Company of Canyon City, OR. Jim specialized in antiques from the mid-west, including horse-drawn wagons. He and his crew also built wagons of all shapes and sizes, up to and including a stagecoach. We decided it would be nice to have a wagon for hayrides. So, Jim and I began looking at various designs, and working over the phone, we came up with our own unique covered hay wagon design. To this day, it is the only hay wagon I've ever seen that was purposely made for handicap accessibility. We had two ramps stored under the bed that could be pulled out to allow for wheelchair access. We also installed a drop-down step system for other passengers.

While Jim and his crew worked on building the hay wagon, I asked if he could extend the front axle eight inches on each end on the mountain hack and put a rubber roller on the side of the bed so that the wheels could be turned more sharply without digging into the side of the bed. I also asked about putting rubber on the metal tread of the wooden wheels. He seemed to think he could do all that. So, I rented a flatbed trailer, loaded the mountain hack, and took it to Canyon City.

The hay wagon design was simple, but not like any I had ever seen before. For one thing, it was a covered wagon. The canvas top was rolled up along the supporting frame so people sitting on hay bales in the center of the wagon could look outside. We had lots of wildlife in Blue Creek Canyon, so we wanted people to be able to watch for the deer, elk, bear, and wild turkeys that were easily observable on the hillsides. The canvas cover would provide shade on sunny days and protect the riders from occasional light rains.

Remembering my inability to see ahead of the horses when I was first practicing with the farm implement cart, we designed the driver's padded seat to be high enough to see over the girls. That made me feel much more comfortable when I had a load of passengers. Shirley also helped me out by providing me with a sweatshirt with an orange "slow vehicle" symbol on the back. That was a good idea since we were on a county road for most of our rides. We also hung a slow vehicle sign on the back of the wagon.

Since we were going to be on pavement for most of our rides, we also chose to use air-inflatable tires on the wagon. That came in really handy when I went to Canyon City to pick up the wagon. We also added tail lights in case I would be pulling the wagon on a public road. If we were to pull it with my truck, I needed one hitch for the truck and a different one for the horses.

Both the construction of the hay wagon and modifications to the mountain hack were finished at about the same time. It just happened that the mountain hack could fit inside the hay wagon so I didn't have to make two trips to Canyon City to get them both. I was really taking it easy when I first got out on the highway as I didn't know how well the hay wagon would pull directly in back of our Dodge pickup. A few miles down the road I was on a stretch of freeway and to my astonishment, I was doing sixty-five miles per hour with the hay wagon directly behind me with no sideways movement at all!

It took some help from neighbors to get the mountain hack out of the hay wagon without damaging anything. Then it was time to back the hay wagon into the barn where we would store it between times we would use it. Oooppss! The wagon was two inches too high to get it through the barn door. So I hopped on my ever faithful Sears garden tractor and had Thomas stand on the scraper blade so it would cut into the ground beneath the door. After twenty or so trips across the entrance, we were able to get the hay wagon in the barn.

My original intentions were to have a stall inside the barn for the girls. Surely it would be appreciated during the winter when it would snow and temperatures could easily be well below freezing. Turns out they didn't like being inside any time they could be outside. We had built a shed roof over the area next to the stall and that is where they would stand if it was raining or snowing. This behavior had me rethinking how we could use the barn. We turned the inside stall into the hay storage area since it was right next to where we would feed the girls. That kept us from having to haul hundred-pound hay bales downstairs from the loft or dropping them through the upstairs trap door to the floor below.

When we were first thinking about doing hay rides, Ev had introduced us to the owner of a farm near Dear Park, WA. We went to visit the owner to see his party barn, his horses, and his hay wagon. He had actually turned a hog-farrowing barn into a party barn. Once we decided we didn't have to store our hay in the loft, we decided to turn the entire upstairs into a party barn.

It is a good thing we never thought we would get rich off all the time and effort we put into the horses, the wagons, and the party barn. Shirley and I were both working full-time, so we didn't really want to get into a major advertising campaign to get people to use our party barn and take hay wagon rides. Instead, we invited fellow employees, friends from church, and neighbors to experience what we had available. We really wanted our friends and fellow employees to be our "advertisers" by word of mouth throughout our community. That didn't work out so well. Over a two-year period, we had exactly two paying groups who took advantage of a hay ride and the use of the party barn. We did get a number of requests for us to "donate" a free hayride for a variety of worthy causes, but we chose not to take advantage of those "opportunities."

When our church in Walla Walla was celebrating its hundredth anniversary, we were asked if we would participate in Walla Walla's annual parade over Labor Day Weekend. We agreed to do so. The church had created a banner that some of the teens carried in front of us. Then we loaded about twenty-five younger kids and their leaders into the hay wagon. It really looked sharp.

Since this was my first time to drive the girls before crowds of people, I was quite nervous to say the least. Pretty soon, Pat was bobbing her head up and down, something I had never seen her do before. Shirley was walking beside the girls during the parade just in case she had to help me stop them. She came back to the wagon and reported that I was pulling so hard on the reins that Pat was having problems with her bit. As soon as I relaxed my grip she stopped her head bobbing.

Somewhere during the process of getting started with this entire effort, I wrote a couple of articles that were published in the *Draft Horse Journal* and the *Small Farmer's Journal* sharing our start-up experiences in hopes it would help others who wanted to do something similar.

When the neighbors came for a wagon ride and a potluck, I noticed after everyone was through eating that all of the kids had disappeared and it was just adults sitting around visiting. I looked out at the corral to find about a dozen kids practically standing under Pat and Babe while petting them. The "girls" loved all the attention and were very careful not to step on anyone. However, I did rush out to "supervise" while the kids continued to admire the girls who were soaking up all the attention the kids were giving them.

One group that rented the party barn was from a local church. They were celebrating the fall harvest season. They decorated the barn with corn stalks and pumpkins and treated themselves to a potluck. We had equipped the loft area with a kitchenette with hot and cold water, a serving table (an old ping-pong table covered with tablecloths), a refrigerator, ten round vinyl tables, and forty chairs. We stored the mountain hack in the loft and decorated the walls with lots of antiques. We even added a 1930s wood-burning cook stove, but it was only to add to the ambiance as it was not set up for cooking. The loft looked almost like a pizza parlor with red and white checkered tablecloths. After their harvest dinner, the group had a variety of games available for both children and adults.

The "Walla Walla Fun Club" consisted of a group of people who were in their forties or fifties. They started out with only four couples who had young children at home about twenty years earlier. They wanted an outlet to go out and have fun with adults their own age, unencumbered with their children, so they started their club. It eventually ended up with more than a dozen couples. Each month, two couples were assigned to plan an event for the next month. They had some simple rules. You could not attend their events unless both spouses were in attendance. You weren't told what the future event was, but they sometimes told you how to dress for a particular outing (Western wear when they came to our party barn).

About twelve couples showed up around 5:00 p.m. We took them on a hay ride along Blue Creek Road. When they returned to the barn, a local caterer from one of the more popular restaurants in Walla Walla was set up to provide them a barbecued chicken dinner with all the trimmings. It was only after dinner was over that the two couples who had planned that month's event revealed that they had hired a square dance caller to come to teach them how to square dance. Only two people in the entire group had ever square danced before, so it was a riot watching them trying to figure out when to "dosey doe" or "twirl your partner." They all seemed to be having a fantastic time.

Earlier in the day, the people planning the event asked how late they could stay. We said we really didn't care. We would wait till they were gone, then clean up the party barn. After their ride, dinner, and dancing lesson, they were all gone by 9:30 p.m. I think they were all pretty much exhausted following the square dancing.

We chose not to allow people to serve alcohol at our place, in part due to the higher cost of business insurance if we did, and secondly, we didn't feel it was necessary for people to be drinking before driving a curvy mountain road back to town. When the Walla Walla Fun Club was preparing to leave, one woman approached Shirley and thanked us for not allowing alcohol at this event. She and her husband had adopted four children all of whom were fetal alcohol syndrome children. She went on to say that alcohol could sometimes be disruptive within their circle of friends in the club.

We had quite an age range of people who participated in some of our rides. A fellow Corps employee and his wife actually brought their one-week-old baby on a ride. The oldest person to ever enjoy one of our hay rides was my dad; he was almost ninety years old at the time.

We continued to attend the draft horse shows in Sandpoint every year and twice attended a similar event in Redmond, OR. I had developed carpal tunnel syndrome and was finding it harder and more painful to lift the heavy leather harnesses onto the horses. While at one of the Sandpoint shows, I met Bev of Big Sky Leatherworks who had a large display of harness equipment that their company produced. She introduced me to "biothane" harnesses, a much lighter-weight material that was also much easier to maintain. The biothane harness weighed only about half as much as a leather harness, but seemed to be just as durable as the leather harnesses.

One thing I really liked about the biothane material is it didn't need to be kept oiled in order to keep it pliable and supple. When removing the biothane harnesses after a hay ride, I would take them off the girls, hang them on the hitching post, wipe them with some soapy water, spray them off, dry them, and hang them in the tack room. I didn't mind giving up the oily tack at all.

Two of my former employees had adopted several children. When they came for a hay ride with a group from our church, one of their children, Isaac, a kindergartner, was too afraid of the horses to pet them. After the ride, all the adults and their children headed to the house where Shirley had prepared desserts and drinks for them. Our pastor and I were unharnessing the horses while getting ready to turn them back into their corral and putting the harnesses back in the tack room. While we were both working on Pat, we noticed that Isaac had stayed with us. He had picked up a rag and was wiping down Babe's belly as that was as high as he could reach! As usual, she enjoyed all the attention she could get.

We were nearing retirement and we certainly weren't making any money off our "Blue Creek Belgians" enterprise. It was costing a lot for feed, hoof care, and vet expenses, so we decided to sell the girls and the tack. It just happened that the gentleman we bought them from had obtained some fenced pasture land near town and he wanted to buy them back. We sold them to him for exactly what we had paid to get them about seven years earlier.

My last horse experience was a total disaster. If you've ever heard stories about "horse traders," it probably wasn't a good experience for the buyer. That is exactly what happened to me. I learned of a lady south of town who had some horses for sale. After looking at them and riding them in a round pen, I decided to take them. One was an Appaloosa and the other was a buckskin. They were to be delivered with all the tack we would need. It was a rainy day when the lady (I use that term loosely in this case) delivered the horses to us. She was in a big hurry to get gone, so we turned the horses, Rita and Ranger, into the corral and took the tack into the barn. She was gone before I got to look over the tack and see what kind of shape it was in. Some of it looked like she might have picked it up at a dump!

Rita was a very nice-looking buckskin while Ranger was an Appaloosa quarter horse cross. One was supposedly eight and the other about ten. It took me a while to figure out a few things, but when I did, I knew these horses were not for us. I'm almost certain she had them sedated the day we went to look at them. Never having owned riding horses before, we soon learned that neither horse was gentle enough for us to ride them. So, we advertised them for sale. Rita was purchased by a guy in Walla Walla who immediately took her to a vet for a medical assessment. The vet told him Rita was at least twenty-one years old based on her dentition. The new owner promptly returned her to us and we refunded his money.

As a follow-up, I reported the "lady" to the Better Business Bureau, the county sheriff, and the Washington Department of Agriculture. Among other things, it seems she was failing to pay the appropriate taxes when selling her horses. Don't know how that ended up, but hopefully it wasn't all peaches and cream for her.

We were getting ready to take a driving trip to Alaska soon after I retired in 2005, so we really wanted to have Rita and Ranger gone before we left. We didn't want the neighbor kids to have to take care of them while we were gone. Somehow we learned that a Christian boys' camp over on the Snake River was interested in them. We decided to donate both horses to them. The day before we left on our Alaska trip, the camp wrangler came to pick them up. He was a long-time horseman and figured he could use them in his camp riding programs. We later learned that both horses were working really well for him.

As a retiree, I'm in a new phase of my life. We moved from north Idaho in the fall of 2019. I was happy to leave my snowblower and snow shovel behind. Before moving to Dallas, OR, I was doing an internet search to see if there were any horse rental businesses in the Willamette Valley where I could go for an occasional ride.

I just happened to stumble on the Horses of Hope (HOH) website. They provide equine horse therapy for people of all ages with a diversity of physical, mental, emotional, and behavioral disabilities. I decided to sign up as a volunteer and started working with them in January of 2020. By mid-March, that came to a screeching halt due to the COVID-19 pandemic. We weren't able to start up again until early September.

I volunteered every Thursday morning from 8:30 a.m. until noon. My routine usually started by sweeping straw and poop off the main aisle in front of the stalls. As the clients arrived, I would start helping to get the horses ready for the clients' lessons for the day. Some clients would brush and curry the horse and even help saddle it. Most of the time we had the horse already saddled or had a riding pad and a surcingle (a belt around the horse for the client to hang on to) already on the horse. Sometimes we had to use a powered chair lift to raise the client out of his/her wheelchair, then gently swing them over the saddle, and lower them onto the horse.

The horse was always led by an instructor as we walked around the indoor arena or headed outside for some trail riding. My job was to walk along beside the horse with my hand on the horse near the client—that's so I would be ready to catch the client if he or she started to fall off. Fortunately, that never happened. They call us "side walkers." I would walk two or three miles in the morning doing this. When not assigned to work with a client, I had other chores to do. Every item that a client touched had to be sanitized after use. That includes saddles and game objects such as balls and other toys. I jokingly tell people I'm working on my "HPSC"—that would be my Horse Poop Scooping Certification. I always came home totally exhausted and somewhat smelly.

Most of the horses at HOH have been donated by people who can no longer keep them or if a horse is no longer capable of performing duties it was trained for. For instance, a ranch horse trained to work with cattle might become too old for that kind of active work, but they can still be ridden at a slower pace. Gloria is a miniature horse that is often used just to introduce a client to horses. On the other end of the spectrum are Dalli (a Percheron mare) and Prince (a Belgian gelding); these draft horses are both quite tall and heavy. The other dozen or so horses are of many different breeds and can vary quite a bit in size. Before a donated or purchased horse can be used for client therapy sessions, it is thoroughly checked out and trained to ensure it is compatible with equine therapy work.

I really enjoyed working with the clients knowing that they are benefiting from the equine experience. All the clients were there due to emotional, physical, behavioral, or mental disabilities. We had a three-year-old girl who had a "killer" smile. She was so excited to ride a horse for the first time in her life. She giggled and laughed the entire time she was on the horse. Other clients I've worked with have ranged in age from ten to fifty-four years old. Some of the clients are very difficult to converse with while others will talk nonstop the entire time they are in the saddle. I tell people I think working at HOH is good therapy for me as well as for the clients as I enjoy working with both people and horses. Here is a quote that has been attributed to several different people over the years, "The outside of a horse is good for the inside of a man." I agree.

One client was especially fun to work with. She has some physical deformities that make it necessary for her to use a wheelchair to get around. She was twenty-four years old, well-educated, and even sought after to give speeches regarding working with people with a variety of disabilities. We like to tease each other as she rode the horses. One day I asked her if she had a boyfriend. Her response was a classic: "It's complicated!"

A year into my HOH volunteering, I began to have problems with my right knee. It was probably due to the fact that while walking beside the horse, I was not on the trail, but rather I was walking on uneven ground beside the trail. So in April 2021, I had to give up my Thursday morning volunteering. My family doctor recommended I try some physical therapy. After two months of that, there did not seem to be any improvement to my knee. A couple more months went by and my condition did not improve.

Eventually, an MRI would reveal that I had a torn piece of my right meniscus that was causing the irritation in my knee. It took a couple more months to land an appointment with an orthopedic surgeon in Salem, OR. I met with him on December 3, 2021. I was finally scheduled for surgery on February 18, 2022. Don't know if I'll be able to return to HOH until after the surgery. Later—sadly, I was not able to return to HOH.

TEACHING ENVIRONMENTAL EDUCATION

The summer I graduated from Fresno State, I was fortunate to enter a teaching internship program through the Fresno County Schools and Kings Canyon Unified School District. I took classes at FSC all summer and was required to take night courses during the school year. My school principal, Mr. Vern Bretz, and Mrs. Lemons, a retired teacher, would be my student-teacher supervisors while I taught a fifth grade class and received a full teacher's salary of a whopping $6,000 per year. Wow, that was real money! Together, the most Shirley and I had made so far was $5,800 per year.

I needed to complete thirty college units in two years in order to meet the internship requirements. Upon completion of the internship and the thirty units, I would receive a Lifetime Elementary Teaching Certification. So I was taking courses three nights a week, and to help pay for Shirley to finish her degree, I was working as a janitor for a friend three nights a week from 6:00 p.m. to midnight cleaning offices and businesses.

Beards weren't normally seen on teachers in those days. I had a beard at the time I was to start teaching, so I thought I had better shave it before school started. When I met the other fifth grade teacher with whom I would be working, I was surprised to see that he was bald, but he had a full beard.

I'm not an interior decorator person, so my classroom tended to be rather devoid of the fantastic bulletin boards other teachers provided. I usually put up some background colored butcher paper with those crinkly bulletin board borders and would have the kids do projects that we would post on them throughout the year. More often than not, it would be the students who would come up with ideas to show off their work.

One assignment I gave them was to create a short story that they would write and then share with the rest of the class. Marcelino wrote a story that I still have in my home file cabinet. Keep in mind that this was taking place in rural California in 1970. His story started out with some commotion that began on the school's playground. Eventually, the police were called in and they ended up having to shoot Mr. Hixson! I'll never forget his next sentence: "And everyone lived happily ever after!"

Our school hosted what was then known as a "special ed" class. We spent extra time with our students explaining to them that the "special ed kids" had issues that were often beyond their control and that they should all be treated with the same respect they were to show each other in their own classrooms. When another school came to our site to play football, some of the visiting students were being disrespectful to the special ed kids from our school. This led to a fight between one of my students and a visiting student. When asked what started the fight, my student explained it was because the other student was not treating our special ed students properly! After hearing his excuse, I found it hard to discipline him for getting into a fight.

Due to not enough students entering the fifth grade at my school the next year, I was moved to another school in the same district. I was in a stand-alone classroom known affectionately as the "chicken coop." It was in fact the kitchen and cafeteria of the school when it was built back around 1920. I'm only five feet six inches tall, but I had to duck to keep from bumping my head on the lights hanging from the ceiling.

Although it doesn't get extremely cold in the San Joaquin Valley in the winter, the fog makes it seem a lot colder than it really is. We had one wall heater in our room. The room was so small that my eighteen students pretty much filled the room. When the heater stopped working, I had to threaten the principal that I would call parents and have them come pick up their kids if they didn't get someone there pronto to get us some heat. It worked!

The interesting thing about those eighteen students was that in that class there were three sets of identical twins: Harry and Jerry, Wayne and Dwayne, and Mary and Susan (don't know why their parents didn't give them rhyming names—I thought that was required!).

The following year I moved to the sixth grade at Alta Elementary giving me an opportunity to participate in the district's Science and Conservation program (SciCon). In fact, Superintendent Silas Bartsch told me when I was hired that he eventually wanted me to teach sixth grade so I could be a part of the SciCon program. It mostly entailed taking a trip to the Bob Mathias (former decathlon Olympic champion) Camp near Sequoia Lake for one day in the fall. Then we returned to the camp for a full week of outdoor education in the spring. In between these two trips, there was no curriculum developed to support the program.

During my first year in SciCon, I co-taught an environmental interpretation class for all of our district's sixth grade teachers who were required to participate in SciCon. At that time, only one other teacher in the program had a science background. Through my own research, I discovered that most available environmental study materials for elementary-aged students were coming out of the East Coast at that time. That meant that their materials were focused on the geology, flora, and fauna of the eastern US. Following their patterns of presentation, I began writing materials for use in my classroom so I could turn the program into a year-long activity emphasizing the geology, flora, and fauna of the Sierra Nevada Mountains and the San Joaquin Valley. I really got into this project in a big way.

Mr. Lloyd Geist had been heading up the SciCon program since the district first adopted it. He asked me to help teach other sixth grade teachers some environmental interpretation techniques. We put together a field trip and some classes through Fresno Pacific College. On our first field trip, we stopped along a road where you could see the difference between the fenced pasture lands and the area between the road and the fence. In the tall grasses near the road, Lloyd reached down and picked a purple flower and held it up to the group to see and stated, "I haven't seen one of these in a long time." I was quick to point out, "And now you may never see another one!"

As I mentioned earlier, the primary activity for this program involved a five-day stay at the Bob Mathias Camp near Sequoia Lake in the Sierra Nevadas. To get the kids excited about the five-day stay, we would take a day trip to the camp in the fall. In late fall, it was usually cool enough that snakes were not very active. We would give the students an introduction to the camp and its facilities and talk about some of the activities they would be involved in when we came back the following spring.

On that sunny fall day after the kids ate their sack lunches, my teaching partner and I would have the students go sit by themselves on the side of a grassy slope above a stream. They were to be quiet, listen to the natural sounds of the area, and just relax. We told them to do this for fifteen minutes. Fortunately, this was long before kids that age had access to a watch or cell phone, so they had no idea how long fifteen minutes would be. We chose not to tell them when the fifteen minutes were up. Some students started arriving back at our designated gathering area after twenty to twenty-five minutes. Some didn't show up for forty-five minutes. At the end of the school year when we asked our students to tell us what they enjoyed most about the SciCon program, a majority said what they enjoyed most of all was being alone during the quiet "fifteen minutes" on the hillside during the fall!

For the week at Bob Mathias Camp, each student had to pay $16. Costs were low as some of the school cooks and other helpers volunteered their time. As long as I was teaching in the program, I was also our teachers' representative on the Parent Teacher Association (PTA) board. I managed to convince the other board members (parents) that since every student would eventually get to go to camp as a sixth grader, the PTA should pay half of their fee. Many of our students would not have been able to afford even this small amount if their families had to pay the total amount of $32.

When we returned for the week of SciCon camp in the spring, temperatures were warmer, so it was very likely that we would encounter snakes in the area. So, the first afternoon at camp, we took all fifty-plus students up to a southwest-facing granite outcropping where I knew there would be some rattlesnakes. The rattlers could almost always be found about two to three feet down in the rock crevasses where it was cooler during the heat of the day. It afforded them protection while at the same time, they could escape the hot surfaces of the sun-heated granite. I wanted the students to not only see the snakes but to also hear them so they would always know what that sound was. Students who had their Instamatic cameras were allowed to take pictures of the snakes.

During the course of the week, we always encountered other critters including other snake species. One day while on a hike, a student behind me immediately yelled out, "Mr. Hixson, a snake!" Sure enough, as I looked down between my feet there was a garter snake a couple of feet long with a mouse headed down its throat headfirst. The mouse was still struggling to escape. Once that snake thought it was in imminent danger from a herd of students, it decided to get rid of the mouse as quickly as possible. While we stood there watching, the snake spits up the mouse. The poor little mouse struggled to get its breath as it obviously wasn't able to breathe while descending down the snake's throat. The snake took off in a hurry, so we stood there waiting to see what would happen to the mouse. It eventually caught its breath enough that it began climbing the closest tree. Last we saw the mouse it appeared to be much happier than when we first saw it.

I was always looking for ways to engage the students directly in the study of nature. I came up with an activity called "Pick a Plant to Peruse." On a "dittoed sheet" of paper (again, ask your parents what this is), I listed things to look at on a plant of their own choosing. They were to describe things like the size, color, shape, and texture of their plant's leaves. They were to study the trunks and stems of their plant as well as any flowers, cones, seed pods, or seeds and list their characteristics. The final thing that would really make this "their" plant was the opportunity to give the plant a name that they thought would be suitable for it. Only after they had completed this exercise would I tell them the name commonly used for "their" plant so they could look it up in one of our research materials to see how their personal descriptions were similar or different to those of the scientists who gave "their" plant its official scientific and common name. I would also point out the importance of the scientific name when people were doing research as many plants and animals have common names that vary from place to place. As an example, there are over fifty common names for a mountain lion here in the US.

The last night at camp was always reserved for our "night hike." We walked far enough up the road so that we could see the lights of the towns in the San Joaquin four thousand feet below us and many miles away. On clear nights one could see all the way from Sacramento to Bakersfield (almost three hundred miles). We also spent some time stargazing and checking out the Milky Way with no city lights nearby to interfere with the view of the night sky.

On one of these hikes, a student found a California mountain king snake. What a beauty it was with its colorful red, black, and white ringed body! I managed to capture it to take it back to the main lodge where we had aquariums for studying such critters. As usual, I picked the snake up in the back of its head and headed for the lodge. Unfortunately for me, this little guy was a wiggle-wart of the first order; it eventually worked its head around to where it could bite into the flesh beside my thumbnail. It wouldn't let go until I pulled it free!

We had a rule that a critter could be placed in an aquarium in the lodge for twenty-four hours so everyone could study it, then it was to be returned to the habitat where it was originally found. So, we started looking for an empty aquarium in which to deposit our newfound "friend." All but one aquarium was already in use, so we decided that was the one for us. We did notice a three-by-five-inch card taped on the back of the aquarium, but we just figured someone had made a label for one of the critters that had occupied it earlier in the week. As I released the snake in the aquarium, it began looking for an escape route. It tried climbing out both ends and the back of the aquarium facing the wall. Next, it slithered straight out the front of the aquarium in our direction! After I recaptured our friend, we turned the aquarium around and read the note on the back of it. The card quite clearly stated: DO NOT USE!

The nice thing about a California mountain king snake is that although it looks somewhat like a coral king snake found in the southeastern US, our snake was not poisonous. We taught the kids a way to remember which snake is poisonous and which is not by having them memorize this simple poem about the colored rings in the length of their bodies:

> Red on black,
> My friend jack.
> Red on yellow,
> Kill a fellow.

Besides the spring week in the Sierra Nevadas, I also arranged for a field trip during the winter to the Mendota Wildlife Refuge on the west side of the San Joaquin Valley. It was a winter home for thousands of migratory ducks and geese that traveled the Pacific Flyway from their nesting grounds in the far north where they would spend the summer. On one of those visits, the refuge manager told our school bus driver to pick up the speed a little and honk the horn as we headed down a road through the middle of the refuge. As we did so, thousands of ducks and geese took to the air honking and quacking as they lifted off the water. The kids were totally awe-struck by the sight and sounds as the air filled with waterfowl.

My classroom began to look like a natural history museum over time as students would bring things to add to our classroom collection. I had an ostrich egg and a hummingbird egg sitting next to each other on the back shelf. We had an aquarium full of mosquito fish that one of the kids brought me from a nearby irrigation ditch. Wayne and Dwayne brought in a sparrow hawk that had dived into some tall grass after prey, but it ended up getting stuck in the grass. I always kept a small cage in the back of the room for such critters. We watched the sparrow hawk for a couple of days, feeding it raw hamburger which it took readily. We then took it out on the playground and opened the cage. It finally hopped out and flew straight up before heading to a nearby orchard.

Someone had brought a small garter snake to school, so it was put into the cage in the back of the room. Everything seemed to be going well for it until the night janitor called me at home to tell me the snake was out in the classroom. I had to drive out to school and recapture the snake as the janitor was not going to touch it. I soon had it back in its cage. Apparently, someone had not closed the cage door properly at the end of the day.

We had a lot of ground squirrels on the playground and they were constantly digging new holes all over our play fields. A short-tailed weasel showed up on the scene and saw the playground as a giant smorgasbord of squirrels. It took him several weeks, but by the time he was through eating ground squirrels, they were all gone.

Our school happened to be on the migration route for turkey vultures (TVs as we nicknamed them) as they made their way south for the winter. These large black birds with red heads rely on rising thermal air currents to lift them high into the air. The TVs spiraled upwards in those currents until they reached their desired altitude, then they headed further south looking to catch the next rising thermal. It just happened that our school was about halfway between two of those thermals. When the migration started in early October, we would see only a dozen or so TVs for the first few days. Then one day a huge flock would arrive. We would all go out on the playground and lay down "playing dead" while we watched over three hundred TVs soar by. Over the next few days, the numbers would dwindle until only a dozen would fly by each day.

Oh, yes, I must tell you about our trips up to Kings Canyon National Park while we were at camp in the spring. The first thing we did was wander through the Visitor Center and enjoy the displays. Then my friend, Rob Zink, would present a slide interpretive program about the park with a special emphasis on the Sequoias.

In the General Grant Grove inside the park, there is a tree known as the Fallen Monarch that fell hundreds or thousands of years ago. It was large enough that early arrivers in the area would actually use it as a shelter and a stable for their horses. Even the soldiers who were first assigned to protect the newly established Kings Canyon National Park in the early 1900s used it.

The Fallen Monarch was one of the last stops we made as we took the trail around General Grant Grove. As we were loading the bus to head down to Big Stump, one of the high school cabin counselors approached me and revealed that three of our boys had written their names on the tree with a magic marker. I sent for the three boys to come and look at the work they had done and asked them how they could get their names off the tree. They all thought sandpaper would do the trick. However, we didn't have any sandpaper with us. So, it was time for a short geology lesson. I asked them what happens to the granite these mountains are made of over a long period of time. They came to the conclusion that it often was ground into sand by glaciers or streams. I pointed to the ground where there was an abundance of sand at their feet and suggested they use what was available and get rid of their names from the tree "muy pronto"! As soon as they were through sanding (bare-handed), we boarded the bus and headed to Big Stump.

At our next stop, we were able to hike the trail at Big Stump where we could study a grove of Sequoia trees. The "Big Stump" was a Sequoia stump that was more than thirty feet in diameter. It remained after loggers had cut it down before the area was protected as a national park. It was large enough that the old timers used to square dance on it. The last thing we did before boarding the bus to return to camp was to have a snowball fight. At seven thousand feet elevation, there was always enough remaining for this activity even in mid-spring. The rule was that no one could throw a snowball at you as long as you stayed on the stump, but step one foot off and you were fair game! That meant you were "target material."

It was all my fault when I made the big mistake of convincing my teaching partner, Laraine Miyake-Combs, that she and I should go off the stump and take on all the kids in a grand snowball melee! Boy what a colossal mistake that was! Laraine was always very careful with her hair, but that day it looked like she might have just stepped out of a shower. I had so much snow packed between my glasses and my eyes, I couldn't even find the stump as big as it was! We decided not to ever do that again.

Two years in a row Laraine and I took our sixth graders to Yosemite on a field trip. Our principal and several parents went along to help chaperone. A couple of our school's cooks also came along to make sure we were all well-fed. Our assistant superintendent of schools, John Rogalsky, a certified school bus driver, even volunteered to drive for us. All the volunteers helped keep our costs to a bare minimum.

The first time we went to Yosemite it was just a one-day trip which turned out to be a little too long. One of the school board members who voted to approve the trip had a daughter in that class. At a PTA meeting a few weeks later, he asked me what I planned to do to top that trip the next year. I said, "Would you believe I'm going to go for an overnight trip to Yosemite." And with his support, that's exactly what we did.

The over-nighter gave us a lot more time to see more of the park as we went on several different hikes. John Krisko, a park ranger and Yosemite's Environmental Education Specialist, gave us a good introduction to the park before we set off on our hikes. We had no idea how interesting things would turn out in the next few hours.

Our first hike was along Tenaya Creek in the shadow of Half Dome. At the first bridge we came to, we crossed the creek and headed back toward our camp at Yellow Pine Campground. By this time we were all very hungry and ready to dive into the cornbread and stew our cooks would have waiting for us when we returned. Along the way, a very red adult black bear fell in step with us and proceeded to follow us all the way back to our campsite. My greatest fear was that the bear would get to our food before we did. However, it surprised us by sauntering right on by as if it didn't even smell our very deliciously aromatic food. Whew, what a relief!

After roasting marshmallows and singing a few campfire songs, we all settled into our sleeping bags for the night on the bare ground. The boys were in one half circle and the girls were in the other half. During the night we could hear a bear hitting garbage cans as it made its way through the campground. There were strategically placed larger "bear-proof" garbage dumpsters scattered throughout the campground. These large dumpsters had a square hole cut in one end about four feet above the ground through which you could deposit your garbage.

Well, bears are not stupid. It didn't take them long to learn that they could put their front paws inside the dumpster and pull themselves up until they could do a summersault landing on top of the garbage. Then it was buffet time!

About 3:00 a.m., one of my male students poked me in the ribs and said, "Mr. Hixson, the bear!" At that very instant the bear did its flip into an almost empty dumpster and let out a roar as it hit inside the metal container. It scared me half to death when I heard the roar and the crash inside the dumpster! Since there was very little garbage in the dumpster, we were shortly treated to watching the bear do its exit flip before it headed off to the next hopeful garbage buffet.

Around 6:00 a.m., I was hearing a lot of screaming from both the girls and boys. A coyote had wandered into our sleeping circle! As it looked for an escape route, first the girls, then the boys would start sitting up in their sleeping bags causing the poor coyote to become quite confused about its exit strategy. Finally after several turns inside the circle, it took a flying leap over some of the girls and headed for parts unknown. No doubt it was glad to escape all the commotion and racket the students were making.

Mixed with the waterfalls, granite cliffs, Sequoias, and other wildife we saw those two days, I have no doubt those kids will retain some fantastic memories from that trip for the rest of their lives.

INSURANCE FOR THE FUTURE

Since I had a lifetime Elementay Teaching Credential from California, I really didn't have to work on any other certifications unless I wanted to teach at a different level (middle school, high school, or college) or move into an administrative position. But then an opportunity arose that I thought I should take advantage of.

My female teaching partner, Laraine, was a third-generation Japanese with a master's degree in Spanish literature. During our teaching years, Dr. Wilson Riles became California's superintendent of public instruction. He decided there weren't enough females and minorities in public school administrative positions, so he decided if a teacher could pass the National Education Association's (NEA) test for Public Schools Administration, they could get their administrative credential without having to take the year of course work normally required to obtain that certification. Laraine and I both decided to take the test.

As we were walking into the building to take the test, it suddenly dawned on me that Superintendent Riles would never have approved that particular test if it had even one "conservative" answer on it as he was a dyed-in-the-wool "liberal" educator. Unfortunately, I did not get a chance to discuss my theory with Laraine before we took the test. It did not matter what the question was, I always chose what I thought was the most "liberal" answer available whether it had to do with classroom discipline, reading or math programs, or educational philosophy. As a result, I ended up ranking in the 97th percentile and obtained my Public Schools Administrative Credential. Unfortunately, Laraine answered the questions as she truly felt they should be answered. Like me, she was an educational conservative, so she did not pass the test. It was too bad because not only was she in the "target group" to obtain an administrative credential, she would have been a fantastic public school administrator. I really never thought I would want to become a school administrator, but it gave me another option for future employment.

After I left teaching and began working for the Corps of Engineers in Natural Resources Management, the California Legislature passed a law that said if a person already had an Elementary Teaching Credential and they could pass the College Level English Proficiency (CLEP) exam and an NEA exam in a secondary subject matter area, they could get that secondary credential also. So I took the CLEP and passed it, then took the Secondary Life Sciences exam and passed it. So I then had my lifetime Elementary, Life Sciences, and Public Schools Administrative credentials that I felt I could fall back on if I ever got tired of the Corps, or if the Corps got tired of me.

Shirley and I really did not ever want to move back to California, so I took some coursework and was able to obtain Elementary and Life Sciences Education teacher certification from Oregon also. We thought that someday we might want to settle somewhere in southwest Oregon, perhaps near Grants Pass. Over the years I kept both my CA and OR credentials current just in case I did want to leave the Corps. I'll always have the lifetime Elementary Certification from CA, but with only a year or so to go before retirement from the Corps, I let all the other credentials lapse.

As it turned out, I ended up teaching industrial first aid, personnel management, and occupational psychology through Walla Walla Community College, a state-mandated supervisor training course at the Walla Walla Penitentiary, and law enforcement in natural resources management at the University of Idaho. I also was on the first Corps team that began teaching our enforcement program (called Visitor Assistance) nationwide.

Early in my career, I became a certified EMT and a Red Cross first aid instructor. When I moved to Arizona, I was able to transfer my EMT certification to that state. Later, while working for the Corps in WA, ID, and OR, I continued to renew my EMT certification every three years. However, once I was working at a desk most of my time and no longer functioning as a field park ranger, I finally let my EMT certification lapse in 1987. I enjoyed serving as an EMT as I generally could stay quite calm during emergencies, thus setting people at ease as I provided medical attention to them.

OLE!

You might be thinking this chapter will be about Mexico or Spain, frijoles, burritos, enchiladas, chili rellenos, or Spanish rice (some of my favorite foods), or even bullfighting. You would be very wrong!

I worked for a part of the government that prides itself on being able to reduce any program, work unit, computer system, defensive equipment, education classes, or manpower positions to a simple acronym. I worked for the Army Corps of Engineers (ACE) within the Department of Defense (DOD). Specifically, I worked in Operations (OPS) at the Walla Walla District (WWD) in Natural Resources Management (NRM) which was not to be confused with Resource Management (RM—the money folks). I always liked to point out that while the RM folks only worked with money, we worked with a multitude of natural, human, and financial resources.

OLE was the acronym for Organizational Leadership for Executives. It was designed for GS-12 or higher-graded managers and for military people who had attained at least the rank of captain. It was a two-week course that I attended in Kansas City, MO. At the outset, I realized this was going to be conducted very much like a number of graduate education courses I had completed many years earlier. So, I decided to keep my mouth shut and let others do most of the talking. I just wanted to be a "wallflower" so to speak.

There were twenty-four participants all seated in a large circle so we could see and hear each other. The first thing we did was introduce ourselves and tell something about ourselves that might be of interest to others. I kept my introduction short and simple. One person in the group, a female from Washington, D.C., went a little deep right from the get-go. I'll merely refer to her by her initials, "MC." She told us about an oppressive mother who always told her she was "stupid" and would never amount to anything. Her story seemed to have no ending, so one of the instructors politely asked her to wind down.

According to MC, when she graduated from high school she applied to a number of colleges and universities. Unbeknownst to her, "mother dear" was tossing her acceptance letters in the trash knowing her daughter was too "stupid" to succeed in college. MC finally figured out what was happening and was able to enter college and proceed with her education. She went on to receive both an MS and a PhD. She was now fairly high up in her agency in Washington, D.C.

The course moved along to the point where the instructors broke us up into three groups of eight that we would work with for the remainder of the two weeks. Of course, there was to be a lot of discussion within our sub-groups, often followed by presentations to the other two groups. MC took it upon herself to step up to a flip chart and start recording each group's input much as a facilitator might do in a different situation. By this time the rest of us were getting a little tired of MC's unsolicited domination of the class. Finally, one of the other women, Hildegard, fired a volley at her complaining about her interference in the process. This caused a minor spat that ended with MC leaving the room in tears and in a huff. And this was just the last day of the first week of class.

One of the rules of OLE was that we could not proceed until all members were present. Since I had stayed pretty quiet all week, people thought I just might be a calming influence that could bring MC back to class even though she had said she was leaving for home. Little did I know that I had set myself up for this assignment by remaining a "wallflower" all week. I managed to catch up with her in the lounge downstairs and got her to sit down with me over a cup of coffee. We must have talked for about half an hour before one of our three class coordinators joined us. After much cajoling, we eventually talked her into returning to class.

To further try to include MC, I invited two members of our group of eight and MC to dine together that evening. There were other people I would rather have visited with that evening, but it seemed the right thing to do to keep peace in the "family" (yup, she was a member of our group of eight). So, we did our best to "bond" over dinner.

We had one member of our team of eight who was always the last to arrive for a session and was generally several minutes late. Finally, our group had become tired of her rudeness, so we read her the riot act and told her she needed to start arriving on time so we could finish our tasks earlier. She did not own a watch at that time, but by the next day, she had gone out and purchased one! From then on, we were always able to start on time.

As I mentioned earlier, we were to keep a journal about something important to us during the course. This would be shared with the class coordinators who would write comments on our writings throughout the two weeks. The topic was whatever we wanted it to be. At that time, I was in the process of building a barn, fencing a corral, purchasing harnesses, and in general preparing to purchase a pair of Belgian draft horses. In fact, over the weekend between our two weeks of OLE, a friend and I drove up to an Amish community in northern MO to look for harnesses. We also got to see the tallest Belgian I have ever seen. It was only two years old and was already nineteen hands (four inches per hand) tall. It was expected to be twenty-two hands tall when fully grown!

Back at the course, on Wednesday of the second week, we were given an assignment that began right after lunch. We would be through for the day and free to leave whenever we completed the task. I thought perhaps we could actually finish early that day. WRONG!

The task required each of us to take turns sitting "knee-to-knee" with one other group member, facing each other, and discussing how well we thought we could work together. Eventually, we were to raise our fingers to indicate "honestly" how well we thought we would do working together. Our other team members were to observe and listen to us and then give a digital rating also.

By "luck of the draw," MC and I were the first two to go through this process. I knew from the get-go this was not going to go well! One finger up meant not so good while ten fingers meant we would work well together. I lied the first time by raising four fingers just so I could get it over with. Unfortunately, MC raised 10 fingers. No way! I would have had much difficulty working with this woman. The rest of the group "helped me out" by showing a very low finger count. Then the discussion started again to see why we were so far apart. I became somewhat brutally honest and shared my innermost feelings on the matter (which is what we are supposed to do). The rest of the group agreed with me, which prompted MC to run from the room with a threat once again to leave for home.

It wasn't bad enough that we had gone first, but guess who was sent to bring her back again! Yup, yours truly. I managed to get her back after much positive stroking. We continued into the evening hours while each pair of the group went through the process. We eventually completed this exercise with each of us going through the process with all seven of our fellow group members.

About dinner time, I decided it was time to get something to eat, but we weren't supposed to leave until we had finished the assignment. So, I suggested we have pizzas delivered to our hotel conference room. While one guy placed the order, someone else collected the money. We broke for dinner and then dove right back into the task at hand, never having left the hotel. Needless to say, we did not finish until midnight. MC was the primary reason for the lateness of the session. She just could not figure out why people did not think they could work well with her, despite the reasons we shared with her.

Bless her heart! MC's mother had set the course for her by always telling her how "stupid" she was. One way or another she was going to prove to her mother and the rest of the world that she was not "stupid." Her advanced degrees and the position she held were the end result of her efforts and she insisted that everyone should know the struggles she had to overcome that title (stupid) and achieve what she had successfully managed to do.

Another task we were assigned involved writing a sentence or two that would sum up why we had chosen our particular career paths. I finally settle on: "I want to do good things for the public and good things for the environment. I figure when I'm doing the latter I'm also doing the former." I stuck with that statement for the rest of my career.

This was not the "easy" two weeks I envisioned during our first day of class. I was extremely happy to return home and get back to my NRM work.

LAVA BEDS NATIONAL MONUMENT

During my first year of teaching, I spent much of my "spare" time filling out the federal government's application form known as an SF-171, a four-page document. I had to fill each one out by hand as there was no way I could ever line up all those tiny little boxes in order to use the form in a typewriter (for you young folks, that is the predecessor of the "word processor" and the computer). My objective was to land my first job as a seasonal park ranger with the National Park Service. I was told to send a separate application to every park where I might want to work. It generally took me at least an hour to fill out each SF-171, especially if I was watching a football game on TV while doing so.

The Vietnam War was in full swing as the school year was coming to an end. I was a "lucky" recipient of number 72 in the first-ever Selective Service draft lottery. That would almost guarantee me a free trip to Vietnam! I was instructed to show up at the induction center in west Fresno for a physical. That would be only one of the three days I missed during my eight years of teaching.

I had grown a little soft during my college years and was definitely overweight. The physical took several hours as there were probably close to a hundred of us being looked at that day. One guy made the mistake of smarting off and was immediately ejected from the room with a promise that he was now in the US Army! No one else was brave enough (or should I say stupid enough) to make the same mistake.

About noon, I was ushered into a room that was no bigger than a broom closet and told to have a seat in the only chair available. There was no explanation for this action. Two hours later, someone came and got me. My blood pressure was taken for the second time that day. Next thing I knew I was told I would have to come to the induction center three days in a row for both an a.m. and a p.m. check of my blood pressure.

Whoa! That really threw me for a loop. It would mean missing three more days of teaching as the induction center was about twenty miles west of my home and my school was thirty-five miles southeast of home. I explained my dilemma to the doctor who scratched his head for a minute while he sought a workable solution for my situation. Finally, he asked me when my lunch break was. Turns out it was from 11:40 a.m. to 12:20 p.m. He asked if I could drive the five miles into Reedley (the nearest town) three days in a row at lunchtime and have a doctor's office take my blood pressure. Before the day was over, I had an appointment to do just that. The Army doctor's instructions were for me to have my blood pressure taken five minutes before noon and five minutes after noon. That certainly met the requirement for an a.m. and a p.m. reading. As it turned out, a very good-looking young female nurse took my blood pressure three times and the older male doctor took it the other three times. Three of the readings were fairly high while three were just a little above normal. Care to guess which readings were higher? She definitely was a good-looking nurse!

Once the Army had my results, they rejected me! As the war was becoming less and less popular at that time, I was greatly relieved to not win a free trip to Vietnam. I was already aware of several of my classmates who would not be returning alive after their trips to Vietnam.

Years later I was in Washington, D.C., and visited the Vietnam Memorial across the street from the Lincoln Memorial. A directory was available to help find a specific person listed on any of the dark reddish slabs of granite containing the names of over fifty-eight thousand men and women military personnel killed in the war. I now have pictures of all five engraved names of the men I went to high school with who were killed in Vietnam.

About the same time, I received my invitation to visit the induction center, I received a phone call one evening from Park Ranger Jerry Lee from Lava Beds National Monument (LBNM) asking me if I wanted to come and work there that summer. I almost said, "Yes," before he finished asking the question. As soon as I hung up I ran to the kitchen to tell Shirley what I had done. The next thing I had to do was look at a map to see where LBNM was! Turns out it is in northern California about thirty-five miles northeast of Mt. Shasta.

By the time the last day of school arrived, we were packed and ready to go. I just had to turn in my keys, sign some paperwork, and hit the road. It was five hundred miles to LBNM, so it was a full day's drive before we arrived. We were shown to the trailer we would live in for the summer and started unloading the pickup. I took a nice warm shower to help me relax after the long drive. Shirley tried to take a nice warm shower also, but that was when we discovered we only had a four-gallon water heater. The water from the park's well was quite cold, so she didn't especially enjoy her shower!

At the end of our one-week training in early June, a lightning storm started a wildfire on Caldwell Butte inside the park boundary. It was already dark, so we had to wear a headlamp on our hard hats to see where we were going. We grabbed five-gallon water cans (that we wore on our backs), shovels, Pulaskis, and McClouds (tools) with which to fight the fire. My water can leaked the whole time I carried it, so my back and pants were soaked. It would be difficult to get water to the fire any other way, so we only used the water for mop-up while the other implements were used to knock the fire down and build a firebreak around the burn area.

When I got my first paycheck I was shocked. With overtime, night and weekend differentials, and hazard duty pay, I had earned over $9/hour! Other than teaching, my previous jobs had all been in the $1 to $2.50 per hour range. Not that I wanted to fight more fires, but that paycheck sure looked good!

The permanent staff at Lava Beds was always excited to have the summer staff arrive. Their housing area was thirty miles from the small town of Tule Lake, CA, and sixty miles from the nearest available shopping in Klamath Falls, OR. The staff was small enough that they were ready for "new blood" to arrive each June. We would play volleyball every evening until we could barely see the ball. Then we would often be invited to one of the permanent staff's house for cookies and Kool-Aid, iced tea, or coffee. We usually had several potlucks during the summer. It was always sad when we "temps" would say our farewells and head for home around Labor Day Weekend.

Lava Beds is riddled with lava tubes and the surface of the ground is "pahoehoe" lava (smooth, undulating, or ropy) and "aa" lava (broken blocks called clinkers). The vegetation is a wide range of high desert plants such as sagebrush, mountain mahogany, bitterbrush, yellow pines (at the higher elevations), and hundreds of wildflower species. The wildlife is a spectacular mix of birds, mammals, reptiles, and lots of invertebrates.

Each summer, all of the seasonal park rangers had to prepare and present a campfire program once a week. I chose to talk about the thirty-five-plus species of mammals inhabiting the park. Over the course of the next couple of summers, I wrote a booklet entitled *The Mammals of Lava Beds*. Some forty years later while visiting the park, an interpretive ranger informed me he was very familiar with that document. While it was still in the LBNM library, it had never been published for public consumption.

We spent four wonderful summers at LBNM. We made many lifelong friends, hiked all over the park, took up wildlife photography, and became avid spelunkers exploring all nineteen of the lava tubes open to the public and a few that weren't. I climbed to the top of all seventeen cinder cones within the park and a few outside its boundaries. I had the opportunity to explore Fern Cave containing coastal ferns although two hundred miles from the coast.

Shirley and I also got to visit Crystal Ice Cave which was a series of lava tubes that crossed over each other at varying elevations. Over time, the different levels became connected as floors and ceilings of the various tubes collapsed. To enter, we had to descend an extension ladder, then hang on to a rope while we crossed a sloping sheet of ice before reaching lava blocks we could walk on. On the bottom level, there was an ice dome above a large rock. There was a tradition that required all first-time visitors to the cave to climb under the dome and over the rock. Since it was only slightly challenging, we all made it. Our only lighting sources were flashlights as we tried to minimize anything that would increase the temperature in the cave. One small room could only be entered by crawling into it. The ceiling of that room was entirely covered with ice crystals of varying sizes, but all were bigger than I had ever seen before. We could not stay in that room for long as even our body temperature would soon start melting the crystals.

The campfire programs gave me lots of opportunities to interact with the public in a very positive way. Our audiences were from all over the country and we frequently encountered international visitors. The groups were usually small enough that once we got the campfire going (using dry yellow pine wood we could ignite with a little help from some newspapers and only one match!), we would ask everyone to tell us where they hailed from. It occasionally rained in the evening before our programs so the air smelled of junipers and other high desert plants. One night a lady who had identified herself as being from LA asked what that strange smell was. Before I could respond, another visitor called out, "Fresh air, lady!"

Another night a man from southern California said his reason for bringing his family to Lava Beds was to show his kids the Milky Way. In fact, there were no intruding lights on the night sky within thirty miles and the air was crystal clear, perfect conditions for viewing the Milky Way.

During our first summer at LBNM, we had a sky interpreter from the University of Michigan come to the park and teach us how to do simple sky interpretation. He had a book, *Star Maps For Beginners*, that showed various constellations with lines connecting the stars. Using flashlights covered with red cellophane paper (to keep from blinding us), we would look at those drawings. Then I would project pictures I had taken (using twenty-second exposures) on a screen showing them the same constellations, sans lines, of course. We then looked up into the night sky and located the actual constellations.

The sky interpretation programs were well received and it was fun for me as I learned so much from the people who participated. A lady once told me that Antares in the constellation Scorpio was seven hundred times larger than our sun and sixty thousand times brighter! Wow! I didn't know whether to believe her or not, but later that summer I found that same "fact" in one of the star field guides. Another visitor told us that Vega, a star in the constellation Lyra, located just about straight overhead was 2.1 times the size of our Sun and is the second brightest star in the northern hemisphere night sky. Vega and our Sun are moving toward each other at an incredible speed, but in our lifetime we will never detect that phenomenon with our naked eyes.

Shirley ended up working at the Schonchin Butte Lookout and at the headquarters information desk during two different summers due to people leaving their jobs before the summer was over. She was working in the lookout one day in August as I was on vehicle patrol near the northeastern corner of the park when she reported smoke on Cougar Butte west of the park near Medicine Lake road. We had an agreement with the US Forest Service (USFS) that either agency would fight any fire within a mile of our common boundaries. As a result, our NPS fire crew (including me) and a number of USFS firefighters headed in that direction and began the task of controlling the fire before it spread. A couple of air tankers were called in to drop their pink, goopy fire retardant on the flames. The larger planes each made two drops "spot on." A smaller plane with only one load was seen heading toward the fire when someone yelled, "Hit the dirt!" That person was experienced enough to know this plane was off his target, enough that we were going to get hit even though we had moved over a rise some distance away from the fire. We ended up covered in a pink slurry that looked a lot like Pepto Bismol.

The pink fire-retardant chemicals used for fighting wildfires in the 1970s were later found to be toxic to plants that survived a fire initially. Today's air tankers are still dropping a pink retardant, but the new chemicals actually serve as a fertilizer for the surviving plants and any new vegetation that sprouts after the fire. The pink coloring is used so the air tanker pilots and other fire officials can see where the retardant was applied.

Way back in June of that summer, we had a lightning storm pass through the area and the lookout lady reported that she could see flames near Cougar Butte. It was still raining heavily for a while, so when fire crews arrived in the area, they were able to smell smoke but were unable to locate the source. Two months later in mid-August, Shirley was reporting a fire at the same location. Apparently, lightning had hit a large yellow pine when the June storm passed through and the tree began burning near its top. The subsequent rains that night beat the fire down to where no flames or smoke were showing by the time crews arrived on the scene.

While we fought the Cougar Butte Fire that hot August day, a USFS sawyer was cutting down the lightning-struck tree when his chainsaw came to an abrupt halt when it hit something rock-hard inside the trunk. After the flames had died down back in June, the tree had continued to smolder ever so slowly and over the next two months, the accumulating ash hardened as it moved down through the trunk. As the tree trunk burned lower and lower, the upper branches began dropping to the ground; that is what started the Cougar Butte Fire that day in August. I still have a sample of that rock-hardened ash, but over the years it is slowly crumbling.

I arrived back at our NPS furnished house trailer (8' x 35') at about midnight to find visiting relatives camped out on the floor of our "summer home." I reeked terribly of wildfire smoke, and to top it off, I was covered in the pink, sticky, stinky fire retardant. The shower felt great that night and I did come out smelling considerably better!

There was a train that passed through the Tule Lake Basin every afternoon. During one of our once-a-week training sessions, the USFS called for fire support from us as a train had started a fire in the lower-elevation grasslands. This was very different than fighting a fire in brush and trees. For one thing, a grass fire can really raise a strong wind quickly. The USFS fire crew, with help from our fire crew and park rangers, finally got control of the fire by working on the flanks of the fire and finally squeezing it down at the front of the fire.

The next day, our supervisor decided to hold an "after-event review" to discuss what we did right or wrong and what we should do if we ever encountered another grassland fire. While we were meeting, the USFS called us again to come down and help them out as a train had once again started another fire near the one we had just put out the previous day. The first thing we saw upon our arrival at the fire was that the USFS fire boss's truck had taken a direct hit by an air tanker turning his normally green pickup into that ugly pink color. After the second fire in two days, the railroad was required to have an observation vehicle follow the train as it traversed the valley floor each day during the rest of the summer.

The largest fire we had while working at LBNM was the result of a lightning strike. Lava is very much like glass in that it does not conduct electricity. The lady working in the lookout tower that night saw the strike hit the ground. She said it looked very much like what happens when you pour water on cement—the lava just splattered pieces of the lightning strike everywhere. The lightning had spread over the ground large enough that it ignited our dry summer vegetation over an area about six hundred feet across. Flames quickly moved upslope as the fire began generating its own winds.

I had the afternoon off, so Shirley and I were escorting two of my former sixth grade students on a spelunking expedition. We had heard the thunder while in a lava tube, but we were not aware of the fire as yet. When we surfaced, we saw the fire rapidly moving up the slope in our direction. I knew immediately I had to grab my gear and head for the fire, while Shirley and the girls headed home (an apartment that summer) to await any evacuation instructions. They were later told they had to leave the park as the park housing, headquarters, and maintenance areas were all in the direct path of the flames. The fire had started about 6:00 p.m. and I worked on it until about 2:00 a.m. I was to report back on the fire line at 6:00 a.m. I worked that second day until 6:00 p.m. During the afternoon, we were trying desperately to save the permanent employees' homes and the seasonal housing. I had parked my NPS pickup in front of one of the houses that were later hit by a direct drop from an air tanker. Unfortunately, I had left the windows down on the truck, so when I returned to it the next day, I discovered the inside, as well as the outside, was covered with the dried pink retardant! While it was easy to clean the outside of the truck, that stuff sure was hard to get off the seats, dash, and floor of the truck!

Late in the afternoon, I noticed a USFS bulldozer had been brought in to cut a fire line around the housing. The problem I could see was that a thirty-ton dozer could very easily drop through the roof of a lava tube. We knew where a lot of the lava tubes were, but not nearly all of them. Also, fighting fires in NPS areas has some requirements for the protection of the natural features that the USFS wasn't necessarily encumbered with on the lands they managed. I notified the chief ranger who put a quick halt to the dozer work. Not only would it have left a tremendous scar on the lava, but it could definitely have resulted in endangering the life of the dozer operator.

Two new developments during the day were welcomed sights. First, a firefighting crew of prisoners had been brought in to help us. They would be camping out at night on the lawn between our two apartment buildings. Second, the USFS had brought in one of their portable kitchens to prepare hot meals for us; that was certainly a welcome sight! I didn't have to be told twice to get in line for some pork chops, veggies, bread, and cold drinks. At 6:00 p.m., while holding my plate out to receive a couple of pork chops, my boss approached me and said I would be providing guard duty around the apartments starting at 7:00 p.m. and continuing until 2:00 a.m. I wolfed down my hot meal then headed for a hot shower and my NPS park ranger uniform.

I was also told while eating dinner that two NPS park rangers from Crater Lake would be occupying our apartment for a couple of days. They were brought there to provide traffic control. So, I ended up crashing at one of the permanent ranger's home until I had to report back for more fire line work starting at 6:00 a.m. I don't remember when I got off duty that day, but I went home to my empty apartment, showered, and crashed again. Sometime that day, the Crater Lake park rangers had been released to go back to their park. Shirley and the two girls also returned that day. Things were gradually getting back to a somewhat "normal" schedule. The prisoners were gone and the USFS portable kitchens were taken elsewhere.

It was interesting to look at the landscape after the fire. There were many small "islands" of unburned vegetation that would be able to reseed the burned areas. Some of the trees and shrubs were "cooked," but not killed by the heat. Some of the larger trees burned near the ground, but their tops seemed to be surviving quite well. Many would ultimately survive.

Lest you begin to think that all we did was fight fires all the time, let me share some of the other things we did. I already mentioned our campfire programs. That was always an enjoyable time as the high desert environment cooled down each evening. Many nights people would hang around after the program to talk to the ranger or to other attendees. A lot of our visitors were returnees who had discovered the park during past travels and had returned to enjoy spelunking, joining ranger-led hikes, or just relaxing in a very quiet and restful campground.

One night after my "Mammals of Lava Beds" interpretive program, a family asked me where they could see a live porcupine as they had never seen one. I advised them to get in their car and head toward Gillam's Bluff at the north end of the park. I could just about guarantee that they would see a porcupine somewhere along the park's main road if they headed out right then at about 10:00 p.m. They saw me at the information desk the next morning and told me they actually saw a porcupine as they left the campground. They were indeed happy campers.

I enjoyed patrolling in the park in our NPS green pickups equipped with seventy-five-gallon water tanks in case we had to put out a fire. I often carried my camera with me so I could take pictures of everything from antelope, to bighorn sheep, to wildflowers, and general landscape photos. In those days I was using film (ask your parents, they'll know what that was) cameras and I was paying for my own film. That could be a very expensive habit. I remember taking a bunch of shots of an antelope one day as it stood stock-still posing for me. Undoubtedly, it knew that my film had not caught on the winding spool. By the time I figured that out, the antelope was long gone. I've never been that close to an antelope since.

We had limited law enforcement authority, but we did enforce the portion of the Code of Federal Regulations that pertained to NPS areas. I did not issue very many citations during my four summers at LBNM, but most of those that I did issue were for speeding. We had lots of deer and a fair amount of antelope in the park during the summer. People don't realize what hitting a deer can do to their car and their vacation plans, especially when the nearest tow truck and repair services were thirty miles away. It would be nice if people could just slow down and enjoy the park at a safer speed. I stopped a pickup one day where several teenagers were sitting on top of the cab. Once they were inside the bed of the pickup, I allowed them to proceed. We used to have a saying that when people enter a national park, they enter a state of "vacation-mind at rest." In other words, they seem to think that anything they do will have no negative consequences.

While on an afternoon patrol, I received a radio call from Pam Edens who was working in the Schonchin Butte lookout advising me that she was watching a family loading lava rocks in the trunk of their car. They were later driving toward me as I was heading to look for them. Pam let me know when the car was approaching so I could turn around and pursue them. They were very nice people. I asked them if they were removing anything from the park. They replied that they were not. I asked if I could look in their trunk and they allowed me to do so. That really surprised me. Since they had been so nice, I asked them to help me load the rocks in my patrol pickup and I would return them where they came from. I don't think they had a clue how I knew they had the rocks. As I drove back to the place where they had obtained the rocks, Pam told me where to stop and unload them. Mission accomplished.

One of my favorite activities involved the "Explorer Hikes" I was privileged to lead once a week. We were allowed and encouraged to take park visitors to areas they were unlikely to visit on their own. I always went somewhere I had never been before. That made it a discovery hike for me as well. Of course, that meant I really had to study up on the vegetation, animals, geology, and history of the park so I could interpret what we were finding.

I also gave a walk around Mammoth Crater every couple of weeks. It was on the west border of the park near the highest elevation in the park. One summer we were able to watch a prairie falcon nest below the rim of Mammoth Crater as the mother was raising a single chick. The last day we took a hike there, the single fledgling flew across the crater and landed not twenty feet from us. While its mother was in a near panic, calling the young one to get away from us, all of the hikers were busy getting once-in-a-lifetime pictures of the prairie falcon fledgling up close. Would you believe, I was the only person there without my camera? All I could do was take mental pictures as I studied the bird through my binoculars.

Lava can be very unforgiving if you take a fall or bump your head on a stalactite in one of the caves. I still have scars on my left wrist from having tripped on some aa lava and then trying to catch myself with my left hand. We had a prematurely bald-headed college-age spelunker who raised up a little too fast in one of the caves and carved a fairly good-sized gash in the top of his head. Gave me the opportunity to practice my first aid.

Mushpot Cave was adjacent to the park headquarters. It contained a small theater near the entrance where we showed a movie of some of Hawaii's volcanic eruptions to give people an idea of how Lava Beds was formed. There was often a bat or two hanging from the ceiling that we could observe and talk about after watching the film. Past the theater area, an asphalt-paved trail continued downslope through the cave for about four hundred feet. It was well-lit with light bulbs strategically placed along the way.

While working at the information desk one day, I received a call from our maintenance foreman asking me to make sure everyone was out of Mushpot Cave as they were going to have to shut the power off for a few minutes while they performed some maintenance on the electrical system. That meant leaving the trail unlit until they finished their chore.

I rushed into the cave and hiked all the way to the end of the trail where I found four young college-aged men just as they were about to head back up the trail. I informed them that the lights were going to be going off for a while, so they needed to proceed to exit the cave quickly. At that very moment the lights went off! When you are four hundred feet into a gently curving lava tube and the lights go off, it is as dark as you will ever see it. I had not brought a flashlight with me as I expected the maintenance crew would not turn off the lights before I informed them that everyone was safely out of the cave.

So . . . there I was in pitch-blackness with four park visitors. I asked if anyone had a park brochure and a match. Someone produced both. We lit the brochure only to find out it burned a blue flame that was of no value as the only thing we could see was the blue flame. So . . . plan B kicked in. I had everyone hold hands and walk a single file. It was easy to feel where the asphalt trail was as the moment you started to step off it, one would encounter the clinkery surface of aa lava. There were two low-ceiling areas in Mushpot Cave where one needs to bend way over at the waist to avoid hitting your head on a lava stalactite. Using my left hand to find those two low spots, I held the hand of the guy closest to me to lead the group out of the cave.

Each of the young men held the hand of the person ahead of them so we wouldn't lose anyone. I don't know how long it took us, but we at last made it safely to the entrance. Just as we surfaced, the lights came back on. I later suggested that power should only be turned off after verifying that everyone was out of the cave!

Lava Beds was an excellent place to prepare for a career as a park ranger as we received training in interpretation, safety, law enforcement, firefighting, interpersonal communications, and public relations. Being there really enforced my desire to make a career in the NPS. However . . . life happens and not everything turns out the way you thought it would.

ROB ZINK–INTERPRETIVE PARK RANGER, MY MENTOR AND CLOSE FRIEND

I first met Rob Zink on a visit to Grant Grove in Kings Canyon National Park. While working weekends at the park during my second year of teaching, I got to know him quite well. He was the best interpretive ranger I had ever met. He had designed many of the displays in the visitor center at Grant Grove, especially those dealing with Giant Sequoias. He was also instrumental in working with park biologists to return fire as an aid to produce more young Sequoia trees. When I met Rob, he was the editor of the National Interpreters Magazine. While working with him at Kings Canyon, he had me write several articles for the magazine.

Rob had degrees in geology and forestry and had used that background to his advantage in the field of interpretation. When I met Rob, he was chief of interpretation at Kings Canyon NP. In his earlier years with the NPS, he had worked at Yosemite, Pinnacles, Craters of the Moon, Lava Beds, Grand Teton, and Crater Lake. Before retiring, he also worked at Fire Island National Seashore in New York.

It was Rob's interpretive knowledge, skills, and abilities that first caught my attention. He was a perfectionist in everything he did. I learned a lot from him that helped me throughout my career. One of the first things he helped me with was how to put together a résumé. When I showed him my very lengthy résumé with lots of complete sentences, he handed it back to me with this message written in red on the front cover: "Outline it!" That has paid many dividends for me over the years. When I would see applications submitted to me in three-ring binders, that was exactly what those applicants needed to hear. Simply outline it!

Each year I participated in our school district's environmental education program, I always arranged for Rob to be the interpretive presenter when we went to Grant Grove. I noticed he was using what was then a very new product called a "lapse dissolve slide projector" for his slide presentations. However, since the NPS said they couldn't afford such an expensive item, he made his own lapse dissolve projector based on a design in an issue of *Popular Mechanics Magazine*.

Rob was a great photographer; me, not so great. I was still learning how to use my Minolta SR-T 101 cameras with close-up, wide-angle, and telephoto lenses. He taught me how to take great pictures that would be of a quality that I could use in my own interpretive programs and later in various publications.

The previous summer, Kodak had sent a photographer out to Kings Canyon and Sequoia NPs to take slides for a program they would present in the campgrounds of the two parks the following summer. They could get spring, summer, and fall pictures just by moving to different elevations or to a shady versus a sunny side of a mountain. But—they had no winter pictures. So, while working as a volunteer in parks, Rob gave me film that Kodak was supplying and told me to go take winter pictures for them. Since I had always paid for my own film in the past, I was somewhat stingy with Kodak's film; I didn't want them to think I was wasting their film. The first time we sent three rolls of film to Kodak for their approval, they wrote back and said, "Bracket your shots!" Rob interpreted that for me to mean take three shots of everything; one at the camera's optimum setting, one above that, and one below it. And they wanted me to be less stingy with the film as they had lots more where that came from. Since I was working at Lava Beds during the summer, I never got to see Kodak's end product when they showed their program in the parks. However, Rob assured me my photos were used, enjoyed, and appreciated.

Our friendship grew and Shirley and I began to visit him at his home in the park and in our home. The first time he came to our home on the Kings River in the San Joaquin Valley, he brought us a bottle of wine. We very politely informed him that we did not drink any alcoholic drinks and suggested he save it for a special occasion at his home. A few minutes later, as I was opening a bottle of Martinelli's carbonated apple cider (it looked like a green wine bottle), I noticed a strange look on his face. I had to stop and explain that this was a non-alcoholic beverage.

While we were living at Tuzigoot National Monument in Arizona, Rob had accepted a position as a park manager at Fire Island National Seashore in New York. During his move to the East Coast, he stopped to visit us. That would be the last time we would see him for several years.

When Rob retired, he decided he wanted to relocate out west. After checking out a variety of locations, he settled in Brender Canyon five miles north of Cashmere, WA. He had about fifteen acres that came with a double-wide manufactured home and a large barn. He began to prepare a site where he wanted to build an adobe home. He even went to Arizona to take lessons on how to make adobe bricks. The entire time he lived there he continued to buy items for the new home; things like wiring, door and cabinet hardware, and light fixtures.

Rob also began developing a Christmas tree farm. Our Finnish exchange student, Pauliina Kekkonen, our two boys, Shirley, and I helped him plant his 1,500 young trees. After a few years, he began selling some of his Christmas trees. Unfortunately, Rob passed away before the trees were all sold. When we drove past his former place in 2018, we saw that the remaining trees had grown to a height and shape that would make them ideal for telephone poles.

Once Rob settled into Cashmere, he was close enough that he spent many holidays with us in Walla Walla. Other times, we would go visit him on long weekends. Shirley had given me a Thompson .50 caliber muzzleloader kit for Christmas one year. I'm not very handy at putting together something like that. However, Rob also had a similar muzzleloader kit, so he brought his kit when he came to our house for the holidays. We set to work on our respective kits at opposite ends of our ping-pong table in our basement. Rob was a perfectionist, so he would not let me go from one step to the next until everything was perfect. The metal butt on the stock had to be absolutely smooth where the metal met the wood. If I had been working on my own, that never would have happened. I still have my finished muzzleloader and it is as perfect as anyone could ever want it to be.

Rob always had special gifts for our boys at Christmas time. He gave Matthew a carving kit one year. That was the year we spent an hour or so at the emergency room in the local hospital while the doctor sewed up a dime-sized slice out of the end of one of Matthew's fingers on Christmas Day!

Rob eventually sold his place and moved into another double-wide manufactured home near Plain, WA. After returning home from a weekend trip, we received a call from friends of his in Lynden, WA, that he had passed away in his sleep a couple of nights earlier. He was found by another friend when Rob did not show up for their local HOA meeting where he served as secretary. It turns out, I was his estate executor and primary heir.

Over the next three months, I drove the 250 miles to Cashmere nine times on weekends to accomplish my executor responsibilities. Rob had only one son who had cut off all communications with him. I had to write letters to several people in Europe (Rob's French wife had raised their son in Europe). I never heard from the son or his mother. I had to go to court twice to verify that my lawyer and I had made every effort to reach out to Rob's only living relatives. The first time I went to court in Wenatchee, WA, I was only there for about four minutes; the second time it was only three minutes.

We arranged for our two sons and their wives to join us at Rob's house to see if there were items they would want. They ended up taking several appliances, a dining table set, a chainsaw, some firewood, and other miscellaneous items. Thomas's wife, Tia, was pregnant at the time, so we gave her two huge key rings loaded with keys and asked her to find out what they all went to. Rob had several nice showcase shelves with locking cabinets below them. When Tia finally found the key to those cabinets, we all gathered around to see what treasures they might hold. As she opened each cabinet, we discovered there was absolutely nothing in any of them!

I was told that a lady conducted estate sales every Thursday year-round in Wenatchee, WA, about forty miles from Rob's home. She had a place in town where she would have everything brought for the sale. The Alcoa Aluminum plant in town would allow employees with pickups to assist her on Tuesday of each week to bring the items to be sold to town. She would then place price tags on everything. The deal was she would get 75 percent of the income and I would get 25 percent. That was a super deal for me since I lived so far away. By the way, any items not sold would go to Salvation Army or Goodwill.

During WWII, Rob had been in the US Navy. He was lucky enough to have served in both the Atlantic and the Pacific Oceans on several different Navy ships. He served as a navigator on those ships. He had taken lots of pictures of the ships and was in the process of writing a history of those ships when he passed away. I contacted the Navy to see if they wanted his photos and writings. They didn't seem to be very interested, but I did not want to just dispose of these items due to the quality of his work and the effort Rob had put into that project. So . . . I packaged them up and sent them to: Historian, US Navy, Washington, D.C. No, I did not put a return address on them. I was sure that a historian would be very interested in receiving these materials.

Rob had attended an Officer Candidate School at the US Naval Academy in Annapolis, MD, upon joining the Navy. Upon successful completion of the course, he was presented with a military sword with his name etched on the steel blade. I still have that very special sword.

Rob also had several thousand slides he had taken while working in various NPS parks. Shirley and I went through them and divided them up by the park where each shot was taken. We then mailed, or delivered his slides to those parks. They would be of historic interest to people wanting to know what vegetation, geology, and historic structures looked like years earlier when he worked in those parks.

One hot Saturday summer morning, Shirley and I had worked hard cleaning Rob's house and getting it ready for selling. After taking a load of miscellaneous trash to the dump on such a hot summer day, we decided to drop what we had planned for the rest of the day and went to an air-conditioned theater, and watched the movie "Seabiscuit"!

Rob had put together three large binders of his family history. They were loaded with old family photos and stories of his parents and other relatives. Someone suggested I check with the local Chelan County Museum to see if they might want them. It just happened that Rob had designed and constructed some displays for the museum and they knew who he was. Rob had actually lived in Chelan county for the last quarter of his life. The museum curator was very happy to get these binders as it would help with understanding where one of their citizens had come from and what he had done with his life.

JOURNEY TO ALASKA

The summer I retired from the Corps, my siblings and our spouses decided to have a reunion at my middle sister's (Mary and her husband Kurt) home in Seward, AK. My oldest sister Joyce and her husband Glenn (both retired teachers) had a fifth wheel as did Shirley and I. So, we decided to travel together to Alaska. Glenn's brother, Russ, also joined us. My sister MyrnaLoy and her husband Harvey, and my brother Tom and his wife Becky were still working, so they took just enough time off from work to fly to Anchorage where we would meet up with them. We would then have about a week to visit and see some of Alaska's highlights before everyone would head back home.

While traveling, I kept a daily log of our experiences so that I could later put together a narrative and photographs of our trip to share with my parents who were already in their eighties and unable to join us on this venture. Although the photos are not attached here, the text is pretty much the same that I shared with the folks. They really enjoyed reading about our exploits and seeing the pictures we had taken along the way. The rest of this chapter is the story of our "Journey to Alaska."

As with any important journey in one's life, you always want to start with thorough planning. Since I had already been retired a couple of weeks, I took on the daunting task of plotting our course, studying maps, calculating mileages, locating potential campsites, and looking for special things we would want to see along the way.

Shirley and I left home at about 10:30 a.m. on Thursday, June 23, 2005, with the intent of going only as far as Post Falls the first night. That evening, we experienced our first-ever night of camping in a Walmart parking lot along with a dozen or so other camping units.

The next morning, we traveled to Stoneridge Resort where I had a resort board meeting. The meeting was very productive, but ran a little longer than I expected, so we skipped the swimming pool that afternoon and headed north.

We stopped at Albini Falls Dam (Corps of Engineers dam) in Old Town, ID, where they were celebrating the fiftieth anniversary of the dam. We were able to visit with several Corps friends including one who now lives in Florida after retiring from the Corps in Omaha the previous year. He and his wife sound like they are pretty much on a perpetual vacation. It was quite warm and muggy that afternoon, but the turnout was still good.

Our plan was to meet up with Glenn, Joyce, and Russ at the Walmart near Sandpoint, Idaho. Things went as planned. Shirley had put together an anniversary dinner for Glenn and Joyce before we left home, so that night we celebrated with lasagna, layered pea salad, glazed carrots, green beans, Martinelli's carbonated grape drink, and strawberry cream cheese pie right there in the Walmart parking lot.

In two nights of camping at Walmart, we made at least four trips to the stores for "necessities." They're really smart to let folks camp in their parking lots. Walmart says they just figure the campers are customers that haven't yet decided what they want or need to buy.

On Saturday, June 25, we arrived at Kingsgate on the Canadian border and went through the Canadian customs processing with no problems. We were a little surprised at the curtness of the female Canadian customs officer; maybe she was just having a "bad hair" day.

Our first stop in Canada was at Simon's Antique Store in Yak, BC, where Shirley and I had stopped three years before when we went to Panorama, BC. Simon had not planned to open that day, but he did so for us while we visited for about an hour looking over his "antiques" (also known as "other people's junk") and hearing about the various projects he was planning that would improve his place on the Moyie River. We ended up buying two antiques: a coffee pot and a skillet for our party barn.

Cranbrook offered an opportunity for some major grocery shopping, so we pulled into the largest store in town, the Real Canadian Superstore, and found parking spaces way at the back of the parking lot so we could get in and out easier with our fifth wheels. Just as I started to get out of the pickup, a guy came running up to me to engage me in conversation about our Arctic Fox fifth wheel camper. At that same moment, a cloud decided to open up full bore! The gentleman wanted to talk about our Arctic Fox camper as he was thinking of getting one. However, the rain finally won out as we were both getting soaked. So I dove back into the truck and shut the door. That's when I realized that Shirley had already exited and to escape the rain, she ducked under the fifth wheel by the tailgate of the truck. About then, Glenn ducked under there too as it was now hailing heavily and the parking lot was quickly becoming a lake. I just sat in the truck and laughed at the two of them because they were stuck for the time being. For some reason, Glenn decided to make a dash for the cab of his truck; unfortunately, when he got there he realized it was locked! I would love to have had a picture of his face when he realized what was happening; so back under our fifth wheel he went. The storm only lasted a short while, but believe me, a lot of water came to Earth in those few minutes.

Once inside the store, the shopping was great. We found some "half-baked bread" that we finished baking in the trailer later. We liked it so much with honey and butter that we've looked for and found it several more times in Canada. Their spinach dip was one of the best we've ever had. So, stocked up with food, we headed further north.

We camped at the Fort Steele RV Campground that night. During the afternoon, Glenn taught Russ and me a few things about playing horseshoes—first, and most important, is don't play with Glenn as he'll beat the socks off you every time. After dinner, all but Joyce took a couple of hours' drive looking for wildlife. We found lots of elk and deer, but the highlight of the evening was the sow black bear with twin cubs. The Rocky Mountian background at sunset would have been worth the trip even if we hadn't found any wildlife.

The next morning, we went across the highway to Fort Steele and toured the reconstructed 1890s fort site. They had lots of interpretive displays and a number of people walking around town in period costumes or working in several of the businesses. They were all interpreters willing to tell you their own special story about life in Fort Steele if you would stop and listen. After a less-than-fantastic buffalo stew lunch at the old hotel, we returned to the campground. After dinner that night, we all went wildlife watching and came up with pretty much the same things we had seen the night before, except no bears showed up. We did add wild turkeys and a peacock (!) to our list.

On June 27, we headed north and pulled in to Dutch Creek RV Resort just south of Fairmont Hot Springs, BC. It rained off and on throughout the day. While hiking that afternoon, Shirley found a four-leaf clover; however, it didn't particularly bring us any good luck as it kept on raining. We all piled into our truck and headed for Invermere to do some currency exchanges and sightseeing that afternoon. After stopping at the local bank where we have exchanged US dollars for Canadian dollars a number of times over the years, we took a drive up to Panorama Resort where we had stayed for a week three years earlier. The developers were still adding on to the resort and the "kabillion" dollar homes and cabins were still going up at a very fast pace around the golf course.

We got "ripped off" at a gas station in Invermere. I figured the diesel downtown, since it would be where the locals would buy their fuel, would be the cheapest. We paid 99.9¢ a liter or $4.23.5 per gallon! However, every station we passed on the main highway priced their diesel at 84.9¢ a liter! Since I had just bought about ninety-five liters, that was quite a rip-off (almost $15). I've learned that a liter is 1.06 quarts, so I could then figure out my gas mileage. We averaged 12.2 miles per gallon thus far, but by the end of the trip that had increased to 13.3 miles per gallon.

That evening, we ate at our favorite establishment in the area, the Black Forest Steak and Schnitzel House. They serve excellent Bavarian food complete with apple strudel for dessert. Our waitress, Nadia, was dressed in a traditional Bavarian dirndl; she was an especially good waitress warranting one of the best tips this anti-tip person has ever given.

On June 28, we headed for Lake Louise. It was raining pretty hard off and on. When we got to the intersection to turn into Kootenay National Park, we were met by mud and rocks flowing down the road in town. A Parks Canada ranger blocked the road with his truck and said it could be a couple of hours before they could get a rockslide removed from the road somewhere in the park. After waiting a half hour or so, we decided to go further north and enter the park at a different location. However, the Parks Canada ranger informed us they would re-open the road in just about fifteen minutes. So we parked and waited another half hour or so before they finally did allow traffic to proceed. It continued to pour down rain off and on most of the day. Just after entering the park, we passed four bighorn rams right at the side of the road.

Glenn had a rather exciting experience as he was coming down the long, steep grade preparing to turn onto the Canada 1 Freeway to head north to Lake Louise. I can't begin to tell you how excited he was, but I can tell you that I saw his pickup and camper go past my rearview mirror while we were waiting on the on-ramp and there seemed to be a fair amount of smoke coming from somewhere during that short moment that I could see him. Seems his fifth wheel was pushing him down the very steep grade we had just descended and his brakes were smoking as he tried to control his speed. I understand there was some yelling and panicky screaming happening in his truck at that very moment as he almost missed the turn onto the ramp.

We arrived at Lake Louise about mid-afternoon, dropped our trailer, loaded everyone in our truck, and then drove on up to the lake for a look around. There were hundreds of people there. I found a binocular case exactly like mine, but as I was putting it in my pocket, I saw a lady looking for something and she was carrying binoculars exactly like mine. Sure enough, it was her case. She and her husband were on a three-week "holiday" from Wales. We had a good, short visit with them then proceeded into the Chateau Lake Louise for a look around at all the expensive souvenirs we could not afford. They had some beautiful items made of muskox wool (qiviut). They actually harvest the wool in Canada, then send it to Asia to be made into garments. It is supposedly both the lightest and the warmest of all wools. Because so many of their customers are Japanese, most of the exclusive shops in the hotel were run by Japanese women who barely spoke English!

We then drove over to Moraine Lake but only spent a few minutes there due to the rain and the fact that the two cooks (Shirley and Joyce) wanted to rush back to the campers to fix dinner.

We left early on the morning of June 29 and headed on up to Jasper National Park. Along the way, we encountered about sixteen Rocky Mountain goats at a natural salt lick at the side of the road. We stopped at the Columbia Icefields at the summit and later spent some time at Athabasca Falls. That night we camped at Wapiti Campground in Jasper National Park. We went to town to get some diesel where we met a young man who was pumping fuel. He knew where Hixson (yup, they spell it incorrectly), BC, was as he grew up in Prince George near there. When I asked if he was just there for the summer season, he said, "No. I'm working two jobs right now and this time next year I hope to have my own coffee shop." It was good to see a young person with a work ethic and some goals. Incidentally, we got the cheapest diesel anywhere in Canada right there in Jasper: 84.9¢ per liter. They must be bringing it in by rail, thus the lower cost.

We made it to Prince George the night of June 30 where we again did some grocery shopping. We spent the night in a small RV park run by a man from up around the Fort Nelson area who was a forestry consultant until he retired earlier that year. We had a great chat with him and gained some interesting information about Canada's trees and forest management practices. I was able to access my email that night, but could not figure out how to send anything.

July 1 was Canada Day, the equivalent of our Fourth of July. We arrived in Chetwynd, BC, just as their parade was ending, so we missed all the festivities. This little "burg" claims to be the "Chainsaw Carving Capital of the World." Actually, we discovered that just a couple of people had carved most of the wooden statues around town. Lunch was at an A&W that day.

Shortly before Chetwynd, we reached the little village of Taylor, BC. The sign at the top of the hill indicated we would be going down a 10 percent grade until we reached the river at the bottom. I was right behind a two-trailer fuel tanker that was obviously going to do about ten miles per hour all the way down. Rather than have my brakes burn out before reaching the bottom and possibly plowing into the tanker, I stopped partway down at a turnout to let him get well ahead of us. After waiting a few minutes, I proceeded not realizing how far it was downhill to the river. Sure enough, I was gaining on the tanker. To make matters worse, construction crews were working on the bridge at the bottom of the hill so we had to come to a full stop before crossing the bridge. I was much relieved to get off that hill safely. It later turned out to be challenging for our pickups pulling that steep grade going south on our return trip.

We spent the night on the road at a rest area. While there, I had quite a chat with a couple from Ohio who had moved to a cabin they built about ninety-five miles south of Fairbanks, AK. They actually moved up here six years ago and he had just retired from working with the City of Anderson, AK. His wife had been working for the school district. They now live about four miles from the closest paved road, so they can get snowed in occasionally during the winter. Because the area where they live is in somewhat of a rain shadow, they get less snow and what they do get is very powdery dry. Their only source of power is a 4,000-watt generator. While they complained about the cost of gas to run the generator, they were glad not to have electricity, sewer, phone, or water bills since they will now be living on just his Social Security check. They were returning from Ohio where they had just sold their former home. They were traveling in two separate rigs, one of which had a wheel bearing go out; so the next day he had to drive back to the last town (about fifty miles) to get it repaired. We saw them twice later on down the road over the next few days.

On July 1, as many travelers to Alaska do, we spent a night in a gravel pit along the Tetsa River. While waiting for dinner to be prepared, Russ and I walked to the upper end of the pit where we were able to see both a bear and an elk feeding further up the hill. While we were eating dinner, a guy came over to warn us about storing our food that night as there was a big black bear right near us in the pit. Thankfully, we didn't see or hear it during the night.

The next day, we really had the feeling of being out in the "boonies." We saw a number of caribou and came across a small herd of bison resting next to the river. We lunched at a place called Allen's Lookout. It is along the Laird River where bandits used to hang out so they could watch both directions for sternwheelers coming and going on the river. Some way or another they would manage to rob the folks on the ships as they were passing by.

We made the obligatory stop at Watson Lake, Yukon Territory (YT) to see the signposts that people have left from all over the world. Some families have made their own while others have obviously stolen or otherwise "borrowed" official city signs from back home; others have merely left license plates on a post. Some creative people even made signs out of such things as plastic plates, a gold miner's pan, or just plain old cardboard. We saw one city sign from Kennewick, WA, and another from Visalia, CA, two places we were familiar with.

That night we camped at a turnout in the middle of nowhere overlooking the Rancheria River in YT. It was rather breezy when we stopped, but later as the wind died down, we became acquainted with the hordes of mosquitoes that infested the area. To make matters worse, since we parked so close to a tree in order to get a nice view of the river, we couldn't open our slide-out all the way. That meant we didn't have a tight seal all the way around the slide-out which then allowed mosquitoes to come and go at will. They about drove me crazy inside the trailer that night. You couldn't even escape them by pulling the blankets up over our heads as they would nail us right through the material. They were so noisy I got up numerous times during the night, turned on the light, and fly-swatted every one of them as they made their presence known. Somehow, Shirley managed to sleep through all of this and was unaware of my killing sprees during the night. Glenn's weapon of choice in their trailer was a whiskbroom while I stuck with my trusty plastic fly swatter. Glenn said he did not sleep any that night and I'm sure I didn't sleep much more than that. Russ left their trailer and opted to sleep in the backseat of their truck which was more tightly sealed.

We moved on to Whitehorse, YT, the next day and proceeded to check into an RV park for water and electric hookups, hot showers, and internet service. Shirley had read about a restaurant in Whitehorse where we could get such foods as salmon, bison, and other interesting entrees. So we ate at the Klondike Rib and Salmon Restaurant that night. Very interesting place; apparently it is one of the oldest establishments in town. We all agreed it couldn't meet any building or electrical codes in the "Lower 48" states. We also all agreed they served fantastic food, some of which we saved for a "leftovers" dinner the next night.

Russ decided to stay in town and walk around some after dinner. The rest of us drove around a little and ended up over at a Walmart. As we were leaving there, here came Russ up the road, walking 180 degrees the wrong way from our campground. Seems brother Glenn, had pointed him in the wrong direction when we left him downtown.

While leaving the RV campground the next morning, I made a startling discovery at the dump station. The handle to release water from the kitchen holding tank was no longer connected although it was still hanging where it should have been. I examined it closely and decided it had merely come unscrewed. Well, try as hard as I could, I couldn't get it reconnected. We went to a local RV repair shop down the street and a guy fixed it in less than a minute. It is always uncomfortable to find something isn't working right when you are a long way from most service facilities. It is a good idea to make sure all of your equipment is in excellent shape before you head for the hinterlands.

By a unanimous decision, we decided to stay an extra day in Whitehorse. We vacated our expensive $25 per night campsite for a more modest, free site at Walmart's parking lot along with about thirty other campers. Yes, we bought several more "necessities" and souvenirs while we were there. That afternoon, Shirley and I took a walk around town on a bike path and ended up at the opposite end of town where they have a small museum adjacent to an old sternwheeler, the Klondike, docked on the Yukon River.

On the way back through town, we stopped at a very old local store that was as cram-packed full of food as any place we had ever seen. They had two kinds of bread there that were named after Bible verses: one was Ezekiel 4:19 and the other was Genesis 1:29. We opted not to buy anything there preferring to amble on down the street and grab a little snack at Dairy Queen. On the way there, we came across two cute little Vietnamese kids out riding their bikes while mom walked along behind. They were wearing all the requisite safety gear from head to toe. Their mother said she was from Vietnam and that she speaks three languages fluently (Vietnamese, Chinese, and English). We coaxed the kids into posing for some "bike safety" pictures.

We stumbled upon Joyce at DQ where she was taking a break from her walk around town. Right around the corner was a very strange site. It was a three-story, high-rise log "cabin"; it looked like it might have been built without any plans.

We also stumbled across a Western store and a fruit stand on a side street. We saw Walla Walla Sweet Onions for $1.29 per pound. Having been shipped so far, we expected the price to be double that. We made a short stop for more grub at the biggest store in town on the way back to the trailer.

When we first started planning this trip, a number of people told us we needed to purchase *The Milepost*. This book, rewritten and printed anew each year, turned out to be an invaluable resource as we traveled along. It also had lots of information about the towns, burgs, villages, and wide spots in the road along the way. Other brochures and pamphlets were also valuable, but *The Milepost* was by far our most consulted printed material throughout the entire trip. The accuracy of its information was of great value throughout the trip. We used it every day.

Along the way, Shirley and Joyce put together some pretty good evening vittles. We've had barbecued pork chops and chicken, lasagna, tossed salads, leftovers from our restaurant meals, tacos with chili rellenos, hotdogs with baked beans, and other assorted goodies including strawberry, blueberry, and huckleberry pies, layered chocolate and butterscotch pudding desserts, fruit cocktail, cookies (some homemade), and cherry and blackberry cobblers. Breakfast was usually done on our own. We generally had something light, but we've splurged a couple of times with bacon and eggs, cinnamon rolls, or blueberry muffins or pancakes.

The roads were fairly good up until the time we left Whitehorse, then they started falling apart. We had gone through some minor construction a couple of days earlier, so we took advantage of a car wash at the Whitehorse RV park and washed our rigs. Unfortunately, there was construction on the road northwest of Whitehorse, so by the end of the next day it looked as though we had never cleaned our rigs.

Somewhere west of Whitehorse, we came upon what we thought was a herd of wild horses. Upon closer examination, we noticed each was wearing a bell hanging from its neck. It seemed a strange place for domestic stock to be running loose.

At Kluane Lake, the road was an absolute mess due to construction. Once we got past that, we found a beautiful little campground, Congdon Creek, near the lake, so we pulled in for the night. We liked it so much we stayed the next day and night also. We attended an interpretive program the second night; it was presented by a woman who was native to the area and what Canadians call a First Nations person. While there, we met Edwin and Helga, a couple from Germany who were traveling all over Canada and Alaska. They come every year and travel around North America. They have a nice pickup and fifth wheel that they will store in Vancouver, BC, until they come back next year. We have run into them a couple of times since and got to visit with them again.

We did a lot of walking, resting, eating, reading, and bird-watching at Kluane Lake. We had a little rain and quite a bit of wind, but it was worth staying there due to the beauty of the surrounding scenery. Our boys would have loved this place as it had the greatest quantity of high-quality "skipping stones" we have ever seen anywhere. The shore was composed mostly of flat round rocks that would skip nicely across a smooth body of water. Unfortunately, the water was too choppy to get any really great skips while we were there. On the return trip, I decided to take the boys each one "perfect" skipping stone which we placed in their Christmas stockings that year.

At Donjek Creek, we stopped at "Buckshot Betty's" and bought a huge cinnamon roll. Turns out her real name is Carmen and, unfortunately, the rolls turned out not to be that spectacular.

We finally hit the Alaska border and sailed through US Customs. We had a much friendlier US Customs agent than the one we had when we entered Canada. We only went a couple of miles further that day and landed at Border City RV Park for the night. We had Wi-Fi service, so I was finally able to not only receive emails, but I could also send them. We visited the Tetlin National Wildlife Refuge visitor center that afternoon where I purchased a new bird guide, *The Sibley Field Guide to Birds of Western North America* by David Allen Sibley.

Glenn had a flat tire the next morning, the only one either of us had all the way to Anchorage. After we changed the tire, we mosied on down the road. We encountered an eight-mile stretch of awful rough unfinished road that jarred us for about forty minutes. Fortunately, it was on a Sunday so we didn't have to contend with construction crews and their equipment.

At Glennallen, we visited a small visitor center and learned about "diamond willows." We had been introduced to this wood a number of years ago at a furniture store in Sandpoint, ID, where a man had made a beautiful floor lamp out of a branch. We learned that there are actually about five species of willow that produce the "diamond" effect where branches grow from the stem. It seems a fungus attacks the stem at the point where a new branch protrudes. It leaves a beautiful red diamond shape around the new branch. When polished, the bulk of the wood is very yellow while the "diamond" is a deep, dark red. The effect makes for some creative carving and furniture-making opportunities.

The last 150 miles before Anchorage provided some spectacular scenery as we passed glaciers, high mountain peaks, huge river deltas, and a few million more black spruces. The road was steep and often barely hung to a cliff. It was kind of a shock to arrive at Palmer and find ourselves on a six-lane freeway heading for Anchorage! We passed some very rich-looking farmland complete with bright green crops but had to watch the road rather than the scenery.

Suddenly, we were "there" and somewhat lost as we made our way through the big city of Anchorage to the Old Seward Highway. We finally found a Walmart where we intended to spend one night. They were somewhat unfriendly as they didn't allow campers to stay in their parking lot. So we went to the Sam's Club (also owned by Walmart) parking lot across the street and spent the night there with about ten other campers.

The next morning, we found a Dodge dealership where I could get my oil and oil filter changed. What surprised me was that I paid the same that day for this service that I paid for it in McMinnville, OR, a week or so after we got the truck back in December 1997. I had fully expected it to cost at least twice as much. So, I was pleasantly surprised.

While we did that, Glenn was getting his new tire and having his tires rotated. We also found a post office and got rid of thirty or so postcards Shirley had written along the way. We also mailed off a package for Tia's (our daughter-in-law) baby shower.

We met a most interesting man (probably at least seventy years old) at the post office. While waiting a very long time for service, he told us about his mining claims that his mother had filed many years ago. Both he and his mother were born in Alaska. He now works the claims during the summer months. The claims are about four hundred miles from Anchorage, but he would not divulge where they were. He's got a little cabin he stays in on-site. He uses a dozer and a front-end loader to work the shore of a creek looking for gold.

This miner takes the equipment out in about October and brings it back in March. There are no roads to the area, so he drives his equipment up a frozen river, then up the frozen creek to his place. He says it is just like driving on a highway when it is frozen at least a foot thick. He sells his gold in Dawson City where he exchanges it for gold bullion; as long as he doesn't exchange it for cash or something else, he doesn't have to pay taxes on it. He has found a couple of nuggets that ranged from three to four ounces which he sold for several thousand dollars each; jewelers will pay more than the going price for gold if they can make it into expensive jewelry. He and his wife now live in an assisted living apartment in Anchorage, but he was headed back out to the claim to work it until about September. He is a ham operator and carries a small radio with him at all times while working on his heavy equipment; in case he tips his equipment over, he can call for help via a repeater on a nearby mountain. He told us he had actually tipped it over several times in the past, but he's never had to have anyone come and help him as he got it upright again by himself.

Russ, Shirley, and I went on a mission to find an RV campground for us to relocate to that night. We learned very quickly that the local RV salespeople didn't seem to have a clue where the local RV campgrounds were. They apparently know the campgrounds out in the boonies, but not near their homes. We finally found several, but they were either filled or did not meet our needs. So, we stayed at Sam's Club again that night.

While out and about, we found an antique store where we bought a few small items including a collection of stories by Robert Lewis Stevenson (*Robinson Crusoe, Dr. Jekyll and Mr. Hyde*, and others). The store owners go to our northeastern states every few months and buy enough antiques to fill a shipping container. After shipping the container by rail to Seattle, it is brought to Anchorage by ship. Their store was so jam-packed with antiques, we could not figure out where they would place another item.

We called Kurt and Mary (brother-in-law and sister who live in Seward, AK) and told them we would stay here until the others (sister from Texas and brother from California and their spouses) flew in the next day. Four more people would have made our rigs too uncomfortable, so Kurt and Mary needed to bring one of their cars up to Anchorage to help transport the newcomers to Seward. They wanted to come to Anchorage anyway as they had some shopping to do. There's not much competitive shopping available in Seward. The couples flying in weren't due to arrive till after 1:00 p.m. the next day so we planned to be there to meet them. Then we could all caravan down to Seward together later that afternoon.

We made a trip across the street to the Anchorage Walmart later in the day and after we were through there, Walmart was probably very happy to have us staying nearby. Shirley bought a number of Alaska souvenirs and I bought myself a nice new bright red windbreaker/raincoat with a hood. It is a little heavier and longer than anything else I had, so I thought I would get quite a bit of use out of it since it had been raining about two of every three days so far on this trip.

When we returned from the store, we found we had new neighbors adjacent to us in the Sam's Club parking lot. Dogs were heard yelping inside their motorhome. Pretty soon, a lady got a kennel fence out and set it up between her unit and ours (about a dozen feet apart). She then proceeded to bring fourteen Scotties and a mutt out to relieve themselves in the kennel on the hot asphalt between their unit and ours. We were afraid we would hear them all night, but they took them back inside. We didn't hear much out of them once the owners drove off in the car they were towing. Because of the hot asphalt dog potty area, we had to close our windows on that side of our RV to avoid the stench.

The next day, Tom and Becky and Harvey and MyrnaLoy flew in to Anchorage. Kurt and Mary showed up at the airport just as Glenn and I arrived to help transport their baggage. Turns out their plane left Portland, OR, early and they arrived even earlier in Anchorage, so they and all of their luggage were at the curb waiting for us when we drove up.

After some serious food shopping, we all headed for Seward. It was quite windy around the Cook Inlet and it was raining off and on as we made our way down the Kenai Peninsula. But, as usual, it was a very pretty country to travel through.

Kurt and Mary have a rental house that was to be sold later in the month. It was only about two blocks from their new home, so we ended up setting up camp with the two fifth wheels in their rental house's front yard while others used the house for sleeping, cooking, eating, and general socializing. It was within easy walking distance of the main touristy part of Seward, so we did a fair amount of walking to and from "downtown." Being on the waterfront, it smelled like a waterfront was supposed to smell—like dead fish and rotting seaweed. The seagulls were doing their best to rid the area of the dead fish.

Glenn, Harvey, Tom, and I purchased our fishing licenses for our big charter fishing outing on the Cook Inlet planned for Friday. Some of us just purchased a one-day fishing license while others bought a week-long license since they wanted to do some river fishing as well. Glenn hadn't planned to go but Kurt was planning to join us. At the last minute, Kurt decided to let Glenn have his place as Glenn decided he really should go while in Alaska.

Wednesday morning, Harvey, MyrnaLoy, and Glenn decided to try to tackle Mount Marathon, the 4,300-foot mountain overlooking

Seward. I cannot begin to describe for you what they went through that day. Apparently, MyrnaLoy had an anxiety attack while Glenn and Harvey proceeded ever upwards. While the rest of us watched from the house with our binoculars, we saw MyrnaLoy stop while the guys kept going upward. Harvey had promised MyrnaLoy he would return within forty-five minutes, so he had to turn around before reaching the top. Glenn tried a route going straight up a talus slope that was beyond his capabilities. We had radio contact with Glenn just before he made the final push toward the top, then the radioing stopped abruptly. Glenn finally turned around and headed back down not realizing he had lost his radio somewhere higher up. Once he realized it was missing, he suddenly decided he didn't really need a radio anymore. The three hikers made it home quite worn out.

Later, we read about the Mount Marathon race held each year. Seems the record was up to the peak and back to the bay in forty-three minutes and ten seconds. Our three "mountaineers" had just spent about six hours trying to make it to the top and back. None of us believed anyone could do it in that amount of time, but when they shared their experience of a young lady running down the mountain, perhaps a few "masochists" can do it. None of our group wanted to try it again any time soon.

While the hikers were returning, the rest of us went over to Kenai Fjords National Park and hiked to the base of Exit Glacier. It was interesting staring into the blue of the cracks at the head of the glacier.

That evening, all but Glenn, Joyce, and Russ took a dinner cruise on Cook Inlet. We were on a boat for about an hour before being dropped off at Fox Island for a nice salmon dinner at a gorgeous log lodge. We then took another hour and a half to get back to Seward. Along the way, we observed sea otters, a humpback whale, Stellar sea lions, puffins, kittiwakes, cormorants, bald eagles, and many other species of sea birds. It was a beautiful evening to be on the water with the mountains rising all around us and a number of glaciers visible along the way.

The fateful day of the fishing trip finally arrived. Glenn, Harvey, Tom, and I had signed up. The evening before, we packed enough food and water in an ice chest to fully equip the French Foreign Legion for a week-long trek through the Sahara Desert. We had sandwiches, bananas, snacks of cheese and crackers, gorp, and assorted other foods to keep us alive. We arrived at the dock by 7:30 a.m. and returned to the dock by 5:30 p.m. Sounds easy enough, right?

The captain's first mate showed up to work late with a can of high-caffeine Red Bull in his hands; others later identified the liquid in the can as beer. It took us two hours to get to our fishing spot in the Gulf of Alaska. The sun was out, hardly a cloud anywhere. The seas weren't particularly high, but riding backwards in the cabin with my back to the sun was beginning to take its toll on me. We were told to dress warmly in layers as it could be cold getting to our fishing spot. Inside the cabin, it just kept getting warmer and warmer as I peeled off layer after layer of clothing.

I finally stood up and looked forward to getting rid of the queasiness I was feeling. However, Captain Arnold lit up a cigarette about that time—not good in the warm enclosed cabin, but at least he tried to hold it out the window most of the time. I asked how much farther we were going. He pointed to the farthest point of land on the horizon and said, "Right there." Took us fully another half hour to arrive at his "secret" hot fishing spot.

Once we arrived, it was time to start catching fish. Captain Arnold's trusty, mousy "First Mate," Dan, had already baited the hooks and had things ready for us to go to work when we stopped on a gently rolling and rolling and rolling and rolling sea. I lasted about fifteen minutes before deciding I had to go inside and try to keep my breakfast down. That didn't last long; lost it all and then some. I was in the cabin and trying to use the wastebasket for a catch basin. I was immediately chewed out by Captain Arnold—it seems one is supposed to discipline oneself to heave over the side of the boat, not in the boat! Everything I did just exacerbated my problem. I did try fishing one more time, actually holding a rod in my hands for about five more minutes.

At one point, Glenn handed me his camera and wanted me to take a picture of him while he was reeling in one of the two halibuts he caught that day. However, the back of the boat was small, there was a pole in the way, at least two other people were crowded around him, and he had never given me instructions on how to use the camera. He did tell me he found out later that I had left the camera on "video" and it had run continuously until all the memory was used up. The rest of the day, I spent lying on berth "A" in the cabin trying not to "upchuck," but each time we moved to a new "hot fishing spot" and the boat stopped to allow the seas to take over their rolling motions again, I would dive out the cabin door, grab the closest railing and do my thing. The only real sympathy I received was from Tom; after he heaved a couple of times himself, he handed me some water and a paper towel to clean myself up. Then he went back to fishing with the others. I told the captain at the end of the day that it was one of the most "memorable" days of my life and you could also substitute the word "miserable" in the same sentence. I thought I would die before we got to shore. We had many good chuckles and jokes about that day when all was said and done and we had recovered from seasickness and lack of fish catching. Tom shared with us later some of his innermost feelings about Glenn coming into the cabin and eating a peanut butter sandwich next to him at a time when he was not feeling especially chipper.

So, for $198 of charter fishing fun and another $10 for a fishing license, I got miserably sick for ten hours while the rest of the group didn't catch enough fish to shake a stick at. Harvey and Tom had each brought an empty ice chest (from Portland on the airplane) with the intention of quick-freezing their catch and taking it home full of frozen fish. I think the little bit of fish they caught was delivered to Tom in Glenn and Joyce's camper freezer. Harvey took one ice chest home—it was full of sewing material that MyrnaLoy had purchased at a fabrics store.

Saturday found us driving over to Homer in a caravan. We spent the night at the Bidarka, a Best Western Hotel. We went out to the Homer Spit (the absolute end of the road on the Kenai Peninsula) that evening and found a place to have some fried seafood and other greasy edibles. Nothing to write home about.

Harvey and Glenn tried their hands at fishing in "The Hole" (a large pond) on the spit later that night with no success. The next morning, they were told only Alaskans were allowed to fish there.

That day, Harvey, Kurt, Tom, and Glenn decided to stop at several places along the Russian River to fish on the way back to Seward. The gals all rode together and stopped to do "gal" things along the way. Russ and I took my truck and stopped at several places along the way to sightsee and look for wildlife.

Our fishermen had their usual amount of luck—I think their licenses were defective. It seems their equipment was Kmart quality while the "professionals" along the river were using Bass Pro Shop quality equipment. When Harvey wandered too close to the "professionals" with his equipment, someone asked what he was doing there. The duct tape on his rod obviously labeled him as an "amateur." Harvey merely replied that he was looking for his grandson (non-existent!), then hightailed it out of the area. We're still trying to figure out how Harvey managed to snag the steering wheel of a park ranger's boat that was parked at a dock in the river!

Monday, Mary had to work a couple of hours to get her payroll out at the Sea World Aquarium where she was the comptroller. It did not help her to discover the aquarium computer system was down that day. We were supposed to hear from her at noon that day whether Kurt and she would be able to go with us as we traveled north to Denali National Park. We finally got word about two o'clock and by three, the rest of us were on the road. Tom, Becky, Harvey, and MyrnaLoy borrowed Kurt and Mary's van for a few days of sightseeing before flying home. They spent the night at a Ramada Inn while the rest of us ended up "camping out" one more night at the Sam's Club's parking lot in Anchorage.

I had told the others I planned to pay for this trip with money I would find on the ground along the way. While in Anchorage, I made my greatest find—a five-dollar bill all wadded up in the middle of a busy intersection crosswalk. That pushed my total find up to about $6.01 at that time! By the end of the trip, I had only found $6.44—about a thousandth of the cost of the trip!

On July 19, we filled up with diesel before leaving Anchorage. That was the cheapest diesel we had purchased since leaving the Lower 48—$2.19 per gallon. It was raining as we left town and continued to do so off and on during the day. Our first opportunity to see Denali (formerly Mount McKinley) was a bust due to the cloud cover. Since the non-campers in our party drove up later that day, they were able to see the mountain once the rain moved out.

Sometime after leaving Wasilla, AK, we came to a wide spot in the road that had a brand-new post office and a "Mike's Mart." Mike has a definite phobia against organization and cleanliness although he did have all of his rental videos in one little cubby hole at the very back of the maze he refers to as a store. He had everything in the way of "junk" (and I don't mean antiques) that one could possibly NOT want. He had an impressive collection of moose and caribou antlers which were scattered hither and yon. I asked if he ever sold any of the antlers. He said, "No, I've been saving them since birth." I guess he meant his birth. He had two reindeer in pens out front that probably would not have pleased the SPCA or the agriculture inspection folks. Shirley said two women in that burg had spoken to her and neither one had any teeth! Must have been a really fun, rough, and tumble place come nightfall!

We saw some beautiful terrain before getting to Denali. At Cantwell, we stopped for some milk and I also grabbed a small (very small) bag of Ritz peanut butter crackers. I handed the clerk a five-dollar bill as she was asking if I wanted a bag. I said, "No," but she proceeded to bag the half gallon of milk and crackers anyway. I was waiting to see if she needed more money or if I had some coming back. She looked at me and said, "Oh, that covers it." Nothing was priced in the store, so I had the feeling she thought five dollars would be about right for me! Well, at least I found a quarter in the parking lot on the way back to the car.

Mary had made reservations for three campsites at Riley Creek Campground in Denali National Park. Upon our arrival, we discovered that that didn't mean you actually had a site assigned to you. We still had to drive through the campground and find our own sites. As it turned out, each rig ended up on a different campground loop about as far away from each other as we could get. That evening everyone migrated over to our campsite where the cooks put together a spaghetti dinner. Russ bought some firewood, so we enjoyed a campfire that evening.

The next day was our big day in Denali National Park. We had reservations to take the bus trip into the park so we could observe wildlife and see the highest mountain in North America. It was a beautiful sunny day—we were told it was the first such day they had had in about three weeks. The wildlife cooperated, except for the moose. We saw seven grizzlies (including one sow with a cub), five wolves (including two pups), hoary marmots, arctic ground squirrels, Dall sheep, caribou, snowshoe hares, a pair of gyrfalcons, northern harriers, magpies, ravens, white-crowned sparrows, bald eagles, ptarmigan, and lots more. Denali was spectacular; you certainly did not have to guess which mountain it was at an elevation of 20,308 feet. Everything was bright green and there were tons of wildflowers in bloom. The bus took us sixty-three miles into the interior of the park on a gravel road.

Our driver, Ralph Oliva, was definitely afflicted with adult attention deficit disorder (AADD). He talked nonstop the entire nine-hour trip. He drives a school bus in Heally, AK, during the winter. He told us he suffers from seasonal affective disorder (SAD) during the winter, so has to use special lights to help him overcome his depression during the long nineteen-hour winter nights.

Speaking of Alaskan nights—there isn't much "dark" up there at night in the summer. I took a picture of a sunset at about 10:30 one night and it would be another forty-five minutes or so before the sun was completely set. If you wake up during the night, there is just less light; it isn't dark. No need to bring a lot of flashlights with you when you go to Alaska in the summer as there is always some light twenty-four hours a day. Fortunately, it didn't affect us too much as we still did get to sleep when we turned in for the night. On the downside, we forgot to go to bed at a decent hour some nights if we were visiting or playing games with our fellow travelers. We still got up at about 6:00 to 7:00 each morning.

After sleeping through a 29°F night and having breakfast in our campers, we all went to a sled dog demonstration in the park. The lady hosting the demonstration was the first pregnant NPS ranger I had ever seen. She is the only park ranger I've ever seen who was allowed to leave her shirt tail untucked!

The sled dogs did not fit my image of what they should look like. Most were fairly long-legged and looked nothing like huskies or malamutes. However, it was very obvious that every one of them was anxious to get in harness and take off running. You could tell that was all they wanted to do. We were allowed to pet and hold some of the new sled dog puppies. They were very friendly and cuddly. After the "Introduction to Sledding" show, several of our group had their pictures taken on a sled with dogs attached, but the dogs were resting peacefully since they were tied up. We then went to the visitor center where we viewed their orientation film—it was very well done.

By then it was time for the "flyers" in our group to head for Anchorage so they could catch their plane back to Portland, OR, at midnight. So after they left for Anchorage, the rest of us proceeded on to Fairbanks about ninety miles further north.

The last twenty-five miles to Fairbanks slowed us down as there was considerable road construction taking place. We tried following a local map of the city, but that just took us off in the wrong direction. A helpful person from a fire station came out and helped us find our way when we inadvertently blocked his driveway while turning around and trying to figure out where we were. We ended up at the Chena Marina RV Park for the next two nights. Fairbanks would end up being the furthest north we would go on this trip.

On the first night in Fairbanks, we relaxed a little and planned our next day in town. We were next to the Chena River which served as a takeoff point for a number of fly-in fishing and hunting guides. Just across the river, not a quarter of a mile away was a small airport. When the seaplanes took off from the river they sounded as if they would come right through our camper. In spite of the seaplane activity, there were occasional ducks on the water and we even saw a muskrat swimming along the shore. The last plane I heard take off that night was at 11:30 p.m. while the sun was still up!

On July 22, all seven of us went up to the University of Alaska Museum and spent most of the morning viewing their very well-developed displays. The museum covered both the natural and human history of Alaska. We then moved downtown to watch a Native American program at a city park. We thought we were going to see the Eskimo games, but we ended up watching intertribal dances for an hour or so because we didn't realize everything else was happening inside the building next door. Shirley had a reindeer sausage "dog" and I had a buffalo bratwurst "dog" for lunch. Very interesting—probably would not have guessed them to be anything other than beef or pork if we hadn't been told otherwise.

After lunch, we went to the U of A's Large Animal Research Station (LARS) for a tour. At LARS, we participated in a one-hour interpretive program about their research on muskox and reindeer/caribou. The latter are actually one species; reindeer are merely a domesticated form of the caribou and are raised mostly in Scandinavian countries. The muskox underfur is extremely valuable due to its light weight and ability to hold in heat. It was interesting learning about both species' natural history.

That evening, Joyce and Shirley needed to do laundry, so Glenn drove them around town for about an hour looking for a laundromat. The first one they found would do the laundry for you—too expensive. The second was temporarily closed for three days. The third one was open, but there was no hot water available—they used this one anyway for $3.50 a load!

Saturday morning we all headed across town to North Pole, Alaska—yes, there really is such a place. Guess what it is. Yup, a tourist trap! Tons of Christmas trinkets for sale and a couple of reindeer outside for the guys to watch while the ladies shopped. After a fast-food lunch, it was time for Kurt and Mary to head back toward their home in Seward while our original party of five began making our way back to our homes in the "Lower 48."

We headed out toward Tok, AK—the first town you encounter if you drive to Alaska and the last town you leave when driving out of the state. On the way there, we stopped to take a look at the Alaska pipeline where it crosses the Tanana River. We were surprised at the muddiness of the river. Although there was a boat launch ramp along the shore, you could not see the bottom of the river. The river was flowing at a pretty good pace. There is no way I would have tried to launch a boat right there.

Right under the pipeline were a fur shop and another shop selling diamond willow sticks and burl sticks. We bought some of the diamond willow for our friend Larry in Walla Walla as he had taken up wood carving recently. I wanted to buy an arctic fox fur to hang in our camper since it is an Arctic Fox fifth wheel, but I was unable to convince Shirley that it was an appropriate souvenir.

We managed to see six moose that afternoon, including one mother who sent her not-so-young youngster into the woods and then stood and made threatening glances at us several times before also escaping into the woods. Most of the highways we have traveled in Alaska have a wide swath of vegetation removed on both sides of the road. When you get to the trees, perhaps fifty to seventy-five feet from the road, you can barely walk through them as they are so thick. We've watched wildlife disappear into the woods and within just a few feet, they are totally out of sight. It is easy to see how an animal could shoot out of the woods and onto the road quickly without time to react if a wide buffer zone was not kept clear.

We camped that night in a gravel pit somewhere on the Canadian side of Tok. The next morning, we made a stop at Border City where we had spent a night on the way north. It would be our last chance to fuel up at American fuel prices. We discovered that the prices have continued to climb throughout the last month. One place told us they were to raise their price by ten cents a gallon the next morning.

On the 25th of July, we drove a little over 250 miles and landed at one of our favorite stops on the way up, Congdon Creek Campground on Kluane Lake in the Yukon Territory. It was cloudy and rained some. The lake was up a few feet making it difficult to get out to one point I had walked to the first time we were there. Again, it was too windy to take advantage of the superb "skipping stones" that lined the lake.

I rose early the next morning and went for a walk. While my main pursuit was to look for birds in the immediate vicinity, I did manage to find a flock of about fourteen Dall sheep on the mountain to the southwest. It is unbelievable where those animals can climb to and that they can actually find enough forage up there to keep them alive and healthy.

As we left Congdon Creek, we encountered the construction zone we had gone through on the way north. The young lady who stopped us until traffic could proceed was from Newfoundland. She hasn't decided what she wants to do, so when a friend found her a job flagging on this construction site, she decided to take it. The workers all live in portable dormitories that are provided since they are so far from any town. The construction company also provided all their meals. So, I imagine young people with nowhere to spend their money could probably save quite a bit working ten-hour shifts from April to October.

Later in the day, we encountered another construction zone. The stretches of torn-up roads have a way of coating your vehicle with very sticky, gritty soil that doesn't even wash off well with a pressure washer. I'm just glad I hadn't washed the truck and trailer again before hitting the two construction zones that day. A van flew past us in one of the construction zones just before a flagger stopped us. I mentioned to the flagger about what the van driver had just done since his vehicle sent gravel flying everywhere. She informed me that she had seen it and already told him it is illegal to pass in a construction zone and fines double in these areas. I managed to lose the cap to my sewer hose compartment in one of those rough areas, but fortunately, the hose stayed with us. It cost a little over $15 to replace that little piece of rubber in Whitehorse, YT, the next day.

That night, we ended up camping at High Country RV Park in Whitehorse once again. Remembering our great meals at the Klondike Restaurant, we decided to eat there one more time. After dinner, we dragged Glenn, Joyce, and Russ through the little Riverside Market that we had visited the last time we were in town. With their narrow aisles and tall shelves, I couldn't imagine what it would be like to keep the shelves stocked almost to the ceiling.

On July 26, we drove to Mukluk Annie's where we camped for free along the shore of a large lake. It wasn't anything special since it was just an open dirt area with some picnic tables. We had started to camp at a provincial park a few miles back down the road, but the mosquitoes chased us away. While taking a walk along the shore, Russ and I found a sandpiper with one tiny chick. We also came across some sizable moose tracks along the shore, but didn't see a moose.

On the 27th, we took a short walk out to Rancheria Falls via a boardwalk. The ground was covered with lichens, moss, and more kinds of mushrooms than you could shake a stick at. The falls were well worth the short walk to see them.

Along the way, the five of us started playing various games while camping in the evening. Since Glenn and I lost a game of cribbage to Shirley and Russ, we had to buy them an ice cream cone (I don't know who started this "gambling" thing—I think it was Shirley!). So we stopped at an RV resort in the middle of nowhere to pay up. The lady didn't want to admit she had ice cream, but we mentioned that her sign said she had it. So, she removed the newspapers that were hiding the ice cream containers and served us black cherry and maple nut ice cream cones. She says she doesn't like to mess with the ice cream so she keeps it covered, and she only serves it when she's in the mood! We had a nice visit with her before proceeding on. She said that particular area doesn't get much snow in the winter although the temperatures can drop into the −60°F range.

Somewhere along the way, Glenn and Russ found out that if they would forage for wild berries (blueberries, raspberries, and strawberries), Shirley could turn them into some scrumptious desserts. So as soon as we parked out in the boonies, they would head out foraging for the contents of our next dessert. We could not keep up with their ability to supply berries so they had to start leaving some for the wildlife and birds.

On this particular night, we found a gravel pit in which to camp. Glenn turned on his generator, popped a cassette into the DVD, turned on the TV, and there we sat in the middle of absolutely nowhere watching the first half of *Cleopatra* starring Liz Taylor, Richard Burton, and Rex Harrison. It had been about forty years since I last saw that movie—I probably wasn't supposed to have seen it then!

The next day, at Contact Creek, Russ went into the store and came out carrying a "free" calendar with lots of nice wildlife pictures on it. Since it was free, Shirley wanted me to get one also. Well, I felt a little strange going in and just asking for a free calendar, so I picked up a candy bar, paid $1.25 for it, and walked out with my "free" calendar. It was only when I got back to the car that I realized that it was a 2005 calendar—I thought it was a 2006 or I would not have even bought the candy bar. As it turned out, that was our only expense for the day.

That day was one of our best for viewing wild bison as we saw three separate groups that included calves, cows, and bulls. It is hard to imagine how big they are till you have one up close to your car and you're trying to get a picture of it. We were surprised at one place to see only a calf and a bull together—there was no sign of the mother anywhere near the calf.

We went on down the roadways and pulled out along the Tetsa River for lunch. While there, Russ and I explored a little road across the highway from where we were eating. Turns out the road came right back out to the highway in just a couple hundred yards. We ran up a half dozen or so grouse while walking along the road. We decided this would be a great place to camp for the night, so we moved the rigs to the new site and settled in. It was nice because we were away from the highway and no one could even tell we were back in the woods as they drove by.

Shirley had us all participate in an assembly line to produce enchiladas that we would have for dinner the next night. It was quite an assembly line operation. We all wore our aprons so we wouldn't get our good traveling clothes dirty! I even wore the camouflage apron I was given at my retirement luncheon; the rest of the group couldn't even see me as I chopped up the olives! Much to Russ's surprise and disappointment, the enchilada making was followed by a great meatloaf dinner. He didn't realize the enchiladas were for the next night's dinner. Dessert that night was a blueberry cream cheese pie that Shirley made from blueberries that Glenn had picked a few days before. Actually, they were huckleberries, but everyone was happy thinking they were blueberries, so we left it at that. That night we watched the second half of *Cleopatra*; that may have been the first showing ever of that film along the Tetsa River!

On the 29th of July, we passed by Muncho Lake again. It is a beautiful lake that pretty much fills the entire valley. The road is right down next to the water and there are steep cliffs that climb abruptly on the other side of the road. We stopped at a log lodge where we had seen a huge wall-mounted wood-carved map of the area that I wanted to photograph. While there, a man asked if we owned the Arctic Fox fifth wheel out front. He and his wife had an Arctic Fox bumper hitch trailer and were thinking about trading it in for one like ours. They had been on the road since early May and also traveled all the way to Alaska. Although they were from Reno, NV, they had purchased their trailer in Pendleton, OR. We suggested they check out the place we bought ours in Pasco, WA.

As we were leaving Muncho Lake, we saw and photographed six Doll sheep along the side of the road. They were on one of the very impressive alluvial fans that came out of the steep mountains above the lake. These alluvial fans were massive; they were almost all cobblestone with practically no vegetation growing on them. Some were a half mile or so wide before they reached the lake.

A little before noon, I pulled off to the left at a pullout to get a picture of a beaver dam. I called Glenn on the radio as usual to let him know we were stopping. I got out in time to see Glenn slowing down to pull off the road. As he did so, there was a lot of smoke trailing him, then a huge "bang"—I thought for sure he had just blown his engine as the smoke stopped almost immediately. Turns out the right front brake on his trailer must have locked up coming down the last hill, so that tire had been sliding along on the pavement for a couple of miles before it wore a hole right through the tire.

As the tire was being changed, Russ noticed that some critical lug nuts for holding the wheel on the axle were missing—two of five bolts were gone. Glenn was able to improvise a fix using some nuts and bolts from his satellite dish tripod. Later, they would learn that more lug nuts were missing on other wheels; one had only one of the five bolts still in place! Russ, the only really mechanically inclined person in the group, made a repair at the site of the blowout and packed the bearings with grease before we took off again.

About nine miles down the road, Shirley noticed in the rearview mirror that I had left one of our cargo box locks on the top edge of the pickup bed. How it rode there on this very windy road that long without falling off we'll never know.

We stayed at the West End RV Park in Fort Nelson, BC, that night. I tried washing the pickup and fifth wheel; I managed to knock some of the dirt off the surface, but the next morning it really didn't look like I had washed it at all. We were not really impressed with this park. If it had been in the States, I'm sure a health department would have closed them down as there seemed to be a lot of sewage in the standing and flowing surface water throughout the campground. It really needed some cleaning up. The laundry room was really dirty and you had to prop a chair against the dryer door to keep it closed. I was able to download email messages that night, but the park's server would not allow me to send any.

We enjoyed our previously prepared enchilada dinner that night along with wild strawberry and raspberry shortcakes. Our friends Herschel and Nancy Henderly had given Shirley a Bisquick cookbook when they stopped by our place in June. Shirley used it several times on this trip. Luckily, it contained a recipe for shortcakes.

After fueling the next morning, we stopped at an IGA store to stock up. They had some really good apple fritters that we helped to get rid of. Then, Glenn and Russ decided to work on the trailer wheels some more. After they finished, we decided we needed to go back and replenish our apple fritter supply. Unfortunately, they only had one left, so we let Russ have that one. I decided to get some peaches and nectarines—they were both tasty and very juicy, better than what we can usually get back home.

Right next to the store was a laundromat that advertised that they had buffalo meat for sale. We bought a frozen package which we planned to hang on to till we got home. As we drove away, we noticed that this same laundromat was also some sort of a "love web boutique." We hadn't seen any sign of that while in the place and the saleslady certainly did not look like someone who would work in a Victoria's Secret store!

Later that day, we came upon a rather large black bear as it was grazing on a patch of clover at the side of the road. It paid no attention to us as we took several good pictures of it before proceeding onward.

That night we camped at a pullout that had a fantastic view of a valley and mountains to the west. At 10:30 p.m., the sunset was a bright orange and purple due to the clouds. Shirley had already gone to bed, so I got her up to be able to enjoy the sunset also. Later that night, at about 1:30 a.m., I awakened to something I had not experienced for over a month and a half—total darkness! A quarter moon was just starting to rise in the east, but it was truly darkness. Since we were traveling mostly south at that time, our nights continued to be a little longer and considerably darker.

The next morning, we observed a species of bird we had never seen before; they were pine grosbeaks. The males are very bright red. We also saw several pine siskins. Both species were eating something on the dirt surface where we had parked.

As we were traveling near Buckinghorse River on July 31, we came across a cow and bull moose at the side of the road. It would be the only bull moose we would see on the entire trip. We also saw three bucks that day; we were just getting back into deer country finally.

A short way down the road, we met a couple at a pullout who were from Kansas City, MO. The man had lived with his family on the Yukon River until he was ten. His father had worked for a trading company there for many years and finally decided he needed to move his family back to the Lower 48 so his kids could get an education.

All through Alaska we had seen a book entitled *Tisha*. It is about a woman, Ann Purdy, who taught in a one-room schoolhouse on the Yukon. The KC man told us that this woman was his second grade teacher at Eagle, AK. When his father decided to leave AK, he built a raft and put his family, their belongings, and an old pickup on the raft and set out down the Yukon River until they could reach a point where they could head south on a real boat. The Kansas City man said there was no reason why they shouldn't have drowned riding such a flimsy raft.

That night we stayed at a rest area we stayed at on the way to Alaska. It was just about fifty miles west of Fort Saint John at Alcan Highway mile 80. It was a nice little spot with restrooms, picnic tables, and lots of tall shade trees. However, I did note that many of the larger trees had died and many more had already been removed. We dined on soup, cornbread, and another berry cobbler as a result of Glenn's berry-picking efforts. We played dominoes until retiring for the night at 10:30 p.m.

The next morning, we had to climb the 10 percent grade coming out of Taylor, BC. The climb really heated up both rigs since the pull lasts several miles. Near Farmington, we stopped at the Van Han Apiaries and bought several types of honey. To our surprise, Chris Van Han, the lady we were talking to is the sister of Lyle Hanson, a vice president of Baker Boyer Bank near our home in Walla Walla, WA. She gave us a short note to deliver to him once we arrived home. We did as she requested.

Dawson Creek was our next fueling point. Both coming and going we stopped at the "Gas Bar" which is affiliated with the Extra Foods grocery store across the parking lot. For every liter of fuel purchased, we got seven cents off our grocery bill. Since I would get about ninety-plus liters every time I filled up, it was a nice little rebate on the groceries. That store also was where I got introduced to Oh Henry! Bite-Size candies. They became my friend for the rest of the trip. I would allow myself three for every hour of driving; that way they would last for a while.

Dawson Creek was both the beginning and ending of the AlCan Highway. From Dawson Creek to Fairbanks, all distances were measured from Dawson Creek. In the Yukon, they had kilometer markers that also measured the distance from Dawson Creek.

As we headed south, we found a rest area next to Sundance Lake. The lake was probably fifty acres in size. It was a little noisy at the rest stop since it was so close to the highway and twice some rowdy folks shot past our units at very high speeds on a motorcycle and a four-wheeler. If we had stepped out of our camper, there was no way they could have stopped in time to miss us. After dinner that night, we played a round of Balderdash and dominoes.

The next morning, we were hearing loons out on the lake. I went for a little walk to observe them and any other waterbirds that were present. A man stopped to see if the fish were biting that day. Seems he fishes there frequently, so he was able to tell me a little about the lake. It is quite shallow, about seventeen inches at its deepest. It is stocked with trout, so the fish and game folks installed a bubbler in the middle of the lake to allow oxygen to get into the water when the lake freezes over during the winter. Apparently, the ice is about a foot thick, enough that people drive their vehicles onto the lake for ice fishing. He said it is frozen from late November to about March.

191

We spent the next night at Tudyah Lake Provincial Park. The picnic tables had assigned numbers, you just picked out a spot on the grass to camp wherever you liked. While Shirley and I hiked near the lake, we are fairly certain we saw a bittern fly up out of a reedy area across the lake. We also discovered some of the tiniest frogs we've ever seen. They were all over the place in great numbers. Some on the road were considerably flatter than others! We barbecued pork chops for supper that night; another in a long line of great dinners. We also had a good supply of mosquitoes later in the evening, but we were able to escape them inside our campers; it was nothing like our earlier experience at Rancheria River.

While playing dominoes that night we heard an unwanted creature gnawing behind a cabinet in the Fitzgeralds' trailer. The next morning, we had evidence of a mouse having visited them. That prompted us to buy a couple of mouse traps which we baited with cheese and peanut butter. Apparently, our "guest" did not appreciate our hospitality, so we never heard or saw it again.

Somewhere between Chetwyn and Prince George on the following day, we had just crossed a railroad track when we noticed a number of people out picking some kind of berry. We radioed to Glenn and Russ to see if they wanted to stop and do some picking; they were just about out of their truck with buckets in hand before we finished the conversation. Shirley and I also got into the spirit of the picking. We later had another huckleberry cream cheese pie to get rid of some of the berries.

In Prince George, I had to do a money exchange. The lady in the bank was most friendly and wanted to share with me all the neat things to see and do around Prince George and on the highway to Prince Rupert (we weren't going there). While Joyce and Shirley did some grocery shopping, Russ and I went down the street to a station to fuel up our truck and refill both my propane tanks. I asked if they accepted Discover credit cards. They indicated they did, so I radioed Glenn so he could also come down and fuel up. While we were filling our tanks and Glenn was gassing his rig, the lady came out of the station and said she had made a mistake, they don't take Discover anymore. It didn't bother me, but it was not going to set well with Glenn, so we asked her if she had told him yet. When she indicated she hadn't, we cautioned her to let him know gently. Fortunately, Glenn found out they were affiliated with Shell Oil Company so they accepted his Shell credit card. She offered us each a free cold drink for making the mistake; while Glenn didn't take anything, I took the opportunity to have a strawberry-passion fruit Fruitopia drink—enjoyed it so much, I've had several more since, plus we've tried the strawberry-kiwi which is also a good warm weather drink.

On August 3, we camped at the Canyon Creek RV Park in Hixon, BC. Yup, they spell it wrong, but we still felt a special affinity to the place. Russ had developed the skill of getting a hug from all the women he met along the way. The lady running the campground was sitting on her riding lawn mower the next morning when we started to leave. She jumped off the mower and gave Russ a big hug before we left. We stopped at a small store in town for some free Hixon Falls postcards, then visited the antique place out back. I managed to find a fur trappers trap that I thought would look good in our party barn back home, so I bought it. Shirley also bought a teacup and saucer. Apparently, the gal working the store doesn't sell a whole awful lot as she couldn't find her receipt book when we were ready to make our purchases. As we were leaving the antique store, Russ stopped at the door and set his free cup of coffee on the steps (he had a knack for getting free ice cream and coffee along the way) and called out to the lady inside, "Wanda, we're leaving now!" She promptly came to the door and gave him a huge hug!

We stopped at the Hixon Take Out to see what it was about. Joyce, Shirley, and I each tried a Hixon Burger or the Single Hixon Burger. I didn't want fresh onions on mine, so the cook sautéed them for me. They were fantastic flame-charred burgers. If you're up that way, you've got to try one. The only reason Russ didn't get a hug there was because Hilda's (the cook and proprietor) husband was there having lunch at the same time. Hixon is an unincorporated village of about five hundred people; seems most eat at the Hixon Take Out quite frequently. We were able to glean quite a bit about the community from a number of locals who were surprised to hear our last name was Hixson. I took a picture of my Hixson burger, and every time I see it on my computer I say to myself that it was the best burger I've ever eaten!

Down the road at Williams Lake and Quesnel, we encountered some pretty bad air pollution. Seems both areas have several sawmills that put out quite a bit of stinky smoke. I met a lady the next day who said that Prince George often has the worst pollution of the three towns in the area due to their larger mills. However, we happened to be there after a two-day wind storm that had pretty much purged the valley of most of its bad air.

As we moved south toward the Fraser River Canyon, the temperatures started to soar. We experienced our first 80°F+ temperatures of the entire trip that day. This was a very arid, desert-looking steep-sided canyon that seemed to trap hot air. The air quality wasn't looking very good either. We did get to see some bighorn sheep in the canyon as they were crossing the road and headed straight into a small village.

We stopped at Lac La Hache Provincial Park that night. Glenn and I took advantage of the opportunity to go down to the lake for a refreshing swim. Shirley (a non-swimmer) served as a lifeguard on shore while Russ was introducing himself to a young lady further down the beach. We liked the campground enough that we decided to stay another day. Fortunately, it was not as hot the second day, so we just lazed around the campsite, relaxed, napped, and read all day after a breakfast of pancakes topped with huckleberries. Shirley and I did go on a walk that was supposed to take an hour, but due to the mosquitoes, we were able to do it in a mere twenty minutes. Along the way, we caught a glimpse of a fox.

As we proceeded south, we realized there was a very large wildfire in the Fraser River Canyon. We observed several helicopters ferrying water from the river to drop on hotspots and we saw a number of firefighters scattered throughout the canyon. There were flames clear down next to the railroad track just across the river from us.

On August 6, we spent our last night in Canada at the Wild Rose RV Park just west of Hope, BC. After dinner, we went for a walk in town to see their chainsaw carvings. Both Chetwynd and Hope claim to be the "Chainsaw Carving Capital of the World." We had seen the carvings at Chetwynd, so we decided we should check out Hope's.

As we were walking up Hope's main street, we saw a couple of businesses that were apparently on fire. Before we could walk closer to be certain that was what was happening, the fire units started arriving. Since most of the fire crew appeared to be volunteers, it seemed as though the initial attack on the fire proceeded extremely slowly. While there, one of the owners, an older lady in her bathrobe showed up. Unfortunately, she was of course helpless to do anything. It was quite a while before anyone from the crowd stepped forward to comfort her and walk her over to the paramedics who were standing by. It appeared as though both shops would sustain serious smoke and water damage. We ended our evening with ice cream treats at the local Dairy Queen.

The next morning, we stopped at the Mintor Gardens about twenty miles west of Hope. It was a gorgeous day to walk about the gardens and enjoy the flowers and other ornamental vegetation. They've done a beautiful job developing the gardens. After lunch there, we proceeded to Burlington, WA, where we spent the night at a KOA campground.

Getting across the border was quite an ordeal that day. It took us one and a half hours just to get to US Customs with other cars constantly trying to cut in front of us. One guy almost took off my front bumper as he cut in. We endured the silly questions they ask—What do you have in there?—while pointing at the camper! Why did you make this trip? Do you have any fruits or vegetables? We had our IDs and birth certificates checked, then headed for the first gas station to fill up on lower-priced US fuel. It is a good thing I had stopped and bought about five gallons worth just before we sat in the long line at the border as you have to keep your engine running the entire time in order to keep up when the line moves.

Well, we got our fuel, then we waited and waited and waited for the Fitzgeralds to catch up with us. We were less than a mile from the border. It just happens they were computer-selected for a thorough inspection of their pickup and trailer. They were placed in a room with no restrooms and told to wait there. They were not allowed to use their radio to contact us to tell us what was happening. One customs lady told them to sit in a certain place, then another customs agent asked why they were sitting there—he said they would never get waited on as long as they were seated there. About forty-five minutes later, they caught up with us and we headed on down to Burlington.

We were about five miles from our kids' so after we dropped the trailers at an RV park, we loaded into our pickup and headed to Thomas and Tia's place. We had a great visit with the kids including a delicious pizza dinner. Our other son and his wife, Matthew and Heidi, were just getting back from a weekend at Leavenworth, so they were also able to join us.

Next morning, we took the Fitzgeralds up to see Matthew and Heidi's place. After a short visit, they took off for Tom and Becky's at Battle Ground, WA. Our caravanning days had finally come to an end. We took our trailer up to Matthew's and parked it there for the next two nights while we did things with all four kids and our one-year-old grandson, Briley. Heidi, Tia, and Briley took us to Padden Lake for a picnic. Afterwards, Tia took Briley home for his nap, but Heidi, Shirley, and I walked completely around the lake (2.5 miles) with Heidi's dog, Sage, towing Heidi. Matthew barbecued his famous fiery-hot buffalo wings that night for dinner. For our taste, they would have been better if not quite so fiery!

Tia, Heidi, and Shirley picked a bunch of blackberries and some apples and peaches which they worked at canning the second day we were there. I got to help entertain Briley while they were busy in the kitchen. Matthew, Thomas, and I played croquet that evening using the "house rules of the day." They tend to set the course up as more of an obstacle course and allot points as they proceed through the game. Believe me, it is quite challenging on a sloped and bumpy lawn.

Under cloudy and somewhat drippy skies, we headed down the road for our last 340 miles to home. By the time we got to Ellensburg, it was sunny and starting to heat up again. Fortunately, when we arrived home at about 5:30 that evening it was only about 80°F.

We left on Thursday, June 23, and we arrived home on Thursday, August 11, exactly fifty days of a very fantastic vacation. We had driven 6,801 miles and purchased over five hundred gallons of diesel along the way. The good news is that we were able to average 13.3 miles per gallon even pulling the trailer. It was truly an exceptional once-in-a-lifetime journey. Two years later, we visited Alaska again via airplanes, buses, trains, and the ship, Ruby Princess. I'll save that story for another day.

DREAMLAND

Dreams have always fascinated me. My earliest dreams often involved my parents or other adults asking me a "yes or no" question. I frequently would reply out loud with my answer, waking myself up in the process. I would then be confused because there was no one there talking to me.

Many a time I would have a dream in which there would be people from all different times of my life. Perhaps someone from our church, along with a high school friend, or a former fellow teacher. These people would have no connection with each other in real life, so I would be telling myself that this couldn't be happening. That usually caused me to wake up and wonder how these people ever ended up in the same dream.

I've thought about people who are generally considered to have cognitive or mental illnesses who "hear voices" that tell them to do things that are not always appropriate to act upon. Are these "voices" merely an exaggerated form of dreaming? I know in my dreams people actually carry on fictitious conversations which must be generated by my own brain.

One dream I have had several times over the years involves my attendance at a conference or a professional training course. In these dreams, it is always the last day of the session and I am frantically packing my suitcase since I have a flight to catch within an hour. I have no idea why I had not packed the previous night or early that morning. The problem I am confronted with during the frantic packing process is: I can't find my flight tickets or my itinerary. On some occasions, upon arriving at the airport I'm told I'll have to take a train since I don't have a boarding pass. By this time, I'm usually conflicted enough that I wake up and try to figure out what was going on.

In the past few years as my brain is aging, I've come up with a series of dreams that usually causes me to react physically, much to the chagrin of my wife. I might be having a conversation with a friend when a dog attacks my legs, so I begin kicking at the dog to scare it away. Unfortunately, I am actually kicking my legs in bed! That's why Shirley isn't too happy. Other times I've dreamed someone is trying to grab hold of me to do me great bodily harm, so in those cases, I start hitting back at the perpetrator! Again, Shirley has objected to my reactions to my dreams. Actually, I'm not too thrilled about them either. It is scary to wake up and realize your actions were caused by something your own brain has created.

The following is truly a random access memory. I have no idea where it came from. I was enjoying a very deep sleep when a dream crept into my head. They say dreams only last for a couple of minutes, but this one had to have lasted longer.

It seems I was attending a conference of land managers from a mix of state and federal natural resource agencies. I had just taken a seat at one of the large round tables at the front of the room and took a quick look at the meeting agenda. Lo and behold the first topic was to be on feral hog management on public lands. That wasn't so bad, but the presenter of that topic was to be Phil Hixson! Whoa, that set me back a notch or two as I had NEVER had to deal with a wild hog management issue on any lands I had managed!

Almost immediately, the moderator of the session kicked things off by introducing me and my topic of discussion. I was still in shock having just learned I would be addressing this topic. I tried to indicate to the moderator that there was a mistake and that I should not be leading this session. Next thing I knew, he had handed me the microphone and walked away. Placing my hand over the mic, I whispered toward him that I don't know anything about this topic other than what I've read in magazines and journals and seen on TV. He left me standing there waiting for me to begin my "talk," but then my teaching skills took over.

I have taught numerous classes to adults during my career. When doing so, since the students are adults also, I can usually assume that someone in the class will know the answer to a leading question I might ask. In first aid classes, many students have taken a similar class previously, so if I ask them how to perform a certain procedure, someone will know the correct answer. Then all I have to do is praise them for their answer and reinforce what we are talking about, often relating something from my personal experiences. I have used the same method when teaching a "Law Enforcement in Natural Resources Management" class at the University of Idaho, in "Personnel Management" and "Job Psychology" classes at Walla Walla Community College, in our "Young Married Couples" classes at church, and in training and conference sessions with the COE. This method keeps me from "lecturing" to the participants.

So, as my dream progressed, I began asking questions. The first was: Have any of you ever dealt with feral hog management on the lands you manage? Several people raised their hands, so I asked one of them to relate that experience to the rest of the group. Although I don't think my dream included that person's answer, it triggered my brain to kick into gear and start asking the group more questions. How did the feral hogs come to be on public lands? How quickly has their population increased? At this point, I related having seen a sow pig at a Shaker farm in the northeast who was nursing twelve piglets at one time (this is a true statement that my mind dredged up from the depths of my subconscious). Do you allow the hunting of these animals?

Eventually, the moderator called for a short break. During the break, I noticed one of the managers in attendance had brought in a potted cactus plant that was probably going to be part of his presentation later in the conference. When we got back together, knowing that feral pigs were found in many of the southwest parks, and in Hawaii, I asked that gentleman how these animals have affected endangered species on the lands he manages. I was really on a roll now. Questions were popping into my head at an alarming rate. I had not "presented" a thing to the group, and yet they (and I) were learning a tremendous amount of knowledge pertaining to the management of feral pigs on public lands.

Then, BAM! Right as my alarm went off at 6:00 a.m., I found myself not at a conference, but wide awake in my bed at home. Even though I was awake, I continued thinking of other questions I could ask that would elicit more thoughts on how to manage feral hogs on public lands. Suddenly, I realized it had all been just a dream, brought forward from somewhere deep in my brain as just a random access of my memory, and apparently from a creative part of my mind where synapses and neurons were piecing together a very entertaining scenario that never happened. I was in hog heaven knowing I really had not been put on the spot!

CANOES, PADDLES, AND LIFE JACKETS

My family was not into boating of any kind. I can remember only a few times we were near a lake or pond where a row boat was available to us. We weren't really good at paddling a boat, so I'm afraid we got fairly wet while learning how to row the boat and keep it heading in one direction.

The second summer we were at Crater Lake Nationa Park, we learned that several of the summer staff had gone to Eugene the week before and purchased canoes and accessories. Because several bought them at the same time, the proprietor gave them each a $100 discount. I contacted the store owner and he agreed to give us the same discount, so we headed to Eugene to buy a seventeen-foot Grumman aluminum canoe. Of course, we had to buy a couple of beautiful wood paddles, life jackets, and devices to be able to carry the canoe on top of our pickup and camper shell.

Shirley is a non-swimmer, so we were careful where we went the first time. It happened that the University of Oregon had a small stream on its campus that was just right for us first-timers to begin to develop our canoeing skills.

Later, we ventured out into the waters of the Upper Klamath National Wildlife Refuge. We eventually moved on to the upper reaches of the Deschutes River southwest of Bend, OR. The river at that point was slow moving with the tops of the banks several feet above our heads. It was a windy stretch, so we couldn't see around each bend in the river. It was interesting to come around a bend and find a female hooded merganser with a half dozen ducklings swimming downstream. The only problem was that since we were several feet below the banks of the river, we couldn't see any other wildlife in the forests and meadows around us.

In 1975, we bought a house that was being built along a side channel of the Kings River in the San Joaquin Valley of central California. There were several reasons to buy where we did: 1) it was out in the country; 2) it looked straight up into the Sierra Nevada Mountains; and 3) it had a beaver dam in the backyard! That beaver dam provided us with a swimming hole in our backyard.

Some of the neighborhood kids didn't like the beaver dam being there, so it wasn't until the next year we discovered they were in the habit of placing a large pole where the beaver built its dam each year. To keep the stream free flowing, they would lift up the pole and destroy the dam so they could float down the river on innertubes. It just happened that the man who owned the lot on the other side of the dam worked for California Fish & Game. We both liked the dam, so the following year we helped the beaver get started on building a new dam by placing tree prunings in the creek before the pole was in place. The beaver took the hint and built the dam the rest of the way. Thus we had a swimming hole available during all the hot spring, summer, and fall days. It also allowed us to occasionally canoe a half mile or so up the channel.

We took the canoe up to Hume Lake in the Sierras on several occasions. I had paddled across the lake from our put-in point when a headwind came up. I was still quite naive about how to handle such a situation, so I sat in the back of the canoe and paddled like crazy against the wind. With me in the back, the front of the canoe was sticking up in the air. No matter how hard I paddled and tried to steer toward the other shore, the wind would catch the front of the canoe and turn it right or left as if it were a weather vane. Eventually,

I discovered it would help greatly if I moved to the center of the canoe to keep the front end in contact with the water.

By this time I was working as a park ranger at Pine Flat Dam just twelve miles up the river from our home. I became friends with another park ranger, Kent, who was also working at Pine Flat. We decided it would be fun to canoe down the river after work some evening. So Kent dropped his car off at my house and rode to work with me that day. I already had the canoe on top of the pickup ready to go.

We started our adventure just downstream from the dam. The plan was to canoe down the river and take the side channel the last half mile or so that would allow us to end up in our backyard beaver pond. The river immediately below the dam had several standing waves that we enjoyed "bouncing" over with no problems. We thought we could handle almost anything the river had to offer after that bit of "rough" waters.

A mile or so below the dam, the river took a bend to the left. There was riprap on the right which supports the road to the dam. The water on the left was shallow and fairly smooth. But the riprapped side was choppy with lots of challenging-looking waves, so since we now thought we were "pros" at river canoeing, we decided to take the bumpy route. We did fine on the first wave or two that hit us as the river hit the riprap and bounced back toward us. However, we began to realize that each wave that hit us was causing the canoe to list to the left and it did not upright between the waves which were now coming at us faster than we could row to avoid them.

After five or six of these waves hit us, the canoe tipped over and we found ourselves in the water and under the water. Fortunately, we each had our life jackets on; I'm sure mine saved my life that day! I can still see that canoe under the water for several seconds before the river let me come up and grab a quick breath. I got to do that several times before I saw an opportunity to seize one of the big rocks on the shore with my legs. By now I had grabbed hold of the side of the upside-down canoe with both hands. As the waves continued to pummel me, each one was prying the canoe away from my grasp. About this time I saw Kent floating past me. He had managed to snag both of the paddles and was using them in tandem to stay afloat and move out of the rough water.

I finally had to let go of the canoe about the time my legs were losing their grip on the riprap, but I managed to grab hold of the thirty-foot manila rope I had tied to the back of the canoe. As the river began to widen out, I saw a cottonwood tree ahead of me that had fallen into the river. I swam hard to get to the last few branches of the tree and started trying to pull the canoe toward me. The current was swifter than I thought it was at this point, so while hanging on to a branch of the cottonwood with my right hand, the manila rope was being pulled through my left hand. It began to burn my hand badly enough that I finally decided I might not need a canoe any longer! The rope was finally pulled free of my hand and the canoe was headed downstream still floating upside down.

As I watched my canoe floating downstream, I began to climb through the fallen cottonwood finally making it to shore. By the time I caught my breath and started looking for the canoe, I looked across the river several hundred yards away, and there was Kent with the canoe and both paddles. I yelled at him to stay there while I would run upstream to cross the river on a bridge and would head down to his location. However, by the time I got there, he had paddled across the river to pick me up! Eventually, he saw me on the other side of the river and came to my rescue.

Further down the river, we had to portage around a weir, but the rest of the trip was relaxing and totally uneventful. We were both just happy to be alive. We were able to find the side channel that would take us to our backyard beaver pond.

My brother-in-law Glenn and I decided to canoe down the San Joaquin River below Millerton Dam. It was in a fairly flat part of the valley, so it would be an easy trip both downstream and upstream.

We were approaching a place where there were a number of large rocks that backed the water into a small pond. There was a place between two rocks where the water dropped about three feet to the next stretch of the river. We decided that wasn't much of a drop, so we would just paddle real fast and drop over the small falls.

There was a fisherwoman on the shore that was taking great interest in our endeavors. When she saw what we were about to attempt, she reeled her line in and decided to watch the show. Glenn was in the front of the boat and I was in the back. We were a pretty good paddling team working this way. We paddled as fast as we could so the front point of the canoe would not have time to drop below the surface.

We needn't have worried about that. It seems those two rocks were closer together under the water than they were above the water. We hit those two rocks going full speed ahead—the boat stopped immediately while Glenn flew out of the front and into the water, and I ended up in the middle of the bottom of the canoe! Wow! Were we ever surprised. Oh, and the lady fisherwoman was doubled over laughing her head off at our free "daredevil" entertainment. Once again the rest of the trip was uneventful.

We would visit our friend Grandma Ev up at Sandpoint several times each year. The boys were about four and seven when we decided to take the canoe with us. We drove up to Lower Priest Lake and unloaded the canoe at the state park at the upper end of the lake. From there we could paddle a few hundred yards across the lake to enter the 2.5-mile-long thoroughfare that connected Lower Priest Lake to Upper Priest Lake.

The Thorofare was designated as a "no wake zone," meaning you were supposed to go slowly, not going fast enough to leave a wake behind your craft. We had heard people talk about seeing deer, elk, moose, and even bears along the way. All we saw that day were a number of geese and ducks and an assortment of motorboats, pontoon boats, and canoes. After eating our lunch on the shore of the upper lake, we headed back to our vehicle at the state park.

It wasn't until we got to Lower Priest Lake that we realized a wind had come up. Shirley and I were doing all the paddling so by this time we were getting pretty tired. We had the option of taking the long route along the shoreline, or cutting across the end of the lake as we had done earlier when going the other way. The wind was creating some three-foot-plus waves that were parallel to our direction of travel. While the waves gave us a bumpy ride rocking us from side to side, we finally made it back to our vehicle. Our ride at that time was a

Chevy Blazer. Shirley and I were so weakened by our strong paddling across the lake, we could barely lift the canoe to the six-foot-high top of our car!

About the time our boys were in middle school, we had taken a camping trip to Banff and Jasper National Parks in the Canadian Rockies of British Columbia and Alberta. We were pulling our eighteen-foot Road Ranger camp trailer with our 1978 Blazer. The boys' cross-country bikes were hanging on the car's front bumper with our canoe strapped on top of the car.

At Banff, the boys rode their bikes to the top of Sulfur Mountain while Shirley and I took the easier route via the gondola. They said they had to stop at one place to let a small herd of bighorn sheep cross the trail.

Lake Louise is one of the most picturesque lakes in the Canadian Rockies. While they have canoes for rent on the lake, it was too far for us to carry our canoe from the parking lot to the lake. I'm not even sure they would have let us launch our canoe on the lake. However, about fifteen miles south of Lake Louise in a glacier-carved canyon at about six thousand feet in elevation is another beautiful glacier-fed Moraine Lake in the Valley of the Ten Peaks. It used to be pictured on the Canadian twenty-dollar bill until they created new paper currency about thirty years ago.

We asked permission to drive our vehicle closer to Moraine Lake near the restaurant so we could launch our canoe for a trip around the lake. While we were unloading our canoe, a couple of men with large video equipment approached us and asked if we would mind letting them film us while canoeing on the lake. They said it was for a popular Sunday afternoon TV show entitled *Hymn Sing* broadcasted throughout Canada. While playing hymns in the background, they would show films of popular Canadian sceneries and activities from all over the country. We agreed to let them film us, but we never got to see the results as the show was only shown in Canada. While we canoed around the lake, our boys climbed to the top of a large boulder and timber dam that had built up over the years at the outlet of the lake.

While in Jasper, the boys rode their bikes around Beauvert Lake a couple of times while Shirley and I canoed around the lake once.

We also did some canoeing at Honeymoon Lake, a beautiful and very shallow lake a few miles south of the municipality of Jasper.

It turns out that canoeing can be a great way to relax while exploring the out-of-doors. Or it can provide you with some hair-raising experiences that will be fun to tell your friends and family about someday.

LARRY, CANADA, AND ME

We first met Larry through the Baptist Church in Clarkston, WA, where he grew up. We tired of that particular church and started attending a Nazarene church across the Snake River in Lewiston, ID. We soon discovered that Larry had also migrated to that same church.

We had a mutual acquaintance at the Nazarene church who lived just a few blocks from us. He was the son of a preacher, but he obviously didn't pay much attention to his father's sermons. He befriended us and we became "friends." However, we were never quite sure of his business ethics, especially after I heard him on a phone call with a "client" from near San Diego, CA.

The client had some desert land in southern California and he had our "friend" (I'll merely refer to him as JN) take some soil samples to assay as he suspected there might be some valuable minerals on his land. JN had asked us to feed and water their family dog while he and his wife were going to be away for a few days. He received a phone call from the San Diego man while I was there. JN informed him that the assay report was very favorable, but that he should not reveal the results of the report to any landowners adjacent to his property. JN was proposing that the man buy up as much of the surrounding land as possible before his neighbors became aware of the value of the land.

JN also made weekly trips from Clarkston to the Canadian Stock Exchange in Vancouver, BC. He never discussed those trips with anyone we knew. It seemed like everything he did concerning his business dealings was always "top secret," but he was going to strike it rich one day.

JN shared news of a new company that he was developing called "Hello Pages." People would call this company and ask where the closest car repair shop, bank, dry cleaners, or any other business was located. Sounded like he had come up with a plan to start the company, possibly in Portland or Seattle. JN had developed contracts which he was asking people to sign that required them to pay $10,000 to become a part owner in this new venture.

I happened to mention this plan to our pastor. That's when he introduced me to Larry Bayman and suggested I have lunch with him someday soon. It took Larry a couple of hours to share with me some of the shady dealings he knew JN was involved in, some that had a severe financial impact on Larry.

I wanted to get hold of one of JN's contracts so I could have a lawyer take a look at it. JN came to our house and we sat down at our kitchen table so JN could fill me in on the details of his company and how it was to operate. He finally pulled a copy of the contract out and set it on the table, but not where I could read it. At the time, we were in our early thirties and $10,000 was a lot of money to us. We would have to have invested just about everything we had at the time. JN thought he had me all ready to sign when I suggested we take a look at the contract and get back to him later in the week. I've never seen anyone snatch papers off the table and shove them into his briefcase so fast. There was no way he was going to let us "review" the paperwork until we were ready to sign. Our "friendship" ended then and there.

I was so glad Larry had revealed to me the kind of person JN was. I'll stop right there with my knowledge of JN as what I knew could have gotten me in trouble "accidentally."

Larry is about twelve years older than me, divorced, and the father of one son who was raised by his ex-wife and her subsequent husband.

Larry would spend the rest of his life looking for a good Christian woman to marry, but he has remained a bachelor into his late eighties.

While serving as the temporary chief of natural resources for the Walla Walla District of the Corps of Engineers, I would drive to Walla Walla on Sunday night or Monday morning and drive back home to Clarkston on Thursday night. I was working ten-hour days so I had every Friday off. Larry and I would usually meet for lunch every Friday.

My days of annual leave were building up and I was going to have to use them or lose them. So, since Shirley had already started teaching in early September and the boys were back in school, Larry and I got the great idea of taking our Blazer, camp trailer, and canoe and heading to Canada for two weeks.

We each had some business to conduct on the trip, so we made several phone calls to facilitate our business actions. The first couple of nights we camped out at Grandma Ev's place on Pend Oreille Lake near Sandpoint, ID. On our second night there, something was rubbing up against our camper in the middle of the night. Although we didn't get up to see what it was, we were fairly certain it was a bear getting a back rub.

I was trying to find a place to buy for Shirley's and my future retirement home. Since we really liked northern Idaho, we decided I should look for something near Sandpoint or Bonners Ferry in the panhandle of ID. I actually found a nice twelve-acre site eight miles east of Bonners Ferry that had great potential. It had a grand view of the Purcell Mountains along the British Columbia, Montana, and Idaho borders. There were several signs in the area stating that this was a grizzly and black bear habitat management unit. There were lots of signs of elk and wild turkeys in the area. There were also a couple of old apple trees that remained from a former orchard.

I learned that a former member of our Lewiston church was the bank president of a bank in Bonners Ferry. He was able to provide us with a loan in order to purchase the property.

We headed on north and entered Canada near Cranbrook, BC. At the north end of town where a major east/west highway and north/south highway crossed, there was a huge empty dirt lot at the side of the road. The Royal Canadian Mounted Police (RCMP) were pulling over a number of cars (including us) and directing them into the vacant lot.

Our car and trailer were given a thorough inspection from lights and engine to brakes, and all of the passenger compartments. In the camper, they even opened all the cupboards and looked inside all our food containers including our cereal boxes. Then they had Larry open his briefcase while they went through all his business papers. They had me open my backpack where they found my camera. They proceeded to remove the camera lens to look inside the camera.

When they were all through with us, I asked why they were doing such a detailed inspection. He told us that once a year they gather all the new RCMP recruits and teach them how to do thorough inspections looking for vehicle thefts and non-compliance of vehicle laws, drugs, illegal aliens, and illegal weapons. If you passed all the inspections, you got a little yellow sticker placed on your windshield so you would not get pulled over again.

Before we could leave, we were asked how long we had been in Canada. Since it is less than an hour's drive from the border to Cranbrook, I guessed we had only been in Canada for about an hour. Then he told us to describe the customs agent who talked to us at the border. I replied that she was short, had short light brown hair, and she spoke with a very slight lisp. Larry added what only he would have noticed: "And she's not married. She didn't have a wedding ring on!" The officer laughed as he waved us on our way.

Within the next hour, I discovered my trailer's left turn signal was not working. It never worked again until we got back to Idaho. We never did figure out why it wouldn't work.

We spent a night in the Tunnel Mountain campground in Banff since it had full hookups for the camper. With the main tourist season over, only one loop of the campground was opened. Both Larry and I needed to make a couple of phone calls. About sunset, we finally found a phone booth at the opposite end of the campground—the part that wasn't open. We made our calls and suddenly realized it was already dark and neither of us had brought a flashlight. While standing outside the phone booth, we heard two bull elks fighting very near us. The next thing we knew, one of them was retreating right toward us. I do believe if we had reached our hands out we could have touched the bull as it went by!

The next day as we headed further north, we saw what John Muir described as a "snow banner." That is where the wind is blowing snow off a peak forming a white "banner." It was very beautiful against a bright blue sky.

We camped at the Lake Louise Village campground that night. After dinner, we walked along the river where we found a mink running in and out of the rocks along the bank.

The next morning, we hiked the trail on the north side of Lake Louise all the way to the upper end of the lake. Along the way, we heard a loud rumble and looked up in time to see the entire face of a glacier at the head of the lake drop into the valley below. About a minute later, we saw a cloud of snow floating up from the canyon floor.

We met two young men from Germany who were exploring Canada. They told us they had just seen a "husband" moose! They were obviously still working on their English.

Later that day, we took our canoe to Moraine Lake and canoed around the lake. The lake was so clear you could see a very long way down. The only "wildlife" we saw was a shrew that had drowned in the lake. Even though summer was gone, we could still hear small rock and snow avalanches tumbling down the canyon walls.

At an elevation of almost ten thousand feet, we arrived at the Columbia Icefield. We took a ride on the six-wheel drive bus that carried us out onto the glacier. Larry and I were so interested in the glacial features we almost missed the bus back to the terminal. It was shocking to see the markers downstream of the glacier that indicate where the glacier used to reach. It is indeed receding at a very rapid rate.

We spent the next couple of nights at Whistlers Campground near the municipality of Jasper. I was the "cook" for this trip while Larry usually did the cleanup. So while I would be cooking, Larry would be finding people to visit with. One night, he brought a lady back to our campsite who was actually a graduate of Fresno State, my alma mater! Another evening, he called in a small herd of elk that was hanging about the campground. They surrounded our campsite for a while before moving on to better feeding grounds.

We were walking around the campground late in the afternoon when we came across a herd of thirteen cow elk. There was a young bull elk that was cutting cows out of the herd and moving them away from the remainder. About the third time he did this, a much larger and older bull elk jumped up from his hidden resting spot and headed directly toward the young bull. The race was on as both bulls laid their antlers back on their backs and took off running through the heavy brush. Pretty soon, the older elk returned, collected the three cows that had been "stolen" earlier, and returned them to his harem. Exhausted, he promptly dropped back down to rest in a location where he could keep an eye on his thirteen cows.

Along the way, we encountered pikas (small rabbit-sized furry mammals) on several occasions on rocky slopes. They were busy gathering grasses from nearby meadows. As the grasses turned into dry hay, they would have a supply of food stored for the winter. Their "chinking" high-pitched bark kept us aware of their presence.

When we returned home, Larry had lunch with a church friend who always "knew" everything about every kind of animal. Larry would say we saw mountain goats, and Dave would say he had seen them. If Larry said we saw moose, Dave would say he's seen lots of them. Larry finally had enough, so he said we saw picas. Dave had no idea what they were, so Larry described them this way: They're a little larger than a moose, have a slightly reddish coat, and live in the forests in Canada! That totally caught Dave off guard; I hope he had a chance later to look up picas in a wildlife book.

In October of that year, I was selected to be the permanent chief of natural resources management (NRM) in Walla Walla. That meant we would have to sell our home in Clarkston and relocate to Walla Walla. One immediate problem was that Shirley and the boys had already started the school year in Clarkston. So I proceeded to find a place for us. I thought if we ever had to move to Walla Walla we would have to live in town, in an onion patch, or a wheat field. But we were fortunate to find ten acres in the mountains just ten miles from town. The only problem was we had to develop the site ourselves.

I had already rented an apartment in town while looking for a place for us to live. Once we found the site on Blue Creek, Larry moved into the apartment next door and we began to plan how to develop our place. Larry had always been a builder and a heavy equipment operator. After hauling his heavy equipment to Walla Walla, he was able to clear a lot of the heavy brush from our building site after he bulldozed a driveway from the county road down a fairly steep slope to our lot.

We had searched for and found a manufactured home we wanted to live in. Actually, it was the first one we looked at before we looked at about fifty others in Washington and Oregon. By the time it arrived, we had drilled a well, installed a septic system, had power brought down to the location of the house, and obtained all the permits we needed to move forward.

I have never operated heavy equipment, but one day when Larry got his backhoe stuck in some seriously deep mud, he chained it up to his road grader and instructed me how to operate it. I was only to back up slowly while he would steer the backhoe to dry land. I decided right then that I was probably not cut out to operate heavy equipment!

When not working on our place, Larry kept busy working for other people on various carpentry and building projects in the area. He liked to come to our place to see the birds and other wildlife in Blue Creek Canyon. Shirley and I were on a walk one evening when Larry drove up and told us to jump in his pickup. We turned around and drove about a half mile before he stopped and pointed out a cougar in the tall grasses up the slope from the road. One other neighbor was already there watching it.

This was no ordinary cougar as it was coal black with shiny yellow eyes. It was merely taking a rest in the tall grasses where we could only see his head from his nose to the points of his ears. As a biologist, I wanted to get a good look at the cougar. For one thing, I wanted to be sure it was not hurt or having other health issues. I had Larry and a neighbor (Candy) hike up the hill west of the cougar and hide behind a tree while I hiked further up the hill with my binoculars (we always took them on our walks) where I also hid behind a tree. On my signal, Larry and Candy were to jump up, yell, and wave their arms. I was less than fifty yards from the cougar, so I had a good view of it as it jumped up and took off running through the grass and small bushes. It was totally black with a long tail that it used to help steer him around the bushes. It was a beautiful sight to behold.

I called the local game warden that evening to tell him about the black cougar—but all I got was his voice mail. He called me at my office the next morning and told me he didn't appreciate me leaving my message. He worked out of his home, so his wife actually got the message first. She had told him on several occasions of having seen a black cougar along the WA/OR border when she was quite young. He always insisted there was no such thing in the mountains near us. And here I was, a biologist saying four of us had seen the black cat at the same time. A couple of months later, we heard it had also been seen about thirty-five miles from us near Dayton, WA. If it weren't for Larry's quick actions, I doubt we would ever see it.

While we lived in Blue Creek Canyon, we had several other projects that Larry helped with. We built a three-car garage with the intention of adding an apartment above it. We also were getting ready to purchase a couple of draft horses, so he started building our barn. It was his idea to make it an earth-sheltered barn so that we could have a road up to the back of the second floor where we wanted to store our hay.

When our friend Rob Zink passed away, I inherited his wood carving tools. I decided to give them to Larry as he liked to carve. He went on to win ribbons at wood carving events around the region. His "masterpiece" was a carving of a bull elk head on a door that a doctor paid him several thousand dollars to carve and hang the door! He also builds cabinets and does other beautiful inlaid projects using many different kinds of wood.

Larry has since made Walla Walla his permanent home. He has built houses and apartments in town. He now lives in one of his apartments next to a small creek that winds through town. He has planted a number of trees near the creek improving the habitat along his piece of the creek. Ducks and tree-dwelling birds seem to like what he has done for them.

HEALTH AND FITNESS

Although I was never really an athlete, I did enjoy playing outside a lot in my younger years. I also enjoyed playing sports, but due to my small size, I was often the last kid picked for a team sport during recess or physical education in my elementary and junior high schools.

Earlier I mentioned that I was the manager for both the track team and swim team while in high school. The last three years of high school I was able to swim every day the swim team practiced during the entire school year. My senior year, I was able to play on our school's first-ever water polo team. It would be the only sport for which I was awarded a school letter to place on my Clovis High sweater.

Many of the jobs I had while in high school kept me very active and in pretty good shape. Although I didn't necessarily enjoy bucking hay in southern California nor shingling roofs in the San Joaquin Valley's hot sunny summers, they did keep me physically fit while earning a whopping $1 an hour! Working at Sears as a salesperson for the last four years of college didn't do much for my physical fitness, but by then Shirley and I were both staying fit by hiking in the Sierra Nevadas east of Fresno as frequently as possible.

Upon graduation, I began teaching elementary school and started applying for summer seasonal work as a National Park Service park ranger. I would apply to parks all over the US in hopes of landing a seasonal job that would lead to a full-time appointment with the National Park Service. I managed to find employment at Lava Beds National Monument for four summers while I continued teaching during the school year. I also was able to work weekends (while teaching full-time) at Kings Canyon National Park during two winter seasons. Giving guided snowshoe walks helped keep me in shape. Eventually, I landed a seasonal position at Crater Lake National Park in the summers of 1974 to 1976.

While Shirley and I each weighed 125 pounds when we were first dating, things changed over the years. Since Shirley, a home ec major, was into "experimental cooking," I rapidly became fond of "experimental eating." In the first couple of years we were married, I began to carry around a few more pounds each year.

Being a park ranger was a physically demanding job. Leading interpretive walks and fighting an occasional fire helped me stay in pretty good shape. Shirley and I also did a lot of hiking on our own as we explored the Lava Beds and many of its lava tubes and cinder cones. That helped me to shave off a few pounds.

It wasn't until I was preparing to return to Crater Lake for my third summer that I was told I would have to participate in the Cooper's Aerobics Program. Dr. Cooper, an Air Force doctor, had developed a program to help keep military people in shape. Its major element involved running one and a half miles in under twelve minutes. We were also told we would have to pass the US Forest Service's "Step Test" which entailed stepping up on a bench fifteen and three-fourth inches high and then stepping back down. In order to step up and down at the rate of twenty-two and a half steps per minute, a metronome was set at ninety beats per minute. We were to keep pace with it for five minutes. Fifteen seconds after we finished, a monitor would take our pulse for fifteen seconds. Using some calculations, a final score was presented.

During the school year, I lived at an elevation of 350 feet above sea level in the San Joaquin Valley. So a couple of months before returning to Crater Lake, I started running one and a half miles every morning.

This is where my "experimental eating" habit began to "weigh" on me. I definitely lost a little bit of weight, but I would never see 125 pounds again.

A number of my sixth grade students were wearing nice-looking pairs of blue suede running shoes in those days. They told me they got them at Sears. So I promptly purchased a pair and started running every day. I had only been doing so for a few days when I sprained my right ankle. A week later, I started running again and promptly sprained my left ankle. Upon closer inspection of the shoes, I realized that the soles of the shoes were not nearly as wide as the top of the shoe. Even stepping on a small stone would cause one to twist an ankle. I asked my students if that ever happened to them. They said it did, but they wouldn't tell their parents for fear they would have to take the shoes back to the store! That's exactly what I did. With the purchase of a more stabilizing pair of running shoes, I kept up my efforts to get in shape before returning to Crater Lake.

Arriving at Crater Lake for the summer I continued my daily runs, but then I was at 6,500 feet above sea level and all of my running was uphill and downhill. Finally, the big day came when we had to prove we could do the one-and-a-half-mile run in under twelve minutes. My best time at that elevation had been ten minutes and fifty seconds up until that day. We were to run around the Steele Circle housing area three and a half times to complete the one and a half miles (it was about evenly uphill and downhill). We split into two groups of rangers and fire crewmen. I chose to go with the first group just to get it over with. Of course, I ended up with the "jackrabbit" runners who took off and left me in the dust! One ranger was six feet four inches tall and weighed in at about 210 pounds. I was surprised to catch up with him on our last lap. I not only passed him, but I decided there was no way I was going to let him beat me, even though this wasn't supposed to be a competitive race. I never looked back, but I could hear his size 14 shoes pounding right behind me. I not only beat him, but I also ran my fastest ever one and a half miles finishing at a "brisk" 9:40—a full fifty seconds faster than I had ever run it before!

A few days later, we had to perform the Step Test. Again I surprised myself. I achieved a score of 57 putting me in the "Superior" category!

Eventually, I landed a low-grade park technician position with the Corps of Engineers at Pine Flat Lake just twelve miles from our home on the Kings River near Centerville, CA. Six months later I moved up a grade to a park technician job with the NPS at Tuzigoot National Monument in Arizona. While in those positions, I faithfully continued to run at least one and a half miles most mornings. I always ran in the morning so I wouldn't come up with an excuse not to run later in the day. Also, the mornings were generally the coolest part of the day for running.

Moving to Clarkston, WA, to assume a park ranger position with the Corps of Engineers in 1978, I began running a mile and a half or three miles each morning. As I moved up in rank from an assistant natural resources manager to a full natural resources manager, my jobs became more desk-bound. That led to me putting on more and more pounds until I peaked out at a little over 200 pounds! Eventually, we moved to Walla Walla when I became the district natural resources manager and I continued to run, but not on such a regular schedule. And, yes, the "experimental eating" continued.

While heading home from a Christmas trip to my folks in Clovis, CA, we had a vehicle accident when a young lady not familiar with driving on snow skidded her little Toyota Tercel out of her on-coming lane and across the front of our much larger Chevy Blazer. I didn't realize it until later, but I had torn a muscle in my neck. Every time I tried to run after that, it really aggravated my neck. So, I pretty much gave up running after that.

In 1997, we bought two Belgian draft horses. They were full-blooded sisters and a great matched pair. We planned to use them for hayrides and parades. About once a month, a friend of ours from our church would deliver a couple of tons of hay for the "girls." My job was to pull the bales to the back of the flatbed truck where Brian would pick them up and stack them in the barn. One evening he arrived just as we had started dinner.

At fifty-two years of age, I went on out and performed my usual duty, but something didn't feel quite right. When I went back in the house to finish my dinner, I told Shirley I must have been allergic to something in the hay as my chest was feeling tight and I wasn't breathing quite right. However, within a short time, everything was back to normal.

Later that month we were in Panorama, BC, and doing some mildly strenuous hiking in the Canadian Rockies when I began to experience the same chest pain I had while unloading the hay, only this time it was more severe. As a former CPR and first aid instructor and an EMT, I recognized the "elephant standing on your chest pain" I had spoken of so often in CPR and first aid classes. As soon as we returned home, I had a visit with my doctor who sent me to the hospital for a series of tests. Sure enough, I was having a critical heart issue that needed tending to promptly.

On August 12, 2002, I was at Sacred Heart Hospital in Spokane having an angiogram when the doctor administering the test pointed out that I had two 90 percent blocked arteries and two 100 percent blockages. Two days later, I was scheduled for a quadruple bypass.

Shirley was waiting to hear the results of my angiogram when she was approached by a female hospital chaplain. The chaplain said she had some very sad news for her. When she started telling her the news, it became obvious to Shirley that the chaplain was talking about someone other than me. After the chaplain profusely apologized, she immediately left the room.

Dr. Nisco was scheduled to perform my surgery. He came to see me in the hospital to talk about what he would be doing. He had the best "bedside manners" of any doctor I had ever encountered. While sitting on my bed talking to me, I asked him about the "DaVinci Surgical System" I had heard discussed on NPR a week or so earlier. This new system would allow doctors to use computers and special equipment to perform less invasive surgeries. He explained that he was actually one of the doctors working to perfect that equipment.

Later, after my surgery, Dr. Nisco was talking with Shirley when she asked him what kept me from having a heart attack. He said there were four factors that played a role: 1) he doesn't smoke; 2) he doesn't drink alcohol; 3) he exercises regularly; and 4) he eats well. I guess all that experimental eating was paying off!

On August 14, I was scheduled for surgery at 10:00 a.m. However, I got bumped by someone else and didn't start getting prepped until about 1:00 p.m. By then, they were in a hurry to get me ready, so two nurses busily shaved me from the tops of my feet to my chin—suprisingly, they left my beard intact!

The anesthesiologist came in to run some tests on me to insure I was not going to have any problems with the anesthetics he would use. My last comment to him was, "I want you to guarantee me that I won't be there while this is happening!" I did not want to have any memories (random or otherwise) of the actual surgical procedure. When it was time to take me into the operating room, he injected me with something and told me to start counting backwards from ten to one. The last number I remember saying was seven.

My surgery lasted about four and a half hours. I finally awakened briefly in the intensive care unit. That's when I first noticed that Matthew was there with Shirley. I asked him how long he had been there. He said he had been there about ten minutes. I quickly faded out again. When I re-awakened, I saw him standing there and asked him again how long he had been there. Again he responded, about ten minutes. One more time I faded out and re-awakened to ask him how long he had been there. Somewhat annoyed, he gave me the same answer for a third time. Seems he was getting a little tired of giving the same answer each time.

I continued to fade in and out for several more hours. When it was time to move me to a recovery room, I was told I was going to be placed on the sixth floor where they usually placed heart patients. Since I had already spent one night on the eighth floor following my angiogram, I asked if I could go back up there as I already had met several of the nurses, and more important than that, I could see the medic helicopters landing and taking off from the hospital just a floor or so above me. Surprisingly, they allowed me to go to the eighth floor.

During the bypass surgery, the doctors actually cut my sternum in two with a small electric saw. Then they spread my chest wide open so they could work on my heart. My lungs and heart were stopped during the surgery, so the doctors connected both my circulatory and respiratory systems to machines that kept my blood oxygenated and flowing throughout my body until the surgical process was completed.

Bypasses of the heart arteries are made with veins taken from other parts of one's body. A hole was poked in my left groin and another just above my left knee. From there they were able to extract a vein that could be used to make a bypass. A hole was also poked just below my left knee and another lower on my left calf where they took another vein. They also used an artery in my chest that was then connected directly to my heart. Although my chest scar is quite noticeable, the four holes in my leg are hardly visible.

Because my lungs had been stopped for several hours, they had lost some of their elasticity making it harder for me to take deep breaths. So the next day I was told to inhale a white milky gas that would help re-elasticize my lungs. I seem to have an overactive epiglottis as every time the gas hit my throat, I would choke and my epiglottis would divert this "foreign" substance away from my lungs. One nurse was even "yelling" at me to suck harder so it would reach my lungs. I tried, but to no avail. To this day my lungs don't have the elasticity or the capacity that they once had.

That same day, they started having me get out of bed and walk the hallways while dragging along my wheeled IV drip device. My heart rate was monitored during my walks, and on the second day of walking around, I was told to slow down as I was going too fast.

Being in a hospital was truly an otherworldly experience. I had two tubes sticking out of my chest sucking fluids from around my heart and lungs. That machine gurgled under my bed twenty-four hours a day. There was also a wire inserted close to my heart in case they had to give me a shock to get it beating again. When people see my chest, I tell them the long scar was a knife wound and the two holes near my heart were caused by bullets! The last day I was in the hospital, a doctor came in and pulled the wire and the two tubes out of my chest and merely placed a Band-Aid over the holes! He said they want those wounds to heal from the inside out, thus they would not stitch them up.

The doctors monitored my blood sugars the entire time I was in the hospital. To do so, they had to collect all my urine for testing. Shirley was holding my collection jug for me one night when I thought I was urinating for almost five minutes. She asked me several times if I was through, but I kept telling her, "No!" Finally, she told me she thought I must be through. I told her I knew I was still "going" because I could hear it in the jug. That's when she told me I was merely hearing my "gurgling machine" under the bed! She was right.

For the most part, I liked all of my male and female nurses. However, when they came to get me at midnight the second night to go take X-rays to show the doctor the next morning, I refused to go as I really needed to get some rest. I sent them away and they didn't return until 6:00 a.m. in plenty of time to have the X-rays ready for the doctor.

One male nurse came on duty about midnight each of the last three nights I was in the hospital. He would come in and check all the medical devices, give me any meds I had to take, and ask if there was anything he could get for me. Then he would turn off the light, leave the room, and shut the door. He continued to monitor all the medical devices I was hooked up to, but he would not let anyone bother me till early the next morning. Finally, I started getting some undisturbed sleep!

Most of the nurses were very cautious about giving me my medications. However, one of the male nurses seemed to be adding something to my IV often and was giving me more meds than I had been given previously. I asked that he not be my nurse again and the hospital honored that request after I told them why.

It wasn't until about my third day of recovery that I was told to take a shower. I was still hooked up to a breathing tube that would allow me to get all the way to the bathroom without disconnecting. I got rid of my "backless" hospital gown, closed the shower curtain, and sat down on the chair provided in the shower. I was resting from the "long walk" to the shower (maybe ten feet) when I heard the bathroom door open, then the shower curtain was thrown back, revealing me merely sitting there doing nothing. There stood one of the female nurses who promptly told me to get off that chair and start taking a shower! Seemed like "boot camp" had just begun.

I finally got even with that nurse on the last day as I was preparing to leave the hospital. My clothes had been packed away in my backpack since entering the hospital, so they were quite wrinkled. When she came in, I tossed her my shirt and said, "Go iron this." As she turned away with it, presumably to go iron it, I told her I was only joking. If I remember correctly, she threw it back at me!

A friend from my natural resources staff in Walla Walla, Jimmie Brown, knew that we had driven to Spokane for the surgery in our Dodge pickup. He also knew it would be a rough two-hundred-mile ride home in it. So he was kind enough to drive to Spokane from Walla Walla to swap our pickup for his much smoother-riding Lincoln sedan for Shirley to drive me home. Fortunately, the hospital had given me a pillow to hold against my chest while riding in a vehicle or if I started coughing. Squeezing that pillow on those occasions really helped relieve the sharp pains where my sternum was trying to heal. That pillow and I became best friends for several months, especially when traveling by car!

On the way home to Walla Walla, Matthew was driving his own car and we were following him. He hadn't eaten for quite some time, so he pulled off at the Taco Bell in Ritzville, WA, for a bite to eat. While he and Shirley had gone into the restaurant, my cell phone rang. Knowing that only my family would have that number, I answered with, "Hello, this is the Ritzville Taco Bell. How may I help you?" I was surprised to find out our pastor in Walla Walla also had that number and he was calling to see how I was doing! Talk about embarrassing!

Soon after we returned home, Shirley returned to her teaching job, so we asked a member of our church just to come out and spend the day with me while she was gone. The next day, my nephew, Jeff, arrived from Battle Ground, WA, and "babysat" me for the next week. While he was there, he helped me get started on my walking assignment. We had a one-eighth of a mile loop gravel road between our house and Blue Creek. So I started by walking it once each day. Over the next few weeks, I kept increasing my laps until I could do one and a half miles nonstop.

I started back to work after about three weeks, but only went in for three hours a day the first week. Over the next couple of weeks, I gradually worked back up to eight-hour days. In the twenty-six years prior to my heart surgery, I had not used even one day of sick leave. During this medical event, I had just used about 320 hours of leave.

Our offices were divided into cubicles with walls about five feet high. I had a cubicle that was big enough to have a separate table and a few chairs for meetings. I was lucky enough to have a view of the Pataha Mountains to the east of town. The panel between my cubicle and the windows was only desk-high, so I could look out the windows easily, especially while I was on the phone (often for the majority of the day). Being on the third floor, I was able to see over most of the buildings in town.

The day I returned to work for the first time after the surgery, I found masking tape establishing some planned reconfigurations for my cubicle. Staff members told me that the Logistics people had changed their rules on what size cubicles people at various grade levels could have. Not only was my cubicle to be cut in half, eliminating room for the table and chairs, but they would also raise the wall to five feet so that I would no longer have the beautiful mountain view! I immediately went to my boss to ask what was going on. He didn't know, so he suggested we go right downstairs to Logistics to find out why this was happening. Just as we stepped on the elevator, another member of my staff stepped in with us and explained that two other members of my staff had placed the tape in my cubicle and made up the story about shrinking my office space. I guess that was their way of "welcoming" me back to the world of weird government regulations! I would not have been the least bit surprised if Logistics really was planning to shrink my office.

I mentioned that my blood sugars were being constantly monitored while in the hospital. They reasoned that if they could control my sugar levels in the hospital there would be a lesser chance I would become diabetic in the future. However, six years later I was diagnosed as having type 2 diabetes.

The first med I was given to control blood sugar levels was metformin, a common drug used by many diabetics. I was to take only half a pill each of the first two days. It just happened that I had a board meeting at Stoneridge Resort in north Idaho the first day I took half a pill. I didn't seem to have any reaction to it so I took the other half of the pill the following morning.

That was the Saturday of our annual resort meeting where all resort owners are invited to attend. We usually have 100–150 people packed into our resort gym for that event. This meeting usually lasts only a couple of hours. About halfway through the meeting, I began to feel quite sick. The second the meeting was over, I raced to our resort room where I promptly started throwing up and having diarrhea. Every muscle and joint in my body ached. I had a terrible headache. Every time I had an emergency trip to the bathroom I would stop in the kitchen to take a drink of water to stay hydrated, but that just seemed to lead to more trips to the bathroom. Things began to calm down by Sunday morning as we were returning home to Walla Walla. At 8:00 a.m. on the following Monday, I was at the doctor's office with my metformin pill bottle in hand. We decided those pills were not for me and I was given a different prescription.

Since that time, I've gone through several different meds to find one that was right for me. About two years ago, I was placed on a drug called Invokana. Its job is to help my kidneys take more sugar out of my blood. One requirement is that I have to drink more water than I usually would. Over the next year, I lost about forty pounds. That alone made me feel better, but I still have to be careful about the foods I eat to ensure I'm not getting too many carbohydrates and sugars. Sure does mess up my "experimental eating" habit! Now I have to stick with tasting diabetic-compatible foods. I sure miss the other foods!

On September 25, 2014, I had surgery on my left arm to repair torn cartilage and clean up some signs of arthritis. I had been playing pickleball and/or swimming every day prior to the surgery. I was supposed to wear a very clunky, uncomfortable sling on my left arm for about six weeks. After eleven days, I took it off and never put it back on. Within a few days, I started swimming again using modified strokes so I would not impede the healing of my shoulder. Soon I was also playing pickleball again.

In 2018, I swam one hundred miles doing a half mile each time I swam. In 2019, we were moving from Stoneridge in Idaho to Dallas, OR. Upon arriving here, I learned that the City of Dallas has a beautiful aquatic center that was built back in 2002. I joined up for a whopping $225 per year and began swimming five days a week. That year I managed to swim 115 miles at seventy-two years of age.

When the COVID pandemic hit, the State of Oregon forced the aquatic center to close in mid-March 2020. They were later allowed to reopen in September. However, just a few weeks later it was forced to close again and has remained closed for a couple more months. Due to the closures, I was only able to swim fifty-four miles in 2020. With fewer closures in 2021, I was able to swim seventy-one miles that year.

On August 14, 2022, I celebrated twenty years since my quadruple bypass surgery. Fortunately, we've not had any more closures recently, so I am back to swimming half a mile Monday to Friday each week.

NATURAL RESOURCE MANAGEMENT IN THE CORPS OF ENGINEERS

While still in college, I subscribed to *Audubon Magazine*. There were many very detailed articles that dealt with a wide variety of Corps of Engineers (COE) projects around the country. My heart was set on working for the National Park Service, (NPS) so I had no interest in going to work for the environmentally "insensitive" COE. I continued teaching and working seasonally in hopes I would eventually land a permanent job with the NPS.

I took the Federal Service Entrance Exam (FSEE) as often as I could in order to better my scores. After they changed to using the Civil Service Entrance Exam (CSEE), I continued taking that test as frequently as possible.

My problem was that I was not a veteran. The mid-1970s was about the time the war in Vietnam was winding down and the job market was flooded with veterans seeking employment back home. Although I might have scores of 99 across the board, a 10-point veteran's preference would move a person with scores of 89 across the board even with me and therefore bump me from any job that the veteran applied for.

About the same time, the government was under pressure to hire more women, minorities, and disabled people. I did not fit into any of those categories. I had been working at Kings Canyon National Park for a couple of winters when they were going to hire a permanent park ranger. At the same time, Sequoia was going to hire two permanent park rangers. Since Kings Canyon and Sequoia National Parks were both under the same administrative office, Sequoia selected their two rangers first. My friends at Kings Canyon were fairly certain they would be able to select me. However, since Sequoia did not hire anyone from the three targetted groups listed above, Kings Canyon was told they had to hire a disabled person. The ranger who had to tell me this news was so disappointed that they could not hire me that he actually had tears in his eyes when he shared the news with me. So, I kept on teaching sixth graders and working for the NPS as a seasonal park ranger.

In the mid-1970s, I began hearing about the COE starting to hire park technicians, park rangers, and natural resources managers and were starting to develop a Natural Resources Management (NRM) program at their lake projects around the country. But my steady "diet" of *Audubon Magazine* articles made me shy away from applying for COE jobs. The number of people they were hiring in the 1976–1977 period was steadily increasing. So, in 1977 I took a chance and applied for a "Subject to Furlough Park Technician" position (GS-4) at Pine Flat Dam on the Kings River. That was only twelve miles from our home on the Kings River. I was hoping to use that job as a springboard to obtaining a permanent job with the NPS.

I was selected for the job at Pine Flat and resigned from my teaching assignment in mid-March to assume my new position. My first assignments were strictly working with the maintenance crew helping to get the parks and boat ramps ready for the upcoming recreation season. One positive thing I got to do was to plant buttonwillow twigs below the high water line. These twigs will grow into trees even though they are submerged for a good share of the year. By May, I was in a COE park ranger uniform and patrolling up and down the lake at the parks, campgrounds, concession facilities, and boat ramps.

The COE park ranger uniform looked almost exactly like the NPS uniforms complete with a "Smokey Bear" straw hat. When people would tease me by saying we just copied the NPS uniform, I would point out that the NPS uniform was actually a spin-off of the old US Army Corps of Engineers uniforms as most of the first NPS superintendents were colonels in the US Army!

A big difference between the NPS and COE park technicians and rangers was that the COE people could only enforce misdemeanors. At Pine Flat, even though I had been a certified law enforcement officer with the NPS and had received some of my training at the Federal Law Enforcement Training Center at Glenco, GA, I was not even given a citation book. If something required stronger enforcement action, I would have to call a park ranger or local law enforcement officers.

Only one of the park rangers I worked with at Pine Flat had any law enforcement background. That person had been with the NPS at an archeological site in the southwest. The rest of the ranger and technician staff had no enforcement training with the COE. One of my fellow park technicians did have a degree in criminology from the University of California at Berkeley, but even he was not given "citation authority."

There was a very windy road that paralleled the western shore of Pine Flat Lake. As I came around a bend in the road one day, the first thing I noticed was a motorcycle hanging upside down on a barbed wire fence about fifteen feet down from the shoulder of the road. I then saw a man climbing up the bank to the road. When I stopped to see what had happened, I saw another man lying unconscious under the motorcycle that was hanging on the fence. I immediately called for emergency response support (this was before cell phones and 911).

I had the man who had climbed up to the road sit down and covered his eyes as he had a lot of dirt in them. I told him repeatedly to keep his eyes covered. However, every time a fire truck, ambulance, or county sheriff vehicle arrived, he kept uncovering his eyes.

The story behind this accident started as the two men left a local bar at Piedra a short distance from Pine Flat Dam. People at the bar reported to the sheriff that they had dumped the motorcycle on gravel in the middle of the intersection before heading upriver. They seem to have been well "lubricated" after their stop at the bar, so they got back on the bike and took off again. It was obvious that they once again had lost control of the bike and ended up in the situation where I found them. I don't remember ever finding out how the driver ended up, but the guy who had climbed up to the road was at one of our campsites the very next day. I stopped to visit with him and learned that he wished he had heeded my instructions to keep his eyes covered. At the time of our visit, he had both eyes bandaged due to the damage his eyes had incurred while moving his eyes around with a lot of dirt packed in them.

My supervisor gave me a design for improvements to our main campground and told me to look at the campground to see if it was feasible to move forward with the proposed development of the site. After studying the drawings and walking the site, I did some checking with the NPS, the USFS, the Bureau of Land Management, and California State Parks to learn what their criteria were for the number of restrooms needed for a campground the size of ours. As I suspected, the COE drawings were calling for three-restroom buildings whereas the criteria from the other agencies called for only two. I submitted my findings on a suggestion form and was informed I might be able to get a cash award for saving the COE a lot of money by building one less restroom. Several months later after leaving the COE, I received a call from one of the Pine Flat rangers telling me they were going with my suggestion, but there was no mention of an award.

In September, I was offered a permanent park technician position (GS-5) at Tuzigoot National Monument near Cottonwood, AZ. It was one grade higher than my position at Pine Flat and I would not be faced with a four-month furlough each year. I accepted the offer and we moved into government housing in the park. Now I am not a big fan of deserts, nor am I really excited about interpreting archeology, so it was not long before I was looking for a job elsewhere, and especially one with a higher grade. My annual pay at Pine Flat had been lower than the poverty level the government had established when President Carter was in office. Fortunately, when I arrived at Tuzigoot I was making $9,959 a year. That was great as we already had one son and the other one arrived just three months later.

I continued to watch for both NPS and COE job announcements and would apply to both agencies. I had applied for a GS-7/9 park ranger position at Clarkston, WA, on the Snake River. I was somewhat surprised when they called to offer me the job. However, I was still holding out hope to land a job with the NPS, so I turned the offer down.

Six more weeks in the AZ desert and the hot weather was arriving. That helped me reassess my decision. So I finally picked up the phone and called to see if the job in Clarkston, WA, was still available. To my surprise, I was told they had readvertised the position, but if I wanted to accept it I would be hired. They said they were really disappointed when I declined the job offer earlier. When I went home for lunch, I told Shirley that I thought we were going to be moving to Clarkston. Sure enough, I received a call the next day confirming my acceptance of the position.

It took us two days to drive to Clarkston from AZ. We spent one night in McCall, ID. It was such a beautiful area we were hoping Clarkston would look like McCall. The closer we got to the Snake River Canyon, the lower we dropped in elevation. By the time we arrived in Clarkston, we realized the interior of the Snake River Canyon was basically a grassland with occasional riparian vegetation.

We settled into Clarkston and soon purchased a new home in what was known as the Clarkston Heights. It was on a bench a few hundred feet above the river and the main part of town. Our office was at the confluence of the Snake and Clearwater Rivers. The office had only been built and occupied a couple of months earlier. I shared an office with the assistant resources manager and a park technician.

Stan Vanairsdale was the natural resources manager (NRMgr) at that time. He had formerly served on the maintenance crew at Albeni Falls Dam near Old Town, ID. Stan let my supervisor and me know that he really didn't know anything about natural resources management, so he would rely heavily on our advice. He did reserve the right to override our advice if he thought we didn't have sufficient justification for what we were suggesting we should do.

After my GS-7 year was completed, I was promoted to the GS-9 level which came with another nice salary increase. After a couple of years, Stan was hired to supervise the NRM maintenance crew at Dworshak in central Idaho about forty-five miles east of Clarkston. When he left, my immediate supervisor was offered the manager position in Clarkston. That opened the door for me to apply for the GS-11 assistant manager position. If I had stayed with the NPS I would have been lucky to have gained this level before I retired. NRM being such a new program for the COE, I was most fortunate to be able to advance as quickly as I did.

Our area of management included eight miles of the Clearwater River to its confluence with the Snake River. The major portion of our project included about ninety miles of the Snake River from Asotin, WA, to Lyons Ferry where the Palouse River joined the Snake River.

A primary responsibility in the Lewiston area was the maintenance of the levee system that protected the City of Lewiston from flooding. On the landward side of the levees were ponds that would collect surface water and then would be pumped over the levees and into the river. The levees had an extensive bike path system that extended to Hells Gate State Park on the south end and crossed the Clearwater and continued east for several miles along the river. The result was a linear park that stretched for miles. On the Clarkston side of the river, the bike path extended from the Snake and Clearwater confluence all the way to the town of Asotin. We ended up with twenty-one miles of bike paths and eventually had it designated as a National Recreation Trail. The Lewiston side was known as the Lewiston Levee Parkway.

On our stretch of the river, we leased land to Idaho and Washington State Parks. Hells Gate State Park was on the Lewiston side of the Snake. Washington had Chief Timothy, Central Ferry, and Lyons Ferry State Parks. There were also leased marinas at Lyons Ferry, Boyer Park and Marina, and Rooster Landing in Clarkston. All of these parks and marinas were owned by the COE, but were leased to the state parks and private concessionaires.

Besides managing the facilities we owned and operated, we also had the responsibility to oversee the management of the leased parks and marinas. There were also port districts in Lewiston, Clarkston, and at Central Ferry that we also leased to local entities. There were many things we had to work closely with all of our lessees to ensure lease agreements were being adhered to.

The Corps was developing two interpretive centers on the Lewiston Levee system when I arrived. One was to interpret navigation on the rivers and the other was to interpret the history of the tribal activity in the Snake and Clearwater Canyons. The COE wanted the Nez Perce Tribe to have a lead role in developing displays depicting their history, so I was assigned to work with the tribe's resources manager, Jim, to develop the displays for the tribal interpretive center. One day Jim took me to the sight of a place known to the tribe as "Coyote's Dam." I took pictures to share with the display artist so the interpretive display would look like the actual site.

Jim was a very quiet, soft-spoken man in his mid-twenties. He did not fit my image of a Native American. He already had degrees in physics and aerospace science from a university in Illinois. He called me at home one Saturday and invited me and my family to their school in Culdesac, ID, to observe their tribal dances and songs. It didn't look quite like one would see in Westerns on TV as it all took place in their high school gym. Many elaborate tribal costumes adorned the dancers, drummers, and singers.

We generally had at least two summer interns working for us while earning credits from their respective universities. These were top-notch students who were real "go-getters." One young lady was given the task of coming up with a plan to stop people from sliding down the steep slope of the levees as their actions were killing the grass in the area and what they were doing was somewhat dangerous. Being a landscape architect by training, she came up with a nicely landscaped split rail fence and planter bed that effectively blocked the sliding and created a pleasant feature.

The COE top general came to town to present our district Construction Division with an award for the design of a bridge that crossed the Snake river connecting Lewiston, ID, and Clarkston, WA. The general had flown from Washington, D.C. that morning and landed at Lewiston Airport. My job was to greet him and take the award to be presented later that day to my office for safekeeping until time for the presentation ceremony at Swallows Park later in the day.

The general had a brand new aid, a captain, who was accompanying him for the first time. The general sent the captain into the plane to get the award, but he returned empty-handed. He had inadvertently left it sitting on the general's desk in Washington, D.C.!

Once again I called on our summer intern (the landscape architect) to help us out. We found a picture of the new bridge on a wall in the construction office which would have to serve as the "award" for the day. Most landscape architects have great printing skills. We didn't even know the exact name of the award, but I asked her to print a name (that we made up on the spot) for the award on the front of the picture. She did a beautiful job. To conceal our secret, we kept the "award" facing the end of the table until it was presented to the chief of construction, then replaced at the end of the table. No one ever knew the rest of the story.

Another intern accomplished two things for the Lewiston/Clarkston area in one year. She managed to get our National Trail Designation and was key to having Lewiston designated as a Tree City USA!

Besides their special projects, we also introduced them to park maintenance contract management, patrolling the levees by bicycle, presenting interpretive programs, writing work requests for our maintenance crew, and of course, filling out government forms. Halfway through each summer, the universities would ask us to evaluate the work of our interns. I gave each person a blank copy of their performance form and asked them to fill it out. Next, I would fill out the same form then sit down with the intern and compare their form with mine. On a scale of one to five where one was the best and five the worst, I found that these young people would usually rate themselves at the same number I rated them, or one point lower. I believe the lower numbers they gave themselves were because they rated themselves tougher than I did and they knew what they were capable of doing.

With twenty-eight years of experience with the COE, I'm finding it very difficult to keep each story in chronological order, after all, they are each independent random memories of all those years.

Jim Wolcott was my first supervisor in Clarkston and as I had risen in grade, he was always one step ahead of me. I had the bad habit of saying things like, "At Lava Beds, we did it this way, or at Crater Lake, we did it that way." Finally one day he said, "I don't want to hear how you used to do things somewhere else ever again." Soon after that I learned a quote that I would use for the rest of my career: "Creativity is the art of concealing your source." So henceforth, I would merely say, "What if we did it this way, or have you thought about doing it a different way, etc." So, all of a sudden I was beginning to become "creative" in my own way!

Neither Shirley nor I were excited to live in the Clarkston area, so I began applying for NPS and COE positions in other areas. A GS-9 park ranger position became available near Eugene, OR, a place with lots of trees and not nearly so cold. I put in for the job and was selected. The government does many strange things. As it turns out, I received congratulatory calls from a couple of the people who had also bid on the job before I was officially told I had been selected.

We moved to Eugene and I settled into my downgraded position. My areas of resources management included Dexter, Hills Creek, Lookout Point, and Fall Creek Lakes. Since Hills Creek was leased to the USFS, I would only patrol it once every couple of weeks to see that the USFS was managing the area in accordance with our lease agreement.

I had a GS-7 park ranger who worked for me. He did most of the day-to-day patrolling. I knew he had also applied for the job, but I did not know what a pain in the neck he was going to be until the day I arrived. He was sitting at the largest desk in the room and it was the one with a nice view out the window. To further annoy me, he was smoking a cigar in the office. Right away I decided I need to assert myself in a positive way to establish what our relationship would be.

I immediately told him I was highly allergic to tobacco smoke, so there was to be no smoking in our office. (I later learned he had never smoked in the office before the day I arrived!) The project manager, a highly respected man I had worked with previously in the Walla Walla District summoned me to his office for an introductory session. Before I left my new office, I directed the park ranger to move the large desk he occupied to the location of the small desk, and move the small desk next to the window. I told him I could not care less about the size of my desk, but I would like to be next to the window. I wanted this to be done by the time I returned. Fortunately, he complied! I was extremely happy as I had no idea what my next move would be.

We struggled with our relationship for several months. In the meantime, Jim Wolcott had vacated the GS-12 manager's position in Clarkston and had accepted an assignment at the COE headquarters in Washington, D.C. That meant his position was open in Clarkston. We really didn't want to go back there, so I just kept doing my best where I was.

Soon after Jim got to Washington, D.C., he was helping to put together a team to begin teaching the COE's enforcement classes. Not to make the program sound too much like a law enforcement course, it was called "Visitor Assistance." They wanted a team that would have a representative from headquarters, a division office, a district office, and a field project. Jim knew of my teaching background and that I had taught a law enforcement in natural resources management class at the University of Idaho while I had been working for him. He nominated me to be the field representative.

Our team went right to work to develop a forty-hour course that we would teach across the nation. We had our first team meetings at the COE's training facility in Huntsville, AL. Over the next three years, we would teach classes in Huntsville, Atlanta, Tulsa, Nashville, Saint Louis, Sacramento, and Lake Texoma. I was ever grateful to Jim for honoring me with this opportunity to teach and to travel. Wherever I went, I always took advantage of the opportunity to visit other COE lakes to learn more about how different districts operated the same programs I operated back home.

Each of the Visitor Assistance teaching team was assigned different topics to teach. My session was aimed at how to be an effective park ranger. I always taught on Thursday afternoons after the students (usually forty per session) had been together since Monday morning. The first thing I did was ask everybody to pick up their belongings and move to a new location where they would be sitting next to someone they had not met that week. It was interesting that no one ever said they had met all their classmates already. I would then begin the Park Ranger session by asking the class participants to respond to questions regarding how they handled a variety of situations one would expect a park ranger to encounter from day to day. This usually elicited quite a bit of conversation between the students as people from different districts were often reacting to the situations I posed in very different ways.

One of the goals of having the students relocate in the classroom was to help them to begin developing their own network of people from across the country that they could contact from time to time. When new regulations were sent out to the field, it would be nice for them to be able to converse with someone in other districts to see how they were reacting to the new regulations. As I progressed through my career, I found it very helpful to maintain contacts from across the country to help me find the best ways to develop policies for our field park rangers and natural resources managers. I encouraged the students to maintain contact with some of their classmates when they returned to their respective projects.

I had only been in Oregon a couple of months when I learned that Jim Wolcott was leaving for his new position in Washington, D.C. Since Shirley and I were happy to have left Clarkston, I wasn't really interested in returning to that area even if it meant obtaining a GS-12 promotion. However, I soon began receiving calls from friends who were telling me how stupid I was if I didn't apply for the Clarkston NRMgr position. It definitely would have greatly improved our family's financial situation as Shirley was a stay-at-home mom at the time, so we were relying exclusively on my salary. So, I finally bit the bullet and applied for the job. Out of twelve applicants from all over the country, I was selected!

Five months after we moved to Oregon, we were headed back to Clarkston. I would remain in the manager position there for eight years. It was a challenging position, but I had an excellent staff of park rangers, wildlife and fish biologists, administrative staff, and a very capable maintenance crew.

I had been in the new job for a couple of months when it dawned on me that my staff wasn't really "clicking" with me. Jim had taken quite a liberal approach to management. But everyone knew I was more conservative as a manager. Finally, someone pointed out to me that because Jim and I took different approaches to management, they were waiting to see how I would reverse some of Jim's prior decisions. We finally had a little heart-to-heart talk between myself and the staff during which I told them if a decision Jim had made in the past was proving to be successful, I was not going to change how we operated just because I might have wanted to do something in a different manner. I was focused on future management and had no interest in reversing the decisions of the past manager.

I was fortunate to have Gary Bunn as my assistant manager for several years. He had previously been our project's wildlife biologist who also was responsible for our fish facilities and operations at Little Goose Dam. Gary was from Texas and had a smooth, slow Texas accent that he used to his advantage. In our roles, we often had to deal with people from the public, other agencies, or disgruntled employees. Gary was much better at calming upset people than I ever could. It was great that he had been in the field as a park ranger and a wildlife biologist. His field experience made him a super manager. I was really lucky to get to work with him for a good share of our careers.

Having spent twenty-eight years with the COE, I'm trying to organize my random access memory so that I don't take off on too many tangents, and I definitely don't want to get too technical.

Toward the end of my time in Clarkston, Gary took a job as a wildlife biologist in Planning in our Portland Division Office. It was a great opportunity for him to advance his career. When he left, I was fortunate to be able to hire Jim Buck as my assistant manager. Jim was another fantastic assistant. However, only six weeks into our relationship in Clarkston, I was promoted to chief of natural resources management in the Walla Walla District Office. Yes, it meant another move.

I always figured if I worked in Walla Walla we would have to live in town, in a wheat field, or in a Walla Walla Sweet Onion patch! Fortunately, we found ten acres on Blue Creek about ten miles east of town. We purchased a double-wide manufactured home and proceeded to prepare the site for occupation.

My new job came with a staff of three outdoor recreation planners (ORP), an environmental compliance coordinator (ECC), and a wildlife biologist (WB). Several years later, we added two fish biologists

(FB) to our staff. Our job was to coordinate NRM activities with the six field offices. While much of what we did could be handled via the phone and emails, when it came to issuing directives we had to go through the chief of operations. This was a somewhat cumbersome way of issuing directives as the chief of operations was an engineer with little or no understanding of NRM programs and not always the best interpersonal communicators (that's my opinion—not shared by everyone!).

We generally had an NRM staff meeting every Monday morning. That gave us a chance to share what each person was doing and to coordinate things that overlapped between their fields of expertise. For instance, the ORP might have a shared concern with the WB when Canada geese were becoming a problem in our public parks. The ECC might have concerns about chemicals the maintenance crews were using on wildlife management areas. Sometimes several side conversations would break out as people threw out a variety of ideas on how to handle difficult issues.

Operations Division had recently hired a new assistant chief of operations, Steve Voss, who had formerly been a project manager on the Snake and Columbia Rivers. We were happy to welcome him into the district office as he was the strongest supporter of the NRM programs while in the field.

One Monday morning soon after he arrived in his new position, he told me he would like to attend our staff meeting that day. I was a little concerned knowing how to an outsider it might look like we were a little out of control at times when side conversations would break out between two or three of the staff. However, I used those "side conversations" to listen to what was being discussed and then tried to pull together some of the best ideas that I heard. In the end, we would consolidate our ideas, polish them up, and develop a plan of action to be implemented either in our office or at the field offices.

As the meeting progressed, I noticed that Steve was also getting enthusiastically involved in the "side conversations." As Steve and I were walking out of the conference room when the meeting was over, Steve turned to me and said, "That's about the most productive staff meeting I've ever seen." Wow, was I ever relieved that he was not only a strong supporter of our NRM program, but he even approved of one of the major methods we used to make the program successful.

There was far more "in-house politics" to deal with in the district office. We dealt with fish and wildlife agencies, port districts, city and county governments, state/county/city law enforcement and fire control organizations, highway departments, Indian tribes, environmental agencies, and a plethora of private interest groups in three different states. Whether we were dealing with contracts, real estate, money transfers, future development planning, or any other Operations activity, we were often in conflict with Planning, Contracting, Engineering, Real Estate, or Legal Divisions who frequently seemed to have different ideas on how we should carry out our work. It was not unusual to argue more in-house than with other entities.

The good news is we still accomplish a lot of positive actions due to the dedication of our NRM people both in the district offices and in the field.

I was pleased to see that many of the younger engineers were being exposed to environmental engineering in their college/university programs. They were much easier to work with on our NRM programs than some of the older engineers who obviously were not supportive when it came to environmental issues.

In 1991, I was fortunate to be selected to attend the COE Leadership Conference in Orlando, FL. Besides getting to do a variety of interesting group exercises with some really enthusiastic and highly creative people, we also were exposed to a number of fascinating speakers. One of those people encouraged us to not only lead by example, but to also share with others what we were trying to accomplish through those examples. The following are items I have tried to focus on over the years. While I have long practiced them, I really wasn't verbalizing them for others; people merely had to pick up the example through osmosis! Since 1991, I have shared these thoughts with every employee who has worked for me. For new employees in the district office, I generally do this on their first day on the job. I also share this with all new NRM employees who come into the district for orientation. Below is what I shared with them.

IF IT IS TO BE, IT IS UP TO ME.

The only way any of the following items will work is on a personal basis when a personal commitment is made to follow through on each. They cannot be conditioned by anyone else's commitment to them. They have to be dealt with by you and you alone. No one else can make you do these things; their implementation is 100 percent in your hands. Even if you choose not to implement any or some of these items at this time, keep this list handy for future reference. As you see others attempting to implement them, you may decide to join in the challenge. Please advise me of any additional items that would be a positive addition to this list.

*Encourage people to expand their jobs. Reach out and do more. Don't let position descriptions and performance standards hold you back. Performance standards should be minimums. "People who only do what is required of them are, in a sense slaves. Those who do more are free." (Anonymous)

*Encourage people to become an expert in some aspect of their job so that others will eventually seek them out for consultation on that topic.

*Encourage more cross-discipline teams. Go to the people you need to in order to accomplish a goal. This might mean calling on other Corps offices or other agencies. Form partnerships to accomplish a task.

*Don't ask others "if we can" do things that efficiency and common sense dictate we do. Rather, ask: "How can we get the job done?"

*While working within regulations, look for opportunities to reform regulations that are burdensome, unreasonable, or downright stupid. (Paraphrased from the chief of the COE, General Hatch.) Be very careful when establishing rules/procedures for your work unit that you don't create items that would fit in these categories.

*Constantly work on improving interpersonal communications skills in an effort to be a more effective professional. Work on establishing good, positive working relationships.

*Encourage creativity and innovation. We are constantly being asked to do "more with less"; this can only be done through creativity and innovation. Remember: "The secret to creativity is the art of concealing your source." (Anonymous)

*Encourage mentoring for yourself and others. Seek out mentors. When you see something done well by someone, ask how they did it. When someone "blows it," try to understand what went wrong.

*Be assertive; state your feelings and ideas in a caring, tactful manner. Don't let opportunities to express yourself pass you by, you may not get another chance.

*Write trip reports when you attend conferences and training or go on field trips. Share your findings with others, especially your boss (if you desire to continue participation in such activities). Let them know what you learned or experienced and how that will impact your work. Put your newfound knowledge to work as soon as possible or you are likely never to incorporate it into your work style/ethic.

*Be an ambassador for your discipline. Let others know what you do and why you do it. Exhibit pride in your work. Be "aggressively" assertive when describing your work to higher authorities, visiting dignitaries, and the public.

*Be an encouragement to everyone you work with. We all need an occasional pat on the back or an uplifting word of encouragement. Care about the people with whom you work and be supportive of them. Look for opportunities to reward people (awards, verbal praise, thank you).

*Be a listener and share what you hear with people who need to hear the same thing (boss, peers, subordinates).

*When you have a good idea, it is up to you to implement it or sell it to others for them to implement. Keep the suggestion program busy. Remember: "The idea is in thyself; the impediment, too, is in thyself." (Voltaire, I think.)

*Look for opportunities to teach people to do things for others. Get people to think about someone besides themselves. This is where you'll finally get the last 20 percent a person has to give (studies show people will eventually give up to 80 percent of their capacity whether they are beaten or rewarded).

*Avoid doing things that embarrass us or make us look bureaucratic. Use common sense to the maximum. (Paraphrased from General Hatch.)

*Always strive for perfection. In reality, we all know we'll never achieve it, but the sign of a true professional is one who never stops trying to perfect his/her work. However, keep this all in perspective; don't do it to the point that you are never satisfied with the output of yourself or others. While others are accepting our imperfections, we need to be willing to accept theirs.

*Apply the "Golden Rule" (Do unto others as you would have them do unto you) to the maximum extent possible. If you can't remember that, just treat people the way your mother taught you to treat others! If you want to be treated with respect, be sure to treat others respectfully.

*GOOD LUCK! THE OPPORTUNITY TO ACT IS YOURS; SEIZE IT!

Every year I would set aside a week to take new "key" district employees from Planning, Contracting, Legal, Real Estate, Logistics, Program Management, and Public Affairs Divisions on a tour of the district projects. Sometimes we would even have the deputy district commander along with us. All of these participants could have significant impacts on our work in Operations, especially in the field of natural resources management.

So I would request a twelve-passenger van, big enough to carry the six to eight people I took each week along with their luggage for the last two nights out of town. On the first day, we would travel to McNary on the Columbia River in the morning, then return to Bennington Lake near Walla Walla for the afternoon. At each of the projects, we would meet with the project manager and any of the NR managers, park rangers, and fish and wildlife biologists on staff who were available. We wanted the tour participants to have an understanding of the work our operations people did at the dams, on the water, and on the lands that we managed. We would spend the first night at home in Walla Walla.

On the second day, we would visit Ice Harbor and Lower Monumental Dams. We would start the day by touring parks, levees, and other facilities along the Columbia and Snake Rivers in the Tri-cities (Richmond, Kennewick, and Pasco, WA). In the afternoon, we would visit their fish, wildlife, recreation, and public lands on the two lakes behind the dams. That evening, we returned to Walla Walla once again.

On the third day, we headed for the upper reaches of the lake behind Lower Monument Dam, wildlife mitigation areas, marinas, state parks, and the fish facilities at both Little Goose and Lower Granite Dams. It was here that we spent several hours discussing our fish transport program. We would trap young fish heading to the ocean and then transport them by truck or barges to below Bonneville Dam on the Columbia River. These young fish were undergoing a physiological change called smoltification. Without the dams, they could have made it from the rivers and streams where they hatched to the Pacific Ocean in less than fifty-four days. However, the dams slowed the river and thus the fish could not make it to the ocean that quickly. So, by trapping and transporting them we could help get them to the ocean within the fifty-four-day time frame during which time they changed from freshwater fish to ocean fish so they could survive in a saltwater environment.

We drove on to Clarkston, WA that night and stayed at a local hotel. I always took them to Fazzari's Pizza Parlor for dinner as the two brothers who owned the place were natives of Walla Walla. Plus, they made the best pizzas in the region. Plus, one of the owner's wife was my former secretary when I worked in Clarkston. To this day I've never found another pizza parlor that makes one of their specialties, a "Bavarian Pizza" (Polish sausage with sauerkraut topped with mustard—absolutely fantastic!).

The next morning we would meet with the Clarkston NRM staff before heading out to visit the parks and wildlife areas. We pointed out that 90 percent of the Lower Granite, Little Goose, and Lower Monumental "neighbors" were right there in Lewiston and Clarkston. That meant the local staff spent close to 90 percent of their time dealing with boundary/neighbor issues in the local area.

Later that afternoon, we traveled on up to Orofino, ID, where we spent the night. We would have dinner at a very popular Mexican restaurant that evening.

Most of the people who went on these tours seemed to enjoy the Dworshak Dam and Reservoir part of the orientation trip the most. After leaving the dam, we would head up the fifty-three-mile-long reservoir by boat. This is the only lake we have that is surrounded by evergreen trees. June weather was usually bright and sunny and not too warm, so it was a perfect time to be out on the water.

Dworshak was a good place to point out a "flaw" in one of the COE's directives. We were told we should do "watershed management." That would mean you would need to control all the springs, streams, and rivers that spill into the lake. Unfortunately, we generally owned only about one-fourth mile back from the lake's edge. That means all the forest land that was being harvested between our boundary and the peaks around us was not ours to control. Therefore, the waters flowing into Dworshak were highly polluted with soil sediments that destroyed the breeding fishes' natural nesting sites in the streams and rivers. Forest harvesting, road building, and stream management were totally outside the control of the COE on the adjacent lands. In a perfect world, we would have needed to own all the land to the tops of the mountains surrounding the lake in order to do total watershed management.

When district employees did have the opportunity to visit the dams and lakes, they generally traveled only on the main highways. I made it a point to take them on a number of the "back roads" that I had discovered while working in the field. Several of these roads would give us a spectacular view of the two-thousand-foot-deep canyons below. It would probably be the only time they would get to have those views.

On many occasions, those field trips paid off as the participants thought back to the site visits and the information we shared with them regarding our operations. When the Portland Division Native American coordinator (DNAC) was hearing disturbing reports about how Walla Walla District was dealing with tribal archeological concerns, we invited her on one of these field trips. Our district Native Americans coordinator, Lynda Nutt, happened to be on my staff at that time. She was our main point of contact with the DNAC. Our district commander decided we should take the DNAC on one of our field trips to let her know the truth about our work with the tribes in our jurisdiction. We hastily planned a field trip for the DNAC with Lynda, our district archeologist John Leier, and myself. We pretty much followed the format of our previous field trips so she could get a thorough feel of our district's work.

In a pre-trip orientation for the DNAC in our Walla Walla office, one of our key Human Resources employees told her how much she had appreciated the field trip she had taken previously and assured her she would learn a lot about the work we did with archeology and with the tribes. That certainly got the DNAC's attention immediately.

The DNAC was loaded with questions that had come from our sister district in the Portland Division. We did our best to answer all of her questions honestly, putting up a strong defense for our actions. When we returned to the district office, the DNAC spent about a half hour with our chief of operations telling him how pleased she was with our archeology and tribal coordination programs. She followed that up with a forty-five-minute session with our district commander in which she extolled the virtues of our programs.

While working in the field, I had the opportunity to take many helicopter rides into the Snake River Canyon. We did wildlife counts each year to ensure we were meeting our wildlife mitigation objectives. For instance, we were supposed to provide ample habitat within the canyon to support a deer population of 1,600 between Clarkston and the Tri-cities. The last wildlife count I participated in revealed we had 4,500 deer in that area. We actually counted all deer within the canyon, so we would fly down the river for about five miles, then go up about five hundred feet in elevation and go back the five miles we had just covered. We would do that until we reached the upper rim of the canyon before moving further down the river.

We also flew boundary surveys looking for encroachments by neighboring landowners, illegal grazing on COE lands, and damage to our fences. Occasionally we would have top COE personnel from Washington, D.C., come out for a tour. Since their time in the district was usually limited, helicopters were the primary method of travel. While the Washington visitors were at Dworshak, we liked to take them to the upper end of the lake by boat to show off our beautiful forested shoreline. Then we would put them in a helicopter and fly them back to the dam. This afforded us the opportunity to show them the road building and clear-cutting going on right down to our boundaries. That would bring up the fallacy of watershed management operations when we did not own the entire watershed.

Not all helicopter rides went off smoothly. Most of the biologists and managers who participated in these rides lost their lunch at least once. I had been lucky not to have done so until one windy day in the Snake River Canyon when I noticed the pilot kept looking at the back of the chopper. I asked him if there was anything wrong back there. His reply was, "No. I'm just checking to see how close the winds are blowing us toward the cliff behind us!" It was so windy and rainy that day we set down for about an hour to see if the weather would improve enough for us to continue our survey. That was a perfect time for us to devour our lunches. Shirley had fixed me a thermos of spaghetti that really hit the spot. Back in the air, I suddenly realized I needed to be back on Earth quickly. We didn't get down quite fast enough. While I was frantically trying to open the door (still about five hundred feet up in the air), I launched my spaghetti all over the inside of the door! Once the pilot got us on the ground, he had to take the door off and take it over to the lake to clean it. At least my stomach was empty then, so I could more easily enjoy the rest of the flight that day.

CONCLUSION

While it has been fun reminiscing about my life experiences, I hope you have enjoyed my random memories. I do think I've saved enough for a sequel someday should the need to continue writing arise.

You may want to think about your own random memories that you might want to share with others. In the "olden days," parents and grandparents passed down the stories and lore shared with them from their ancestors several generations removed. It seems we don't take enough time nowadays to share our lifetime of experiences with our children, grandchildren, and other friends and relatives. Much of what we have learned during our personal experiences could be of value to younger generations. At least, they could begin to develop a better understanding of what shaped our lives through our education, personal relationships, career objectives, religious beliefs, and our economic situations.

Just think, you too might have a book full of memories just waiting to be put into print! So, quit procrastinating! Get started sharing your life's experiences before it is too late.

www.ingramcontent.com/pod-product-compliance
Lightning Source LLC
LaVergne TN
LVHW041913070526
838199LV00051BA/2601